UNDERSTANDING

HOW YOUNG CHILDREN LEARN

UNDERSTANDING

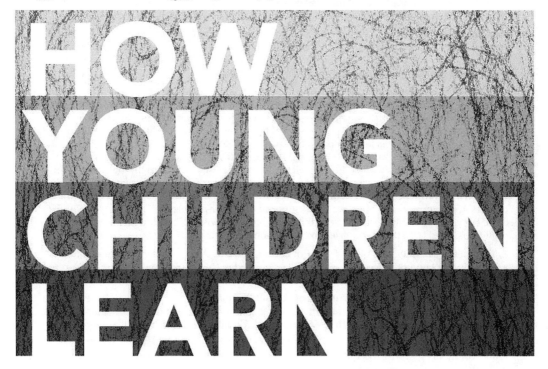

HOW YOUNG CHILDREN LEARN

Bringing the **SCIENCE** of Child
Development to the Classroom

Wendy L. Ostroff

ASCD | Alexandria, Virginia USA

1703 N. Beauregard St. • Alexandria, VA 223111714 USA
Phone: 800-933-2723 or 703-578-9600 • Fax: 703-575-5400
Website: www.ascd.org • E-mail: member@ascd.org
Author guidelines: www.ascd.org/write

Gene R. Carter, *Executive Director;* Ed Milliken, *Chief Program Development Officer,* Carole Hayward, *Publisher;* Genny Ostertag, *Acquisitions Editor,* Julie Houtz, *Director, Book Editing & Production;* Deborah Siegel, *Editor;* Lindsey Heyl Smith, *Graphic Designer;* Mike Kalyan, *Production Manager;* Valerie Younkin, *Desktop Publishing Specialist*

Printed in the United States of America. Cover art © 2012 by ASCD. ASCD publications present a variety of viewpoints. The views expressed or implied in this book should not be interpreted as official positions of the Association.

All web links in this book are correct as of the publication date below but may have become inactive or otherwise modified since that time. If you notice a deactivated or changed link, please e-mail books@ascd.org with the words "Link Update" in the subject line. In your message, please specify the web link, the book title, and the page number on which the link appears.

PAPERBACK ISBN: 978-1-4166-1422-7   ASCD product #112003   n8/12

Also available as an e-book (see Books in Print for the ISBNs).

Quantity discounts for the paperback edition only: 10–49 copies, 10%; 50+ copies, 15%; for 1,000 or more copies, call 800-933-2723, ext. 5634, or 703-575-5634. For desk copies: www.ascd.org/deskcopy.

Library of Congress Cataloging-in-Publication Data
Ostroff, Wendy L. author.
  Understanding how young children learn : bringing the science of child development to the classroom / Wendy L. Ostroff.
    pages cm
  Includes bibliographical references and index.
  ISBN 978-1-4166-1422-7 (pbk. : alk. paper)
  1. Early childhood education. I. Title.
  LB1139.23.O77 2012
  372.21–dc23
                                                              2012017029

22 21 20 19 18 17 16 15 14 13 12   1 2 3 4 5 6 7 8 9 10 11 12

UNDERSTANDING

HOW YOUNG CHILDREN LEARN

Bringing the **SCIENCE** of Child
Development to the Classroom

Preface

I have been teaching college courses on child development for many years in tight-knit academic communities, and my former students often keep in touch. Many of them are elementary school teachers in the area or work directly with children in preschools and early childhood education resource centers. Sometimes when they are visiting and telling me about their wonderful and challenging jobs, they become nostalgic for the past. "I loved your child development seminar—it was so interesting!" they say, beaming. And then I start to get excited and ask them what they use from my course in their daily teaching lives. That's when we inevitably and awkwardly realize that little of the content I had so carefully chosen makes its way into the classroom at all.

I also attend and present at international conferences on child development year after year, where the latest and most revolutionary research on children's learning is discussed by leading scientists. Each time I promise myself that I am going to bring these findings to the teachers and children who could benefit from it. So I put together giant sets of course readings on child development and learning, plowing through theories and ideas written for researchers in scientific journals. One of the greatest challenges that I always face when choosing what to focus on is that the field of child development is so overwhelmed with information. Which theories and studies will be crucial for my students and their students? Inquiry on children's learning over the past hundred years has been flooded with theories (conditioning and behaviorist theories, social cognitive theories, information processing theories, constructivist theories, and sociocultural theories to name just a few). Each of these theories has corresponding and compelling empirical evidence, but little discussion about how and when they should be used. I have often wished that I could somehow distill the mountain of information in front of me down to a handbook of children's learning that would-be teachers could keep with them at all times; a synthesis of the important ideas and findings to reference as they design their curriculum and pedagogy.

This book is my response to that desire. I aim to organize current knowledge on children's learning from the field of developmental science in a way that makes intuitive sense, in the hope that it will be both memorable and useful for my students, and all future teachers. After all, shouldn't this extraordinary knowledge and insight be put to use in the classroom?

Acknowledgments

I want to first thank my colleagues at the Hutchins School of Liberal Studies for sparking my interest in approaching teaching in new ways, and in questioning systems of all kinds, especially education systems. As I read over this manuscript, I can see their ideas about learning leaping off the page. I also want to thank my child development students at the Hutchins School of Liberal Studies and at Smith College, for being game to think like scientists, for challenging me and allowing me to do the same to them. Our classroom seminars germinated the seeds of this book above all else.

Tony Mountain and Buzz Kellogg pored over early drafts of the manuscript and offered suggestions that were especially useful. Brilliant articulators and philosophers both, our many conversations in the hallways of Hutchins over the years profoundly affected my thinking about learning and life.

Margaret Anderson, Charles Atkins, Cécile LePage, Marjan Sobhani, and Roland Vallet read and commented on drafts of this book, and provided unique and helpful perspectives. Carol Berner and her students at Antioch College of New England participated in enthusiastic dialogue about these concepts and offered lots of supportive feedback. Genny

Ostertag from ASCD scaffolded the project from start to finish, transforming the abstract into the applied. And Deborah Siegel, my editor, polished and refined each idea with gentle eloquence.

My understanding of developmental science as a dynamic and emergent process has been shaped time and again by discussions with Robin Panneton, Jamie Cooper, and Megan McIlreavy. Thanks to each of them for keeping my mind in the lab at the same time that my heart was in the classroom.

This project owes great debt to Margaret Anderson, Kelly Wandling, Erika Cellupica, Jane Ostroff-Lin, Carol and Carmen Genova, and Heidi, Susanne, and David Ostroff. It would have been utterly impossible to write without their understanding of (and help with) my children.

Finally, I would like to thank Sonia and Alexei Genova for being patient with a mom who was preoccupied with the many layers of meaning surrounding their learning. But most of all, I would like to thank Rob, who made this possible in countless ways, from the scholarly to the practical. Thank you, Rob, for the 17-year-long conversation that fed this book and all that I am passionate about.

Introduction to Learning, Teaching, and Developmental Science

What if we were to reenvision our school system from the perspective of the learner? Of course, we all know that the objective of education is learning, but for most of the history of formal education, educators' training has been focused almost exclusively on teaching. Children's learning was considered something of an unknown or "black box" until very recently (Gerner, 1981). In the last few decades, however, the field of developmental science has exploded with discoveries of how, *specifically,* learning happens, giving us an entrée into children's minds. We can understand how and when children begin to think, perceive, understand, and apply knowledge. Sadly, few of these cutting-edge findings have made their way into the classroom. The goal of this book is to bridge the divide between the educators and the scientists examining child development. To do so, I believe that we need to train ourselves to think like scientists—who, incidentally, think much like children, always asking *"Why?"* An understanding of children's learning that is grounded in scientific inquiry and research will enable teachers to reinforce and enhance good learning and to offer the best possible educational experiences. This is the solid foundation we need when the weights of uncertain funding, testing, and standards begin to bear down.

In the early 1900s, when most industrialized countries began offering formal, public schooling to children, the curricula were designed for future workers in an industrialized economy. The idea was to groom a workforce that could understand basic instruction while not challenging any fundamental aspects of the status quo. Teaching techniques were based on commonsense assumptions (e.g., that knowledge is a collection of facts and procedures, that the teacher's job is to transmit those facts and procedures to students, and that success at school is determined by testing to see how many facts and procedures students have acquired) (Sawyer, 2006). Some of these techniques are still in place today. Teaching practices that require children to work individually in rows, to compete with others for good grades, to take tests alone, to concentrate for long periods of time without breaks, and to be put into reading or math groups with only peers of matched ability are based upon tradition alone—not at all on evidence of student learning. Children are *not* passive recipients of information, waiting to be filled like empty vessels. Right from the start they are active, exploratory, and involved in the creation of their own knowledge.

What Is Learning?

Learning is very difficult to define. It is the matter of our minds, and includes thinking, becoming aware, imagining, seeing, hearing, hoping, remembering, abstracting, planning, and problem solving (Malone, 1991). Learning is deep in our species, emerging from our desire to take in new information by actively exploring new territory. Learning is a physical phenomenon, occurring in the sensory systems, as energy from light waves and vibrations in the air is converted into electrical impulses that can be interpreted by the nervous system; and in the brain where neurons send out neurotransmitters and forge networks of connections; and in the body where motor patterns are encoded for actions. Learning is also embedded in the world via life experiences, social interactions, and community membership. Because learning occurs at so many levels simultaneously, developmental science (which encompasses the disciplines of developmental psychology, cognitive and linguistic science, developmental psychobiology, and developmental neuroscience) does not privilege any level of analysis over any other (Thelen & Smith, 1996).

The Beginning of Learning: From Infancy to Childhood

For most of the last century, scientists and teachers believed that children are born into the world without much ability to understand it, spending their early days in a "blooming buzzing confusion" (James, 1983/1890, p. 462). After all, other than making messes, babies appeared to just lie around or sleep, with limited behaviors, expressions, and interactions. But now we know that this view is all wrong. Humans learn the most and the fastest during the first few years of development. No time in life is close to infancy and childhood when it comes to the capacity to adapt to new environments, to master new material, and to solve complex problems. "What we see in the crib is the greatest mind that has ever existed, the most powerful learning machine in the universe" (Gopnik, Meltzoff, & Kuhl, 1999, p.1).

Studying prenatal development allows us access to the beginnings of human thought and action. Right from birth, infants pick up on all of the complex sights, sounds, smells, tastes, and textures surrounding them, and they skillfully use this information to guide their perception, attention, and learning (Smotherman & Robinson, 1988). Even before birth, movements beginning in the womb are involved in the development of the mind. The embryo plays a role in its own learning by moving and changing within its cellular environment. Movement patterns of the fetus actually set up brain connections required for learning in early childhood. In one recent study, developmental scientists at the National Institute of Child Health and Human Development discovered that fetuses whose heart rates fluctuated more during the course of prenatal development (as opposed to those whose heart rates stayed relatively constant) went on to achieve higher levels of language and pretend play skills when they were 2 years old (Bornstein et al., 2002).

Brain cells (called neurons) develop and proliferate at the staggering rate of up to 250,000 new cells per minute during the second trimester of pregnancy. Neurons migrate through the neural tube, which bends to form the central nervous system, including the brain and spinal cord. Neurons then begin to grow armlike protrusions called axons, which will connect in networks with other neurons via junctions called synapses. By the time of birth, the infant's neurons will have accrued over a trillion synaptic connections. In fact, areas of the newborn brain are much more highly connected than that of the adult brain. This seems to be an evolutionary adaptation, allowing the infant to assimilate vast amounts of information with ease. As a result, infants commonly experience synesthesia, an overlap of the senses or a blending of sensory information (Maurer, 1993). During early infancy the brain responds to language over both the temporal cortex (responsible for auditory processing) and the occipital cortex (responsible for vision).

Most of what we know about brain development has come from experiments with animal brains or postmortem human brains. Until very recently scientists were unable to access the living brains of human infants and children at all. But new noninvasive technologies are becoming more available. These technologies include ERP, which tracks changes in electrical brain potentials from the scalp surface; fMRI, which assesses changes in blood flow in the brain; and MEG, which evaluates magnetic field changes in the brain over time (Nelson, de Haan, & Thomas, 2006). Even so, studies that directly assess the brains of infants and children are expensive and time-consuming because they can only produce data from infants or children who stay relatively still.

The human brain is first and foremost an efficient organ. When it comes to brain structure, *less is more*. In the typically developing infant brain, neurons and synapses grow at astounding rates and are then pruned back. Those neural connections that are frequently used become strengthened, and those that are infrequently used are cut, resulting in the simplest and best brain possible. During the first year of life, the axon of each nerve cell (the part that connects to other neurons) becomes insulated with a fatty, protective coating called myelin. This speeds up the electrical signal, making communication between neurons fast and efficient. Throughout childhood the brain continues to develop. Brain cells grow and die; they connect and reconnect with one another; they grow additional axons and coat them with myelin (Cycowicz, 2000). As a side note, the brains of autistic children often fail to prune neurons in the brain areas responsible for planning and complex reasoning. They also develop less insulating myelin on their neural connections (Bartzokis et al., 2010; Courchesne & Pierce, 2005).

Thanks to newly developed neuroimaging technology, we now have access to the specific brain changes that occur during learning. Even though all of our brains contain the same basic structures, our neural networks are as unique as our fingerprints. The latest developmental neuroscience research has shown that the brain is much more malleable throughout life than previously assumed; it develops in response to its own processes, to its immediate and distant "environments," and to its past and current situations (Hinton, Miyamoto, & Della-Chiesa, 2008). The brain seeks to create meaning through establishing or refining existing neural networks. When we learn a new fact or skill, our neurons communicate to form networks of connected information. Using this knowledge or skill results in structural changes to allow similar future impulses to travel more quickly and efficiently than others (Squire & Kandel, 2000). High-activity synaptic connections are stabilized and strengthened, while connections with relatively low use are weakened and eventually pruned. In this way, our brains are sculpted by our own history of experiences (Wolfe, 2006).

Processes and Propellers of Learning

Incorporating developmental science research into the classroom means shifting the focus of education from teaching back to learning. In the United States, the content of schooling is determined at the state, local, and national level and is often given the highest priority. Students' ability to remember facts for standardized tests determines how well their schools will get funded. But what children learn depends on *how* they learn. And to figure that out, we need to examine the many levels of the developmental system in which children's brains, bodies, and minds are functioning.

Learning is a complex set of interactive and situated processes which recursively set up the individual's future experiences. Human beings are born to learn. We have evolved over tens of thousands of years to do it efficiently and easily, with all of the stimulation we need already present in our surroundings and our lives. The components of children's learning, motivation, attention, memory, cognition, and action, and the processes that propel and inspire them are the topics of this book. I hope to introduce a new way for teachers to think about learning, based on the perspectives and the findings of developmental scientists.

1

Understanding Children's Motivation

mo·ti·va·tion is the driving desire behind all action and is the precursor and cornerstone to learning. It is no exaggeration to say that children have boundless energy for living and learning. From an evolutionary perspective, behaviors that are important for survival (like eating or reproducing) must be pleasurable to do in and of themselves. Young children *survive* by exploring their world via manipulation, locomotion, language, and social interaction. But they also love doing these things. The immediate satisfaction of "being good at" something also has adaptive significance for cognitive growth. To motivate children and keep them primed for the best learning possible, we must understand how motivation to learn develops.

A Developmental Science Approach to Motivation

Motivation is a readiness (or a setup) to learn. Throughout life we learn incredibly complex skills without consciously trying at all. As the British developmental scientist John L. Locke (1995) notes, infants and children do not set out to learn any of the vast repertoire of skills that they gain in the first years. Instead, they study the faces, voices, and actions of others out of a deep biological need for emotional interaction with those who love and care for them. They simply find themselves in a social and cultural context that values certain skills and uses them constantly. Learning, then, is an unintended bonus. It is a byproduct of wanting to do other things, like receive a smile from your conversational partner or be soothed by your mother's voice.

Across tens of thousands of years of human evolution, certain proclivities on the part of the infant and child have emerged. In the same way, social and cultural mannerisms have arisen around children and in support of their learning. When it comes to understanding where motivation comes from, we should consider both those things that children actively try to master and those things that they just pick up along the way. Children's learning is dynamic and results from the interaction between inborn capacity and experience.

Desire to learn is present even before birth. As their world is suddenly filled with new things to see, hear, smell, taste, and touch, fetuses and new babies develop reflexive behaviors to organize that information and to make meaning from it. Reflexes have evolved to help the young of a species to adapt to its environment. The rooting and suckling reflexes, for example, guarantee that a helpless infant takes in the milk it needs to survive. Sometimes reflexes develop into more complex modes of behavior and set up learning. They are important clues to the development of motivation.

Motivation Propeller 1: Habituation and Novelty Preference

Within minutes of Mr. Frymer turning his back to the second-grade class and beginning to write multiplication problems on the board, Aaron begins to zone out. He fiddles with his pencil and rummages through his desk. It is not until he notices the back of Samantha's neck in front of him that his interest is piqued again. With full engagement and vigor, Aaron begins tearing the corners off of his math worksheet and rolling spitballs.

Beginning in infancy and throughout the life span, humans are motivated by newness, change, and excitement. Habituation, the tendency to lose interest in a repeated event and gain interest in a new one, is one of the most fundamental human reflexes. If the thermostat were to suddenly turn the air conditioning on, you would hear the loud humming sound begin, but within minutes you couldn't even hear it if you tried. Habituation, a fundamental property of the nervous system, provides mechanisms to ignore the environment when it presents no immediate threat or reward, and to focus attention on potentially important new input. Habituation is also an elementary form of inhibition, the complex cognitive maneuver that allows us to override urges. This reflects the function of the frontal lobes of the brain. Finally, habituation is considered to be the simplest form of learning. Habituation is important to understand in relation to children's motivation, because if children are habituating to the learning situation of the classroom, their attention and interest will decline.

Habituation and Learning

Developmental scientists use the habituation response to measure attention, perception, and cognition. Because fetuses and infants cannot tell us about the workings of their minds, researchers must glean what they perceive and understand from behaviors that *are in their repertoire*. Habituation studies can be done in utero, by presenting fetuses with information (often sounds plus vibration) via headphones on their mothers' bellies. The fetuses' responses are then monitored with ultrasound. After many presentations of the same stimulus, fetuses will habituate (stop moving their bodies in response), at which point the vibrating sound will be switched to something new (e.g., a tone of a different pitch). If a fetus moves in response to the new tone, scientists infer that it perceived a difference between the two tones (McCorry & Hepper, 2007).

Habituation can also be used to assess infants' learning after birth. Infants will look at something when they are interested and turn to look away when they become bored. So if we show an infant a repeated display of events until he or she looks away and then switch to a new display (which may be only slightly different), we can determine whether the infant noticed the difference. The habituation response has been linked to both attention and language. Studies have shown that young infants who habituate quickly to complex events have greater vocabularies as toddlers than those for whom habituation takes longer (Dixon & Smith, 2008; Tamis-Lemonda & Bornstein, 1989). Habituation assessments in the first year of life also predict IQ between 1 and 8 years of age (McCall & Carriger, 1993). Rapid habituation reflects the ability to quickly encode an event into memory and to recognize it easily when it is presented again.

Novelty and Learning

After habituating to an environmental event (like the air conditioning) and ceasing to notice it, your attention may be involuntarily drawn to a new stimulating event. The brain is highly responsive to novelty (Wolfe, 2006). The preference for novel objects and events is a very important clue into the workings of motivation. Danish philosopher Søren Kierkegaard (1843/1985) believed that the only way to overcome boredom was to respond to the world like a child: be inquisitive and curious, and marvel at everything. Scientists have explained novelty preference as an efficient way for infants' and young children's immature cognitive system to process information. Once a child has mastered all of the information an object or event offers, paying attention to something new allows him or her to acquire additional information in a short amount of time. It is also a great strategy for getting little ones' attention away from things we don't want them to do. Just yesterday, I used the novelty preference to lure my young son Alexei away from biting the soles of my sneakers (a new and unsanitary habit of his) and toward his wooden train kept high and hidden on the bookshelf. A simple "choo-choo!" sound was all it took to reorient him toward the train, and the sneakers had lost all their appeal. Infants and children have shown a behavioral, perceptual, and emotional preference for novelty across a wide age range, in experiments on memory, language, speech-sound categorization, and number (Diamond, 1995; Lipton & Spelke, 2003; Quinn & Eimas, 1996; Saffran, Aslin, & Newport, 1996).

Infants who lack novelty preference tend to have cognitive delays during childhood. Additionally, novelty preference (just like habituation) is predictive of later cognitive functioning. Infants with a stronger preference for novelty at just 6 months old have better memories, language skills, and motor skills when they grow to be toddlers and children (Colombo, Mitchell, Dodd, Coldren, & Horowitz, 1989; Fagan & Knevel, 1989; Thompson, Fagan, & Fulker, 1991). It follows then, that the desire to learn new things is a deeply embedded part of being human.

Infant novelty preference develops into childhood curiosity and desire for exploration. In order to survive, animals must actively explore. All living things have an urge called "perceptual curiosity," which drives them to examine new things. The newer, more complex, or more unexpected the thing, the more deeply it will satisfy this urge. Nobel Prize–winning physiologist Ivan Pavlov (1927) termed this the "investigatory reflex." When presented with a new, attractive, or surprising object in laboratory settings, children display their drive to explore, which clearly can only be satisfied by attending to, perceiving, or manipulating the object in question. Never-before-seen objects that call to be examined via touching and manipulation (boxes with lights, buttons, and levers, and plants with shiny ribbons on them, for instance) are almost irresistible to a young child.

Exploration in children sets them up to learn. Russian developmental scientist Alexander Zaporozhets (as cited in Berlyne, 1960) discovered that children automatically expose themselves to the important characteristics of a situation. They experiment with anything and everything they can, in preparation for carrying out difficult actions. In a number of experiments in his laboratory, children were trained to press buttons in a certain order (corresponding to lights being flashed) or to push a toy car through a maze. Upon entering the lab, the children would spontaneously do things to acquaint themselves with the buttons, lights, and other features of the apparatus. In fact, they could not be restrained from doing so! In younger children, the most prominent forms of exploration were touching and feeling movements of the hands and fingers. This was replaced by eye movements as the children's age increased. Perhaps most striking, the more time children spent on their preliminary inspection, the less time it took for them to master the actions they were asked to perform.

Remember:

▶ Newness, change, and excitement motivate learning.

▶ Habituation and novelty preference reflect children's ability to encode quickly and correspond to their attention, perception, and cognition.

▶ The brain is highly responsive to novelty.

▶ Exploration sets up opportunities for learning.

How to Enhance Classroom Motivation Using Habituation and Novelty Preference

▶ *Create a secure, predictable structure, with clear expectations and boundaries, from which to divert.*

To avoid habituation and foster novelty in your classroom, you don't have to throw all the rules out the window. On the contrary, children with the most solid foundations are the most willing to explore and experiment with new things. When setting up a classroom full of surprises and newness, do so while ensuring that the students' basic needs of security are met. This will allow them to feel safe to go out on a limb, to try new things and to play with ideas. Clear expectations and boundaries are a crucial foundation from which to springboard into the unknown and exciting.

Austrian philosopher and pedagogue Rudolf Steiner (1919) believed that young children gain great security from rituals and harmonious transitions between events. In the Waldorf model of education, based on Steiner's philosophies, transition routines like songs or candles are used for daily activities and to give a form to the day, providing security for the children. Daily rituals offer an inner, bodily knowledge that can then allow children to adapt more smoothly to change. Likewise, connecting with cycles of the year can provide a sense of predictability for children. Nature, though ever changing, is still recognizable. Teachers of young children also claim that strong routines greatly decrease discipline issues.

Set up daily, weekly, and seasonal rituals in your classroom. Beginning the day with a song, a rhyme, or a check-in with each student creates the predictability and comfort that allows for the exploration and risk of learning. Keep seasonal rhythms in mind when designing lessons, including the less obvious ones such as harvests, solstices, and equinoxes. For example, an interdisciplinary autumnal equinox lesson might include tree bark rubbings, paintings each day using a single fall color (e.g., red on Monday, orange on Tuesday), units on animals who store nuts for the winter, charting fall temperatures, or understanding photosynthesis.

▶ *Locate the drama in the content of the lesson.*

Sociologist James Loewen's work (2007) has shown that American history is full of fantastic, shocking, and important stories to engage novelty preference and avoid habituation. And yet, even elementary social studies students groan when it's time for history lessons. Textbooks present a version of history that is boring and predictable, with every problem easily solved, and with the exclusion of all conflict or suspense. Across curriculum areas, children do get hooked into curiosity when they are shown the drama of the subject, when they are asked to speculate on outcomes of controversies, when they are encouraged to explore mysteries and puzzles, or when they are shown competing answers to dilemmas. This can even be done in math, a field with a reputation for being boring and fixed (but one that is actually filled with controversy, crisis, and change). Sixth grade teacher Margaret Anderson always begins her discussion of square roots with the history of Greek mathematician Pythagoras, and his finding that the square root of two was an irrational number. Imagine the crisis to a civilization based entirely on reason!

Ask children to consider the complexity of the past by exploring vastly different points of view on the same events. For example, before presenting historical "facts" in a social studies/language arts unit on slavery, encourage your students to piece together history from different information sources. You can include such diverse perspectives as slave narratives, excerpts from the autobiographies of slave-owning American presidents like Thomas Jefferson, clips of films that represent slavery, or documents showing that some of the earliest settlers in the United States were from Africa. You might ask the students to write journal entries in different voices—that of a working slave, a runaway slave, a slave owner, a Quaker family hiding runaway slaves, or a slave catcher making money by returning runaway slaves (Czajka, 2004). You could stage a debate or a play as a dramatic finale to this powerful unit. Most importantly, you will be priming the students' minds for curiosity and exploration into new intellectual territory.

▶ *Stimulate, engage, and delight not only your students but also yourself.*

Novelty motivates teachers as much as students. Teaching topics that you are newly energized about or experimenting with new teaching styles can model engagement to your students. As a teacher, you have the unique opportunity to be constantly learning on the job. I have discovered that the most effective courses that I teach (in terms of both student enthusiasm and student learning) are those that are exciting to me. When the content or method is novel, I do have to work a bit harder preparing for each class, but the payoff is tenfold. My passion is sincere, and my students and I are motivated to understand the topics, frameworks, or ideologies together. It sounds like a risky position for a teacher, not being completely secure in how certain assignments or activities will come off. But as radical educator Paulo Freire has said, if we "abandon the educational goal of deposit-making... the teacher is no longer merely the-one-who-teaches, but one who is himself taught in dialogue with the students" (1970, p. 67). Curiosity is not only motivating; it is contagious.

Bring your students along for your next vacation. Okay, not literally. But why not share your interest and enthusiasm with your students by designing lessons on topics that captivate your imagination? Suppose you have always wanted to go to Peru to hike Machu Picchu. You might begin by planning and mapping your route through Peru with the class. Next, you could ask the students to create maps of the region, corresponding to topography, terrain, or climate. They can determine what you will need in terms of food, gear, and supplies in order to comfortably complete the hike. They can then go back about 800 years to understand the Inca civilization and how the geography of the region affected their architecture, transportation, and agriculture. (For example, ask the students to map out a terraced garden plan, which would provide all of the food one Incan family would need for the year). The Incan system of measures can be a lead-in to a math lesson, just as Incan myths can be a lead-in to a clever creative writing assignment—the writing of creation stories. Stories can be depicted in images or even dramatically acted out. Any destination is ripe for exploration from a variety of perspectives. Whether you are planning an actual vacation or just one from your imagination, bringing the children along for your adventures is a natural motivator.

▶ *Surprise the students with your delivery!*

Our brains have evolved to remember unexpected or novel events because basic survival depends on the ability to perceive causes and predict effects. If the brain predicts one event and experiences another, the anomaly will be especially interesting and will be encoded accordingly. Neurologist and classroom teacher Judith Willis (2006) has claimed that surprise in the classroom is one of the most effective ways of teaching with brain stimulation in mind. If students are exposed to novel experiences via demonstrations or through the unexpected enthusiasm of their teachers or peers, they will be much more likely to connect with the information that follows. Willis has written that encouraging active discovery in the classroom allows students to inter-act with novel information, moving it beyond working memory to be processed in the frontal lobe, which is devoted to advanced cognitive functioning. Preference for novelty sets us up for learning by directing attention, providing stimulation to developing perceptual systems, bolstering the emergence of thinking skills, and feeding curious and exploratory behavior.

Plan an outrageous lesson. Use surprise to get your students' attention, and use humor, strangeness, disguise, and drama to keep them transfixed (Pogrow, 2009). For example, at the beginning of a unit on storytelling, 4th grade student-teacher Julie spent the first five minutes of class reading a story about monkeys in the jungle in monotone. She suddenly stopped, slapped her arm, and said a bug had bitten her. She then started reading again, but this time in a wildly ani-mated way, gesturing and imitating the animals' behavior in the story. After a few minutes she pretended to faint.

When the students approached Julie, she exclaimed, "I know what happened. I got bitten by... a story bug!" Julie then asked her students to share their own stories in small groups. When she sensed a lull in their stories, she loudly called, "Look out! Oh no! There is a swarm of story bugs flying into the classroom!" The children excitedly pretended to be bitten, filling the classroom with animated versions of the same stories that had previously been reading. In this way, Julie was able to use surprise to transform her lesson on action verbs in story writing into a highly exciting, motivating, novel event (Pogrow, 2009, p. 92).

Motivation Propeller 2: Confidence

Kelly remembers the exact year when she stopped drawing. At first school allowed her endless time to play with art supplies and create wild, colorful pictures that jumped off the page. She drew hundreds of portraits of her house and her cats. But in the third grade her school began its "Artist of the Week" program, and because Kelly was never chosen, she came to see that her drawings were not so great. The children who won could color in the lines much better than her, and their cats looked more like real cats. Kelly's art and love of learning gradually fell away.

Confidence helps children learn. As adults, we often have a fairly accurate idea of what we're best at, what things come easily and naturally to us. Confidence in our own abilities becomes the first step toward success. On the other hand, if we have had a negative experience with learning, we may label ourselves as deficient in that subject. When we believe that we can't do something no matter how hard we try, we'll soon give up. I have worked with countless students who believed themselves to be "bad at" a particular subject and who stopped engaging long before. Even when situations change (and they would do well), these students lose the motivation to try, a condition called "learned helplessness." Assessing potential success might be adaptive in that it can prevent us from making fools of ourselves, but it can also hinder us from trying and practicing new things.

It is critical that we protect and build children's confidence. In a now-classic study conducted by a San Francisco educator and a University of California psychologist (Rosenthal & Jacobson, 1966), elementary school teachers were told that 20 percent of their students showed unusual potential for academic success (called intellectual "bloomers"). What the teachers did not know was that these students were chosen at random. By the end of the school year, the children who were merely expected to perform better (but were no smarter) actually did show superior academic performance. This was especially true of the youngest students. But even more striking, children who were labeled "bloomers" scored higher on IQ tests, a lasting measure of intellectual potential! Clearly the teachers' continued expectation that some students were destined for success imparted some level of confidence in the children themselves.

Overconfidence

Fortunately, young children's lack of accurate perception of their abilities often keeps them motivated. In study after study, children rate their abilities and proclivities far better than their performance shows. When asked, children overestimate their strength and social standing, their memories, their physical abilities, their knowledge, and their intelligence. In one experiment, 650 2nd through 5th graders were asked to estimate their skills both academically and physically, before trying challenging events. The younger children almost always rated themselves at the maximum, and their ratings decreased linearly with age (Marsh, Barnes, Caims, & Tidman, 1984). In another series of studies, preschool children consistently overestimated their ability to imitate complex acts and therefore tried to imitate behaviors that were often way beyond their grasp. After an unsuccessful attempt at imitating a difficult behavior (e.g., juggling or tossing a ball into a basket from several feet away), the children were equally inaccurate in their assessment of how successful they had been. "How did you do?" the researchers asked. "I did great!" the children replied. Interestingly, the preschoolers with higher IQs tended to overestimate more (Bjorklund, Gaultney, & Green, 1993). As counterintuitive as it sounds, being out of touch with one's abilities was related to higher competence.

In another telling study, kindergarteners, 1st graders, and 3rd graders were given a word recall memory test. The children were asked to estimate how many they would remember prior to studying them. Children with less accurate predictions made greater improvements in word recall as compared with those whose predictions were *more accurate*. Overestimating one's abilities was associated with greater cognitive gains (Shin, Bjorklund, & Beck, 2007). Developmental scientist

David Bjorklund and his colleagues (Bjorklund, Periss, & Causey, 2009) have posited that such poorly developed self-assessment encourages young children to attempt a wider range of behaviors, which in turn lets them practice and improve. An optimistic attitude corresponds with children's active, exploratory, and playful nature, motivating them enormously to learn new behaviors that they would not have attempted otherwise. Just like the *Little Engine That Could* from the classic children's story, success often comes down to confidence.

Visualization as Confidence

One reason that confidence catapults learning is because to your brain, imagining achievement is no different than actually achieving. Research on visualization and mental training has shown that vividly picturing success in difficult tasks actually increases the likelihood of success. This has been shown in sports from darts to Olympic gymnastics, and in the classroom in overcoming public speaking anxiety (Ayres & Hopf, 1990; Straub, 1989; Unestahl, 1983). In one compelling study, students who merely imagined themselves exercising the muscles of their arms significantly increased their strength in the relevant muscle groups. Measures of brain electrical potentials showed that mental training was no different from physical training when it came to parts of the brain that increase muscle strength (Ranganathan, Siemionow, Liu, Sahgal, & Yue, 2003).

Remember:

▶ Confidence helps children try and practice new things.

▶ Overconfidence has positive effects on competence and cognitive gains.

▶ Visualizing success increases the likelihood of success.

▶ To the brain, thinking about doing something is not much different from actually doing it.

In a stunning study, two groups of people who had no experience playing the piano were brought into the laboratory and given a brief lesson on a one-handed, five-finger piano exercise. The first group practiced the exercise on the piano for two hours a day for five days. The second group imagined that they were doing the exercise and visualized as clearly as possible that they were practicing it on the piano. The brains of those who played and imagined playing *both* showed structural changes in the area of the brain related to the movement of the fingers. Equally astonishing, the group that had only imagined playing significantly improved in their ability to do the piano exercise (Pascual-Leone et al., 1995). It seems that being confident that we can do something is linked to motivation and visualization, which feeds success and leads to even greater confidence.

How to Enhance Classroom Motivation Using Confidence

▶ *Provide careful, constructive feedback that encourages students' strengths as well as areas in need of improvement.*

If we teachers can casually receive hundreds of compliments from parents and students, but be devastated by a single insult, imagine the power that criticism can have on a young child! Educator Adrienne Mack-Kirschner (2004) will never forget the time that her 6th grade teacher walked around the room tapping shoulders while the children sang rounds of *Three Blind Mice*. Thinking she was being chosen for singing well, Adrienne sang even louder and more joyfully; she loved singing, just like her dad. *Will the students I tapped*—she held her breath self-consciously, expecting praise—*stop singing*? *You're off key and ruining the songs for everyone else*. Adrienne now laments, "I can recall the exact moment when I stopped singing. Nearly four decades passed before I found my voice again" (p. 4).

Feedback on school performance gives children a valuable gauge of their learning. But given without care and caution, negative feedback can greatly harm confidence and motivation. In order to be effective, feedback on a child's performance should closely follow the behavior or event and it should be as clear as possible. Constructive feedback from teachers should always contain encouragement and should not focus on too many aspects of behavior at once. Positive feedback should let the child know exactly what he or she did well. Instead of saying "nice job," you might tell the child how the technique was effective (e.g., "I see that you used both high-contrast colors and glitter to make the shapes in the painting pop out"). Helping to make a child's process explicit leads to self-reflection and self-confidence, which are both learning enhancers.

During any critique of a child, be sure to comment on his or her process, rather than on him or her as a person. In a revealing study, kindergarteners role-played minor failure scenarios in school (e.g., failing to stack blocks properly or to completely clean up after snack time). Their teacher then critiqued them with either process-oriented feedback (e.g., "The blocks are all crooked and one big mess; maybe you should find another way to do it") or person-oriented feedback (e.g., "The blocks are all crooked and one big mess; I am very disappointed in you"). Then, the children were asked to build a house out of Legos and given the neutral feedback "That house you built has no windows."

When asked to rate their Lego house and themselves, those kindergarteners who had been told that they were disappointing (via person-oriented feedback) rated themselves as significantly less smart and showed little desire to rebuild or fix their houses. Children who had been given process-oriented feedback felt fine about their houses. They rated their Lego creations significantly higher than the others, even without windows. They also believed that they were smart. These children wanted opportunities to try building their house again, this time with windows, thereby finding another way to do it, just as their feedback had suggested (Kamins & Dweck, 1999).

After the next big project, ask students to consider the steps that they went through in their learning process. Perhaps have them represent their struggle toward mastery visually, using drawings or a graph. They should then comment on what worked well, what was hardest for them, and what they might have done differently if the circumstances were different. Written evaluations of the project can have a section for self- and teacher feedback, and the grades and comments can be negotiated during a discussion. Ask students, *Do you feel that this represents the work you did? Why or why not?* and take their assessment seriously.

Children in the 5th grade at the Smith College Campus School end each day by completing a learning evaluation form. They respond to questions such as *What are two things that you learned or practiced today? What is one learning goal that you have for this week? What is your plan to reach that goal? What seems to help you in class?* and *What seems to slow you down?* The children's daily evaluation forms are kept in their desks in a portfolio that they review with their teachers at the middle and end of each term. This way, they become mindful of what they consistently excel at and what they might want to work harder on. Children who get used to articulating their strengths and what they enjoy will retain their confidence and develop the ability to realistically self-critique in time.

▶ *Reward student attempts and intellectual risk taking over "playing it safe" to get correct answers or high marks.*

When I was in the 1st grade, we spent a whole week in March on a special art project, making kites. The large piece of construction paper had to be completely covered in multicolor crayon strokes, which we would then paint over with black. When the paint dried, the crayon wax would begin to show through the paint, magically reappearing. Then we were meant to cut a diamond shape out of the paper and use each of the four corner scraps to make the bows of the kite. I was so excited about my kite that I spent longer than anyone on the coloring part, making each patch as dark and rich as possible for that magic moment they would poke through. When it came time to cut the bows using patterns, I cleverly accounted for all four bows using just two of the corners of the left over triangles. It wasn't easy, but if I turned them just right, it worked. But my teacher, Mrs. Angers (aptly named, it turned out!), valued obedience over initiative and creativity. She forced me to publicly admit that I had not listened and therefore done it incorrectly. Then she made me stand in the corner for the rest of the day. I stood there and cried, humiliated and shamed, my kite thrown aside and never finished.

Risk taking is important to cognitive growth. But all too often, fear of not measuring up, of making mistakes, or of being embarrassed discourages children from taking chances intellectually. Research shows that children who are willing to risk asking questions, sharing tentative ideas, or attempting to do new things also tend to exhibit ongoing interest in the topics at hand. They also exhibit greater confidence and deeper, longer-lasting learning (Beghetto, 2008).

Unfortunately, many of the procedures we associate with learning in school quickly squash creativity. Two of the top creativity killers are surveillance and evaluation. If children feel that you are hovering over them and constantly observing and judging their work, they begin to worry about how they are doing. This can rattle their confidence. Writer and graphic novelist Lynda Barry (2008) claims that asking herself the question "Is this good or does this suck?" plagued her work for years. It was only when she was able to stop asking this question that she could let her ideas flow. Surveillance makes the urge for creative risk taking go deep in the ground and hide. So does overcontrolling. When children are told exactly how to do every step of a project or problem, they begin to feel that originality is misbehavior and exploration is a waste of time. Telling children what exactly they should be doing and how to do it encourages them to simply follow directions by rote. Their wonderful openness for learning will promptly shut down. Likewise, external rewards, competition, and pressure deprive children of the joy and pleasure of creativity. Exercises suddenly become win-lose situations and self-judgment takes over for playful experimentation. Setting unreasonable expectations for a child's performance depletes their confidence, pressuring them to both perform and conform. Innovation, again, goes almost immediately dormant (Amabile & Hennessy, 1992).

Grading is just one of a series of controls used in the education system today. Ultimately, grades say to the learner, "You are answerable to me, the teacher." Lighting children's intellects on fire and letting them come to care about their own education is a much better pathway to lasting motivation. Rather than sorting children into competency categories, why not invite them to love learning and be answerable to themselves? *Would you like to try this?* is a much more effective mantra for long-term motivation than is any carrot or stick approach.

Get children into the habit of taking intellectual risks by inviting them to be comfortable questioning everything around them: ideas, books, teachers, and peers. One great way to encourage questioning is to assign it. The next time you are beginning a unit or lesson, ask the children to come up with 100 questions about the topic. For instance, in a language arts lesson on E. B. White's novel *Charlotte's Web* (1952), the students might begin with questioning the events of the story: *Why was Wilbur in danger?* or *What happened when Charlotte began to praise him?* Then they may begin to ask more analytical questions, such as, *Do animals befriend each other in real life?* or *Do animals have the same kinds of feelings as humans?* They might run out of ideas at 20 or 30 questions, and begin to get creative or even silly: *What if Charlotte had 10 million babies—could they begin to run the farm?* And so on. When they really run out of ideas, they can pair up with someone else to combine their lists and see how close they can get to 100. The more children get in the habit of asking questions, the more likely they will be to stretch their minds and challenge the people and texts around them.

▶ *Let students work and be evaluated in pairs or teams so they have an opportunity to be part of something bigger and to be less self-conscious.*

Russian developmental scientist Lev Vygotsky (1930/1978) advocated for collaborative learning because he believed that meaning is socially constructed. He also discovered that working together allowed children to surpass the levels that they could have achieved alone. When children work collaboratively, they are more likely to get engrossed in the challenge of learning and less likely to focus on achieving good grades. In terms of confidence, peer and group learning can also diffuse the pressure that an individual child can feel to excel. Finally, and perhaps most importantly, a mountain of evidence now shows that collaboration enhances and deepens learning, even on subsequent solo endeavors.

Pair students on tasks that are traditionally done alone. Writing is a great example. Poems and stories can be written serially, with each child seeing only the previous line, adding a line, and passing it along. When the final pieces are read aloud, the juxtapositions can be hilarious! Even short-answer or essay exams can be done in pairs, with the children helping each other remember important information from the lessons they are being tested on. I often ask my students to critique one another's essays and find that they have a hard time expressing what needs to be changed. If instead they are asked to *rewrite* the other student's essay (if the essay they are critiquing becomes "theirs"), they have no problem finding areas that need work. Essays can be passed multiple times, with each student having the opportunity to work with several and to get each one into the best shape possible. In the process they will learn a tremendous amount about other people's ideas, about grammar and structure, and about writing as a process. They will also begin to separate their sense of self-confidence from individual grades.

▶ *Create lesson plans that highlight multimodal strengths, giving each student a chance to shine in some way.*

In the children's book *Horris and Morris Join the Chorus, but What About Dolores?* by James Howe, three best-friend mice try out for the chorus together, but only two make it in. The third mouse, Dolores, is told that she has a terrible voice and finds herself suddenly left out of all the fun. In an impassioned and lonely moment, she writes a letter to the chorus director describing her love of music. The chorus director is stunned to realize that Dolores is a wonderful writer! He promptly recruits her to write the songs that the chorus will sing.

This picture book would make Harvard psychologist Howard Gardner proud. His (1993) theory of multiple intelligences accounts for the wide varieties of abilities that humans are capable of when it comes to mastering their environments. Gardner discovered that traditional definitions of skill, based on IQ testing, limit human potential and creativity. Unfortunately, both our education system and broader culture prioritize linguistic and mathematical-logical intelligence over other types. But where would we be without the artists, architects, musicians, naturalists, designers, dancers, therapists, entrepreneurs, and athletes who enhance the world with equal brilliance? We should place equal merit on the unique ways of thinking in linguistic, logical-mathematical, spatial, bodily-kinesthetic, musical, interpersonal, intrapersonal, and naturalist intelligences (Gardner, 1993).

Teaching students in the modes they learn best (molding lessons to those who are primarily auditory learners, visual learners, or kinesthetic learners) does in fact enhance their learning (Bellflower, 2008; Douglas, Burton, & Reese-Durham, 2008). Additionally, research studies show that all students benefit from being taught in multiple-sensory modalities as compared with teaching the same material via only one modality (Mayer, 1999; Mayer & Gallini, 1990). Teaching complex material using text and pictures, for example, is more effective than teaching the same material using text only (Gellevij, van der Meij, de Jong, & Pieters, 2002).

Whatever topic you are teaching, imagine ways to connect it with words (linguistic intelligence), numbers or logic (logical-mathematical intelligence), pictures (spatial intelligence), music (musical intelligence), self-reflection (intrapersonal intelligence), a physical experience (bodily-kinesthetic intelligence), a social experience (interpersonal intelligence), or an experience in the natural world (naturalist intelligence) (Armstrong, 2009).

In a botany lesson, rather than simply teaching the names and characteristics of trees, go out in the woods and ask your students to pick a tree to be "theirs." They should gather as much information about their tree as they can. You might ask them to draw it, take measurements, or bring a digital camera to photograph their tree. They might be able to find some loose bark or fallen leaves or acorns from their tree to select as samples. Then, back in the classroom, they will put their information to use. Ask the students to pick partners and blindfold one partner. The first child will describe their tree and ask the other to visualize it. They should describe as many aspects of the tree as they can: color, shape of leaves, fruit or pods, feel of bark. If they have collected any physical specimens, a piece of bark or a leaf, they should allow their partner to feel them and get a sense of them. The partners can then remove their blindfolds and attempt to draw the trees they have been introduced to. This will access spatial, visual, verbal, kinesthetic, and interpersonal intelligences.

Next, ask the students to anthropomorphize their trees. After reflecting on the shapes, sizes, colors, and textures, they should imagine what it would be like if the tree had human characteristics. *Would its voice be high or low? Would it be a slow- or fast-moving tree, if it tried to move?* Models of trees can be made from clay and animated with human features, or children can act out their trees' personality in front of the group. They might also write an illustrated story about their tree and its adventures, tapping verbal and linguistic intelligences.

You may also want to bring slices of trees into your classroom. You can find them at local tree removal businesses or mills. Ask the children to calculate the age of each tree by counting the rings and also ask them to map out a story of that tree's life. You might continue with the anthropomorphizing theme by asking the children to invent stories from the tree's perspective. "In the spring of 1955, we had the most rain of my entire life! I gulped down that water and made over 100 extra pinecones by summer." In this way, you can tap verbal, spatial, logical, and mathematical intelligences. Finally, ask the class to find ways of remembering the names of 20 local species of trees. (You might ask older children to learn the Latin genus and species of the trees.) Small groups can use any techniques they want, but students should be encouraged to try rhythm, songs, and visuals to make the memories "stick." This will tap auditory, rhythmic and musical, and interpersonal intelligences.

Lots of lessons can be adapted to integrate more multimodal stimulation. Activities can be applied to almost any area or discipline of study, including group discussion, journal writing, choreography, constructing timelines, putting on plays, making videos, writing stories, making graphs or Venn diagrams, designing posters, emailing experts, sculpting models, or composing songs. Each of these activities integrates skills that children have across their many intelligences. Using the theory of multiple intelligences, you can engage learners on many levels while at the same time increasing their motivation.

Motivation Propeller 3: Play

Six-year-old Peter squeals with glee as the tribes of ants he has been drawing march toward their helicopters. These are rescue ants, in full gear, ready for any emergency that might come up. "Psheeeeeeeeeew!" he says, furiously scribbling the explosion that will cause an avalanche. In come the ants! "Look out below!" And Peter continues this way for almost an hour, his paper and pencil transformed from things to interactive places. He is not at all concerned with the finished product or what others might think. His imagination has transported him from his bedroom to the depths of the ants' miniscule world.

Play is a wonderfully natural and spontaneous setup for learning. Children have an inclination to play as a means of exploring and being inventive, creative, and curious; it is their chief pastime, accounting for a substantial portion of their time and energy and is endlessly absorbing and exciting for them. The motivational forces of play cannot be overstated. Children and other primates play not because they know it will help them learn, but because they have fun doing it. When it stops being fun, children stop playing. Play is the quintessential feature of childhood, sometimes defined as "that behavior exhibited by juveniles." It is also the central activity during the time in development when humans are at their most receptive to knowledge, making it the ideal vehicle for learning.

Play behavior is rooted in evolutionary adaptation; it is ubiquitous among mammals, seems to exist in birds and fish, and is most frequently found in species that have rich behavioral repertoires. Play is also observed in greater complexity among animals with higher cognitive capacities. In order for this distinct motivational system to have evolved, it must serve important biological functions. Peer play lets members of a species bond with each other and enables them to learn to identify one another, to learn acceptable and successful behavior, and to learn to communicate well. These are all crucial skills for the group's survival. Scientists speculate that juvenile play is practice for adult behavior and even suggest that it represents a virtually irresistible drive to acquire the skills necessary for effective adult functioning. Time to play is perhaps the reason that our extended period of childhood exists at all.

Research shows that animals that take longer to reach maturity also play more. Humans (who take the longest to mature and are the most cognitively advanced) spend many years developing complex, symbolic fantasy play as practice for adult roles and socialization. After studying cultures from antiquity to the 20th century, Dutch historian Johan Huizinga (1971) concluded that playing is the foundation for human civilization, including science, law, sport, and trade. Likewise, Russian philosopher Mikhail Bakhtin (1965, 1984) claimed that all cultural innovations have arisen from some element of playfulness.

Children in all parts of the world quickly develop an overwhelming desire to play. First, infants come to perceive the playfulness of their caregivers in their speech, songs, and caregiving rituals. With the onset of smiling at about 2 months of age, infants become partners in playful exchange. Within the next weeks and months, infants begin to manipulate objects and their bodies by sucking, waving, or banging repetitively in exploration. From 6 months of age and beyond, infants spend much of their waking time using their mouths and hands to explore and maneuver objects, including relating two or more objects to understand their unique functions and properties. Young children who engage in more object-oriented play are more successful at simple tool tasks than those who engage in playing with fewer objects (Gredlein & Bjorklund, 2005).

The similarities in object manipulation observed in human and nonhuman primates are striking, suggesting that these behaviors have an evolutionary basis. However, around 1 year of age children's play diverges from that of other primates, becoming more intentional and symbolic. Children begin with imitative play and then move toward more social forms of playing, such as turn taking and role-reversal games, and finally to social-fantasy play, which is uniquely human. Humans are also the only species who plays throughout life, resulting in continued behavioral flexibility and learning.

Play is first and foremost a voluntary activity and by definition involves freedom from clear functions and goals. Children and animals are highly motivated to play because they enjoy it, and that is the power of play for cognitive growth. In play, the child can survey a situation and respond in an unlimited number of ways. A child can hypothesize or imagine many possible *new* situations, while creating responses to them (stretching ideas, theories, and behavior patterns). According to Vygotsky (1978) a child's greatest self-control occurs during play, since play requires acting against real-world knowledge. A child must put aside what he or she already knows about a stick to allow it to become a horse, for example. Because playing is by definition liberated from real-world consequences, children in play can be free to experiment and take risks that they might not take in other circumstances. Such risks are crucial to learning.

Play in Social and Historical Context

More than 2,000 years ago, Plato advocated that the children of Greece be given toys and tools to play with as a means of encouraging their development. However, since the Industrial Revolution, the West has had a mixed relationship with the freedom of play. On one hand, it is considered the opposite of work and is thought of as useless economically, socially, and ethically (being associated with laziness and idleness). Pedagogue and writer John S. C. Abbott, in his 1839 *Guide for Youth to Truth and Duty* cautioned, "If you waste your schoolboy years in indolence and play… in all probability, you will not be successful in any business in which you may engage, and you will live and die in poverty and obscurity" (p. 12). Alternatively, early childhood educators and philosophers of education (e.g., Jean-Jacques Rousseau, Maria Montessori, John Dewey, and Rudolf Steiner) have had a strong tradition of valuing play as essential for learning and development.

Recently our relationship with play has become more splintered. While there has been a huge rise in research on play, children's lives at home and school are increasingly structured with the "work" of getting ahead. Parents receive carefully marketed messages that children need preparation in order to be successful in this world, and fill their every waking hour with achievement-oriented activities. According to one estimate, children's free-play time at home has decreased by one third over the last 30 years due to the (false) belief that specified academic preparation will enhance learning in school (Burdette & Whitaker, 2005). Meanwhile, teachers and school boards, in response to the No Child Left Behind Act of 2001, are cutting free time for more focused study on reading and mathematics. Likewise, the number of schools in the United States with at least one recess period has dropped almost 30 percent in the last 20 years. Recess is one of the only times of the school day for children to talk, run, play, and be with their peers with relatively little adult intervention (Holmes, Pellegrini, & Schmidt, 2006). By limiting or eliminating recess, some administrators and teachers believe that they are enhancing children's opportunity to learn, when in fact they are doing quite the opposite. In response to this misunderstanding, the United Nations High Commission for Human Rights has recognized play as the right of every child based on its importance for optimal development (Ginsburg et al., 2007).

Taking away playtime for more formal "academic" activities may directly harm learning, especially in infants and young children. In a telling experiment, Czech developmental scientist Hanus Papousek (1977) taught infants to turn their heads at the sound of a bell. The infants' training began at birth, at 31 days, or at 41 days of age. Those who began training at birth required more days to learn the behavior than those who began training later. Perhaps even more striking, 8- to 16-month-old infants who watched "educational DVDs" designed to enhance the cognitive development of infants (for example, *Baby Einstein* or *Brainy Baby*), had significantly smaller vocabularies (six to eight fewer words for every *hour* spent watching the videos) (Zimmerman, Christakis, & Meltzoff, 2007). Such findings have led media activists to put pressure on the corporations who market videos as being "educational" for infants and toddlers. In 2009, the Disney Corporation admitted that advertising the videos as educational was misleading and potentially harmful to infants. They offered a full refund to anyone who had purchased Baby Einstein videos during the prior five years.

Passive viewing simply does not engage the infants' sensory systems in the manner that actively exploring the world does. Developmental scientists have discovered that merely having the television on in the background while 12-, 24-, and 36-month-olds played with their toys led to deficits in both focused attention and the quality of play. The effects occurred even if the toddlers showed no signs of paying attention to the TV (Schmidt, Pempek, Kirkorian, Lund, & Anderson, 2008). If we actually allow infants and children the time and space to play, we will find them engaged in testing out ideas and hypotheses that involve imagination and creative fancy; we will find them making rules (which can be changed), and having fun. They will make choices and decisions, negotiate, use ideas and imagination, show independence in thought and action, sustain physical and intellectual engagement, and experiment and investigate with ideas and objects. In other words, playing children exhibit all of the cognitive skills that we consider desirable.

Child-Directed Free Play

Some play advocates have implied that instructors should guide children's play as a means of improving its quality or justifying it as preparation for more productive use of their time. On the contrary, research suggests that *unstructured* free play is especially important for learning. Children's performance on skills differs tremendously when they are left alone to play. In one series of experiments by developmental scientists at the University of Minnesota, preschool children showed significantly less sophisticated language skills when they were playing in a group that included adults. When the same children were allowed to play with only peers, their language was more advanced, more explicit (had more clearly defined pronouns, for instance), and was structured more like a narrative (using more causal and temporal conjunctions like "and then" and "because"). Such language corresponds to higher performance on tests of early literacy. In these studies, children's use of fantasy in play was also more advanced when the adults left them alone. They were likely to take on a wider variety of roles, including playing adults and the teacher (Pellegrini, 1984, 1985; Pellegrini & Galda, 1993).

Children's conversations with adults are less likely to lead to learning, because children are much less likely to question or challenge adults. Researchers posit that when young children are interacting with adults, the adult often does the work of keeping the interaction going. This is especially true when the child struggles socially. Unfortunately, socially struggling children are the ones who tend to want to spend their time with adults on the playground.

The importance of child-directed play cannot be overstated. Play is more advanced when children take the lead. In one study, 1- to 2-year-old toddlers were observed for complexity of symbolic play while playing by themselves or with their mothers. The results indicated that while symbolic play increased during collaboration, mothers who gave directions or offered other instructions had children with significantly less complex symbolic play than mothers who let their children take charge (Fiese, 1990). In another important study, kindergarteners recalled classroom activities from the previous day (including listening to stories, singing, building with blocks, drawing, planting seeds, baking bread, and eating a snack) and were asked whether each was "classroom work" or "classroom play." All activities assigned by the teacher, including building with blocks or singing, were considered "work" by the children. Even those activities that were voluntary but directed by the teacher were called work. The only activities that were considered play were those that the children directly controlled (King, 1979). If we are extra-sensitive to children's cognitive, social, and emotional needs for free play, we will allow them the pleasures of creativity, spontaneity, independence, and the sense of power. Children who play more are happier. They relate better to their peers and have more fun. They also engage more fully in the classroom and do better in school.

Social critics have pointed out the contradictions in spaces claimed to be set up for children's play but actually designed to serve adults' needs. One research team noticed that at Walt Disney World, imaginative play was not only missing from the environment supposedly designed for children but actually *disallowed.* For instance, children who spontaneously began the Mexican Hat Dance on the steps of the Mexico Pavilion's attraction stairway were quickly stopped by park staff and literally steered back into line (Kuenz, Willis, & Waldrep, 1995). Even well-intentioned adult overtures may harm children's freedom to play.

To ensure that adults do not interfere with children's autonomy and freedom (and therefore their learning), Danish preschools often have a room that is only for children with no adults allowed. Whenever I mention this to my students, they panic, images from *The Lord of the Flies* swirling in their heads. Most fear that the children will hurt themselves or others and be unable to handle the conflicts that will inevitably arise. Japanese early childhood educators tend to concur with the Danish. From their perspective, even physical conflicts (like grabbing and pulling toys away from one another) can be valuable learning experiences for young children. Children, they believe, need to be *kodomo-rashii* (which translates to "childlike") first and foremost, and the point of school is to let them learn about the complexity of being social. They argue that nonintervention in physical fights gives children an opportunity to work out their differences without interference, whereas intrusion by adult teachers denies them that opportunity (Tobin, Hsueh, & Karasawa, 2009).

Play and Cognitive Development

It is enormously important for us to recognize that children's cognition develops primarily through play. Vygotsky (1930/1978) claimed that play not only contains all of a child's developmental tendencies in condensed form, but also serves as a source of development in and of itself (because children in play often behave in a manner way beyond their actual age). As children learn to interact with other people and the environment, they also learn to think. Play is related to higher reading levels and IQ scores, and to greater creativity and imagination. Kindergarteners' behavior during free play at recess predicts their academic success in first grade (Hirsh-Pasek & Golinkoff, 2003).

Using a research procedure originally designed for chimpanzees, developmental scientists have discovered that free play enhances problem-solving skills in children. In the experiment, children are brought into a room with sticks that can be joined together to make longer sticks. The children are given no instructions whatsoever, except that they may touch the sticks. After this free-play period, they are then given one or more problems, the solution to which necessitates joining the sticks together to create an extending tool. Results indicated that free play with the sticks made it possible for the children to solve the problems (at times even more effectively than when they were given directions). The more complex their play with the objects beforehand, the more complex the problems children could solve (Cheyne & Rubin, 1983).

In another classic experiment, one group of preschool children was given the opportunity to free-play with four types of objects (paper clips, paper towels, a screwdriver, and a wooden board). A second group was asked to imitate an adult using the objects in obvious functional ways. A third group did not see the objects at all and was simply asked to draw anything they wanted. The children were then asked to come up with ideas for how the objects might be used. Those in the free-play group came up with more totally new and different ideas for each object than those in either of the other groups, indicating that their playful activity fostered creativity (Dansky & Silverman, 1973).

In a third interesting study, a pediatrician and researcher gave a box of wooden building blocks to preschool children from both middle- and low-income families and asked their parents to keep a log of how often the child played with them. Incredibly, after 6 months, the children scored significantly higher on tests of language development than a similar group who received no blocks (Christakis, Zimmerman, & Garrison, 2007).

Play and Socioemotional Development

Free play can act as a buffer to stressful events and anxiety. In one compelling study, preschoolers watched films that were designed to evoke stress and anxiety. Researchers measured their levels of emotional distress (both behaviorally and physiologically) before and after playing, and then compared them with a control group who had not seen the films. The children showed a marked decrease of anxiety after playing, and their play behaviors were related to the events they had watched (as compared with controls). This indicates that playing allowed them to express and thereby reduce their stress and negative emotions. The same researchers examined this phenomenon in a more real-life situation: the transition to preschool. Specifically, they observed 3-year-olds on the first day of preschool and categorized them (based on their behaviors) as high or low anxiety. The children were then allowed either to play freely or to sit and listen to a story. High-anxiety children who chose free play had a greater reduction in anxiety as compared to the other groups. Their play was also more imaginative and solitary than the other groups, indicating that children use creative free play as a conflict resolution mechanism (Barnett, 1984; Barnett & Storm, 1981). Finally, in a striking longitudinal study, adults from impoverished backgrounds were better adjusted socially if they had had opportunities for free play in their schooling (Schweinhart & Weikart, 1997). Nothing can compare to free play as an instrument of learning, least of all formal instruction.

Neurological research indicates that the motivation to play (and in turn, to learn) is deeply rooted in our biology. Play prepares the brain to handle the unexpected and may contribute to healthy brain development. This becomes clear when we examine animal models for human behavior. In one study, rodents placed in environments with running wheels and other play structures showed greater brain development and intelligence than rodents who did not have such opportunities to play (Dugatkin & Rodrigues, 2008). Play behaviors also seem to promote neural development in the higher brain areas (those involved in emotional reactions and social learning). For example, animals that are not allowed to play during youth display social, emotional, and cognitive deficits as adults, compared with those raised normally (Pellis & Pellis, 2007). Likewise, juvenile animals raised with an adult (who they could see, hear, feel, touch, but not play with) showed deficits on tests of cognitive and social functioning. If they were allowed to play with a peer for just one hour per day, no deficits occurred (Einon, Morgan, & Kibbler, 1978).

Remember:

▶ Play is children's prime motivator.

▶ Play enhances self-control and experimentation.

▶ Play enhances children's learning in school much more effectively than formal academic preparation.

▶ Taking away recess and free play harms children's cognitive development.

▶ Play promotes brain development.

How to Enhance Classroom Motivation Using Play

▶ *Develop pedagogies of play.*

Volumes of evidence in developmental science research have shown us that children learn best when they play. With no fundamental difference between playing and learning, the classroom should primarily be a place for exploration, freedom, and creativity. You can use your own creativity as a teacher to find the fun in lessons, transform schoolrooms into play spaces, and encourage children's imagination during learning exercises. Carefully observe children's play expressions and look for opportunities to support or scaffold learning. According to developmental scientists, children should be given opportunities during the school day to engage in both solitary and social play activities, ideally with partners on different developmental levels from themselves. The classroom can provide the space for free play with complete autonomy, while also allowing for activities that children may not otherwise be allowed to do (activities usually engaged in by the opposite gender, for example) and play with partners whom they would not choose on their own (partners of different ages, for instance).

The freedom of playing is a wonderful vehicle for learning because it is self-determined and self-motivated. Psychologists speak of intrinsic motivation (desire that comes from within us, rather than being imposed from the outside) as leading to the most effective, highest-quality learning (Deci, 1972). In order for intrinsic motivation to develop, an individual's actions must be free. Such freedom develops in children only if certain basic needs, such as feelings of autonomy, of competence, and of relatedness, are met.

Begin every new unit or lesson with a session of free play. If you are setting up a science unit on vision, for example, before you begin any formal instruction, fill a table with visual optics objects—magnifying glasses, prisms, plastic models of the eye, old pairs of glasses with different lenses—and just let the children explore them. Another table might be wallpapered with images of optical illusions, views of the solar system via telescope, or close-ups of animals with vastly different-looking eyes. You might have some themed music in the background or project the night sky on your classroom ceiling. If you avoid structuring every second of the day, you might be surprised at the creative responses to new materials that the children come up with. Being allowed to play with tools before being asked to use them not only fosters enhanced problem-solving skills but is also a lot more fun!

▶ *Avoid the high-stakes academic approach with young children.*

Intense approaches to academics are counterproductive for young children. The pressure places them at both short-term risk (e.g., stress, fatigue, loss of appetite, decreased efficiency, psychosomatic ailments) and longer-term risk (e.g., reduced motivation for learning, minimized self-directed learning, harmful social comparisons of intelligence). Attempts to enhance young children's intelligence through vigorous instruction, sometimes beginning in infancy, can be quite harmful. Parents and teachers who feel that children's intelligence needs to be formally sculpted seem to be misinterpreting the research evidence. Developmental science has clearly shown us that the young mind has evolved to be an elegant and efficient system to which learning is as natural as growing.

For example, there are no lasting differences in intelligence between children who go to academically oriented preschools and those who do not. When preschool is viewed as a preparation for kindergarten, the curriculum becomes more adult directed and sedentary as opposed to child directed and filled with play (Egertson, 2003). According to one study, the advantages that children gained in an academically intense preschool (e.g., knowledge of letters, numbers, and shapes) had fallen to baseline levels by the end of kindergarten. However, the negative effects, such as test anxiety, lack of creativity and a dislike of school, were lasting. Students who attended high-stakes school programs as young children experienced more stress, disliked school more, were less creative, and had more test anxiety than their counterparts in less rigorous programs. Any academic benefits gained had equally compelling costs in terms of motivation (Hyson, Hirsh-Pasek, & Rescorla, 1989).

Let the children know that there is much more to school and learning than grades. Notice areas that they are excelling in naturally, and comment on them. For example, *I heard that you were the star kickball player at recess today! Nice job!* Or *That was a hilarious joke that you told during lunch!* When you are making specific assessments of their learning, clarify what the goals of the lesson are in advance, and then reflect with them on whether or not they have met those goals. You might say, *When I planned this lesson, I wanted to make sure that you know the location of the planets in the solar system and how they move together. If I pointed to a planet, would you know which one it was? Can you show me?* Lowering the stakes on most lessons can allow children to develop a more playful attitude toward school, keep their motivation up, and let them learn more.

▶ *Give students choices in both the process and content of learning.*

Children learn best when they have choices. One way to emphasize choice over control is by letting student interests guide the curriculum. Allowing your students to create their own learning goals, and thus to glean their own meaning out of activities, assignments, and free time, sets up a classroom that blurs the lines between work and play. The Montessori education method, for instance, allows children control by making interesting, useful, and captivating materials and spaces that can catch the child's attention. Freedom and choice are not risks in this model—anything that the child chooses to do will be productive and foster learning. The role of the teacher becomes like that of a conductor, bringing together the pieces into a melodic whole (Csikszentmihalyi, 1997b).

Whereas teachers and school boards typically decide in advance what knowledge children should receive based on their age, emergent curriculum is the technique of letting topics for study arise out of student interests and actions. Curriculum becomes what actually happens, rather than what was planned to happen. After all, children design their own "curriculum" all the time, simply by playing in, exploring, and studying the world. In schools inspired by the Italian Reggio-Emilia approach, all lesson plans are tentative and open to change. Reggio-Emilia teachers believe that the interests and inquiries of the child are of equal value to those of a teacher or school board, and therefore let the students invent the topics of study. You can do this by carefully observing and documenting the children's responses to events around them. Then, design instruction from the bottom up. For example, if you notice a construction project going on across the street from the school, bring the children outside to watch the big machines at work. This could lead to a lesson on machines or demolition or local architecture or the layers of dirt underneath them, all depending on what the children show interest in. Reggio-Emilia teachers allow students to work at their own pace, in their own way (rather than by the clock), and to redirect themselves if they are disengaged. The result is a love of learning and an explosion of motivation (Wurm, 2005).

When students feel a sense of control over their own learning process, a much wider range of learning can occur. Furthermore, the brain's cortex becomes more fully functional when an individual exercises choice and empowerment (the cortex is the seat of high-level, meaningful thought processes, including problem solving, creativity, analysis, synthesis, critical thinking, and decision making). Research has shown that students who believe that their learning experience is beyond their control exhibit less cortical activity. In this case the limbic system, which manages simpler skills (e.g., those used for routine), takes over (Caine & Caine, 1994; Erlaur, 2003).

Let the children design their own curriculum. It can be done with even the youngest students and within the framework of very rigid content standards. First grade teacher Lin Frederick has very successfully integrated student-led curriculum into her classroom of 6-year-olds (Nelson & Frederick, 1994). She scaffolds the selection of themes, guiding questions and instructional activities over two weeks with the study of each unit overlapping with the design of the next one.

To use her method, first identify possible topics for the lesson. For example, you might suggest ancient Egypt, local insects, jazz music, or whales. Make sure that the themes you choose sound interesting to the class and that they build on previous classroom experiences and feed future ones. Next, present the themes to the children and provide lots of materials to explore each of them, including books, magazines, and websites. Spend the first week researching and discussing with your class the potential themes, gauging what they already know about the topics and what they are most curious about.

Help the children formulate guiding questions for what they want to learn about. You might develop a specific timeline and outline the sequence and scope of the unit. Ask the children how they would approach answering their guiding questions (including sources they might use, games they could play, and ways they can remember information) to design specific learning activities. Prompt students to think through their suggestions using think-aloud statements. For example, when one of Frederick's students suggested that they could do experiments to learn the names of types of whales, she responded, "Let's think about some experiments we could do to learn the names of whales." The children discussed this and concluded that experiments really weren't the best method of learning the names of whales, and they were guided toward considering more appropriate options (Nelson & Frederick, 1994, p. 74). Designing the curriculum itself is a powerful experience in problem solving, not to mention a major boon to creative, playful engagement.

▶ *Encourage students to generate their own strategies for solving problems.*

Children who come up with their own ways of working through problems learn more deeply. Too much procedural input from the teacher, including the use of "learning tools," can interfere with learning. In one interesting study, 3rd graders were taught an organizational strategy in order to enhance their memories. The researchers found that the mental effort that the children had to expend to use the strategy reduced their mental capacity for the test and did not significantly help their memories at all (Bjorklund & Harnishfeger, 1987).

Problem-based learning is an active-learning strategy in which the curriculum is designed around real, open-ended problems that are approached in small groups, with the teacher as an advisor on the side. Students learning this way are forced to draw upon their own existing knowledge and to investigate the problem to satisfy their own "need to know" (Gordon, Rogers, Comfort, Gavula, & McGee, 2001). In one study, elementary students who used a problem-based learning approach were more curious, thoughtful, engaged, and motivated than peers studying the same science unit in a traditional way (Drake & Long, 2009).

Turn a real-life dilemma into a problem-based learning lesson. Let's say that your students are interested in a class pet. The problem might be that you have to first get the permission of the school administration and each student's parents. The job of the small groups could be to design a persuasive presentation (in the form of a "white paper," a pamphlet, or a poster) directed to parents and administrators. The presentation should specify issues surrounding animals in classrooms. Your groups may want to detail the advantages (e.g., a sense of responsibility) and disadvantages (e.g., the risk of allergies) of animals in schools. They should be sure to cover any logistics that will need to be in place with a class pet (e.g., licenses or plans for school vacations) and to make specific recommendations. The key to problem-based learning is letting the student groups develop their own approaches and strategies for solving the problem. Children will develop flexibility with their own and other's ideas, and will learn to allow room for movement, to listen, to think together, and to play with possibility.

Motivation Propeller 4: Joining the Community

Ten-month-old Diego has been learning Spanish since his ears began hearing sounds, when his mother was only 6 months pregnant. Now he smiles when she smiles and follows the melody of her voice to know when it's time to relax or to get excited. He is also learning to listen when she talks and to babble and coo when she's quiet; they take turns and have little "conversations" all day long. He isn't trying to learn language but just loves the soothing voice of his mother, and he will do any charming necessary to get one of her warm smiles.

Perhaps the greatest motivator and set-up for learning is the one we notice the least because it is so seamlessly embedded in our daily lives—our desire to join the community. Humans have been evolving for over two million years, and living in social groups has been paramount to our species' survival. Like other primates, humans are inherently social, living in complex organizations such as tribes, families, and nations. Social interaction has allowed us to establish complex ways of being together—to develop rituals, value systems, social norms, and artistic expressions, to name a few. Humans have evolved within communities, and the desire to be part of those communities is among our most basic needs. In fact, many neuroscientists now consider the human brain to be primarily a "social tool," meaning that our cognitive skills have adapted for and function in the service of social relationships.

The desire for community joining is so deep a motivator to learn that our lasting learning often occurs without our even noticing. As pioneering education researcher Frank Smith has pointed out, "You learn from the company you keep. You don't learn by consciously modeling yourself on the company you keep or by deliberately imitating other people. You become like them" (1998, p. 9). In other words, most learning is not hard and purposeful, as we tend to characterize it. We are constantly learning and have acquired virtually all of our knowledge effortlessly, including knowledge about who we are, how our (many) worlds function, and how to navigate them. In hunting-gathering societies like the !Kung or the Hazda, children learn through socializing, playing, watching, and slowly doing. All skills are acquired via experience with virtually no formal teaching. The children in turn are not asked to prove what they have learned by explaining or writing; they simply show their learning by doing (Bruce, 2005).

Daily events in our lives can reveal the power of motivation for learning and the power of community joining for motivation. Recently, we were trying to interest our son, Alexei, in new, healthy foods. Feeding after feeding, his dad and I put spoonfuls of healthy vegetables in his mouth, only to have him spit them all over the high-chair tray, practically gagging. We tried sweet potatoes for lunch, but he refused. Several minutes later, we had the same sweet potatoes on our plates and were having a "picnic" lunch on the floor. Alexei wanted so badly to be part of our picnic experience that he reached for forks and napkins, lunging his body forward toward the floor. When I used the tip of my real fork to give him some sweet potatoes, he happily took as many bites as I would give him.

The intense motivational pull of community joining can bootstrap infants and children into new forms of complex learning. For example, the development of walking is a complex motor milestone that involves having enough strength to hold one's body weight on one leg (while the other leg moves forward) and having enough postural control to keep the body centered. This takes a lot of time and effort to learn! But the desire to join the walking community is enough motivation to speed up that learning curve. Research shows that children with older siblings walk significantly sooner than those without, regardless of their height, weight, or gender (Berger, 2006). Walking tends to start at about the same time that infants begin to understand and benefit from access to the social world.

Language Users:
The Ultimate Community to Join

The most powerful example of learning as community joining is the development of language. Spoken language has been coined "the crowning glory of our species." It separates us from animals by allowing us to mentally transcend the here and now. It also affords such complex cognitive skills as symbolic thought and representation. Some developmental scientists believe that thinking itself is only possible due to the representational functions inherent in language.

Learning one's native language as an infant is no small task, and yet it is not directly taught. Developmental scientist Jenny Saffran of the University of Wisconsin describes it this way: "Imagine you are faced with the following challenge: You must discover the underlying structure of an immense system that contains tens of thousands of pieces, all generated by combining a small set of elements in various ways. These pieces, in turn, can be combined in an infinite number of ways, although only a subset of these combinations is actually correct. However, the subset that is correct is itself infinite. Somehow you must rapidly figure out the structure of this system so that you can use it appropriately early in your childhood" (2003, p. 110). Indeed, learning language requires remembering and correctly using a vocabulary of some 80,000 lexical items (words or phrases that convey a single meaning). This includes learning the collection of sounds in one's native language, called phonemes (English has about 44 phonemes; some languages of the world have up to 141). It also includes remembering a set of rules for combining phonemes sequentially in order to form words (of which the average child learns about 20 per day from birth through adolescence!) Finally, learning language involves understanding a set of meanings for those words, a set of rules combining these words into sentences, and a set of rules relating sentences to larger meanings. Once a child has mastered the information and skills, he or she has the ability to understand and speak an infinite number of sentences.

Remarkably, infants from all parts of the world learn to talk effortlessly and at approximately the same time. By about 3 years of age, children speak their native languages in all of their complexity, including all distinctive sound sequences, words that reference abstract ideas or entities, and novel sentences that involve many types of constructions. This is especially striking considering the huge differences in cultural practices around the world, and considering that the languages of the world vary tremendously in terms of phonology, semantics, and grammar (the structure of some languages being significantly more complex than others). But even more striking is the fact that infants learn all of this with very little, if any, explicit instruction!

There are two aspects of the infants' community that support the development of language: first, people around infants engage them in rich, structured speech; second, people around infants constantly communicate with each other. Language begins as an exploratory activity and evolves as a cooperative process between an infant and proficient language users. The desire to join the language-using community actually begins before birth. Infants pick up the linguistically relevant features of their auditory environment in the womb. For example, in one study second- and third-trimester fetuses showed differences in heart rate in response to the presentation of various vowel sounds (Fifer & Moon, 1994). Newborns prefer sounds they have perceived in utero, including, for instance, their mother's voice, a melody, a story read aloud by their mother, and the tone and rhythmicity that are characteristic of their native language (Mehler, Dupoux, Nazzi, & Dehaene-Lambertz, 1995).

People engage newborn infants in a way that is very specific and very informative. Without even realizing it, they are enticing infants to join their community! Parents and nonparents, adults and children from around the world all talk to infants, even though infants cannot yet understand. They put their faces close to infants, look directly at their faces, and make bids for interaction with them. Moreover, they do so in an interesting way: they exaggerate the melody of their speech by elevating the pitch, elongating the vowels, and increasing the rhythmicity. Adults and children also simplify their linguistic information when talking to infants; they use shorter utterances, repeat words, and use simpler constructions of meaning. They exaggerate their facial expressions and gestures, and slow down their actions, both verbal and nonverbal (Fernald, 1989; Kitamura, Thanavishuth, Burnham, & Luksaneeyanawin, 2002). My son Alexei, who is just learning to talk, already raises the pitch of his little voice when talking to babies, dolls, or the ants that have invaded our kitchen. Why do people engage in this type of specific exchange (often called "baby-talk" or "infant-directed speech") with someone who can't even understand them?

Adults may use infant-directed speech, facial expression, and gesturing because infants are small, helpless, and cute. Because they love them, caretakers become emotional in the presence of their infants and thus express themselves in a way characteristic of positively and emotionally aroused individuals. (Think of couples in love that talk to each other in sweet, "baby-talk" voices or the way in which someone's pitch goes up when they share exciting news.) Another reason adults might adjust their speech when addressing infants is that when infants actually do begin to talk (or even to babble), *their* voices are small and high pitched. Adults adjust their own voices to match the anticipated response from the infant. Adults also match the small voices of little children who *can* talk (that is, they speak to them in infant-directed speech). Finally, people may talk to infants this way simply because they have seen and heard other people throughout their lives do the same (although that does not explain how the phenomenon began). Whatever the initial reason, once adults begin to use exaggerated speech, facial expressions, and gestures, they will likely continue to do so because infants love it! When spoken to this way, infants focus their attention, widen their eyes, and smile, laugh, or nod. Thus, a reciprocal relationship forms between the infant and the caretaker. Each one behaves in ways that gives the other a pleasing response, in a dynamic communicative exchange that influences both (Cooper & Aslin, 1990; Fernald & Kuhl, 1987).

Not only do people engage and talk to infants, but they also engage and talk to each other. The environment of the human species is incredibly communicative. Language is our link to both social experience and learning. Thoughts themselves come to be comprised of words, and over time it becomes impossible to describe the detailed contents of nonlinguistic thought. Infants and children pay attention to language structure and content in every circumstance, actively trying to become competent partners in the community.

Infants so deeply desire to join the talking club that they become expert listeners to the complicated stream of speech. An interesting study showed that newborn infants cry with an intonation pattern that reflects the language they heard in the womb. French newborns tended to cry with rising melodies, and German newborns tended to cry with falling ones (Mampe, Friederici, Christophe, & Wermke, 2009). In addition to growing sensitive to melodies of speech, young infants develop very sophisticated mechanisms for understanding the specific sound patterns of their native language simply by being immersed in it. Although none of us remembers doing this, by 8 months of age, we as infants perceived the statistical structure of our language (the likelihood that certain sounds would come before or after other sounds or would be found at the beginning or end of a word). This information allowed us to know where one word ended and another began, since word boundaries are not delineated by pauses when people speak. For example, in the phrase "pretty baby" the child must discern that "pretty" and "baby" are words, and that, say, "tyba" is not. In English, the syllable *pre* comes before only a small set of syllables (including *-tend*, *-ty*, and *-cede*); the probability that *pre* is followed by *ty* is roughly 80%; whereas the probability that *ty* is followed by *ba* in English is only .03% (Saffran, 2003). This is just one powerful decoding mechanism that infants learn without being taught. In fact, if developmental scientists hadn't made us aware of statistical learning, it is doubtful that any of us would have recognized the need to learn to segment the speech stream, never mind understand how to do it! In any case, the daily life of the infant (including active listening to sounds) is nested within the linguistically rich environment provided by the caretakers and the community at large. Language learning is highly adaptive to the helpless infant. By joining the community, the infant accomplishes the job.

Learning to Read as Community Joining

While language emerges before entering formal schooling, learning to read most often occurs within the context of a strict educational curriculum. However, reading too can be achieved seamlessly when couched in motivation for community joining. Six-year-old Scout, the heroine of Harper Lee's classic novel *To Kill a Mockingbird,* was reprimanded on the first day of first grade for already knowing how to read and was told to stop because it would interfere with her learning to read properly. But she was never actually taught to read:

I never deliberately learned to read, but somehow I had been wallowing illicitly in the daily papers. In the long hours of church—was it then I learned? I could not remember not being able to read hymns. Now that I was compelled to think about it, reading was something that just came to me, as fastening the seat of my union suit without looking around, or achieving two bows from a snarl of shoelaces. I could not remember when the lines above Atticus's moving finger separated into words, but I had stared at them all the evenings in my memory, listening to the news of the day, Bills To Be Enacted Into Laws, the diaries of Lorenzo Dow—anything Atticus happened to be reading when I crawled into his lap every night. Until I feared I would lose it, I never loved to read. One does not love breathing (Lee, 1960, p. 19)

Boston College developmental and evolutionary psychologist Peter Gray writes that children can learn to read with the same unawareness and ease that they learn to speak; his youngest brother and son learned to read completely unintentionally by joining communities of readers. For example, at the alternative Sudbury Valley School (where students are free all day, every day to do whatever they wish within a participatory, democratic community), "there are no formal reading lessons; children learn to read because reading is a valued part of their social environment. They see other children reading and hear them talking about what they have read, so they want to read. They play games that involve the written word. Adults and teenagers read to them enthusiastically. They want to hear the same books over and over again until they have memorized them, and then they playfully 'read' the books they have memorized until their pretend reading turns into real reading" (Gray, 2009, para. 16). In other words, children learn to read by joining a community of readers and by spending time with books. They are not learning to read because they desire to be literate—they are simply enjoying the stories. Learning to read is a by-product.

As mentioned earlier, an important characteristic of human development is that developing organisms begin to do things before they can fully do them. Reading can begin as exploration and evolve as a cooperative process between the interested child and the proficient language user. This was clear when my son Alexei was 1 year old. He began "reading" his favorite book, *Goodnight Gorilla*, on his own: he flipped through the pages the way we always have together and exclaimed "Ahhh!" on the page that the zookeeper's wife realizes there is a gorilla in her bed! Hundreds of shared experiences with that book had begun to bootstrap Alexei into the culture of readers. In this case, the experienced reader served as vicarious mind until the new learner could master his own action through consciousness and control.

Vygotsky (1930/1978) termed the discrepancy between what children can do alone and what they can do with assistance the *zone of proximal development.* In terms of both language development and reading, learners co-construct new capacities in cooperation with more learned partners in a rich, structured environment. First, someone in the community shows you what can be done, then helps you with whatever you want to do for yourself. As you become more skilled and more knowledgeable, you can participate more competently and independently in the desired arena and in new arenas as they emerge (Smith, 1988). From birth, children are highly motivated to join their ambient communities. Learning springs from joining in, and children come with an unquenchable urge for both. Like the cartoon characters in the film *Who Framed Roger Rabbit?* (who cannot resist chiming in with "Two bits!" when they hear the musical couplet "Shave and a haircut…"), my daughter Sonia's extreme desire to participate in *The Bumblebee Song* by squeezing and opening her little fingers to the music and singing "Buzz buzz buzz, Ba-buzz" can trump any other situation: getting hurt, falling asleep, or even feeling sick. She wants to participate and make contributions. Children's learning has more breadth, depth, and permanence when the information and skills have a purpose and function or are embedded in the meaningful context of their everyday lives.

Remember:

▶ Our brains and cognitive skills have developed in the service of social relationships.
▶ Community joining is a premier motivator.
▶ Joining the community bootstraps children, seamlessly, into learning the most complex skills of their lives, including language use and reading.

How to Enhance Classroom Motivation Using Community Joining

▶ *Create a learning community in the classroom.*

A learning community is a place where all participants are active and responsibility is shared. Students come to learn via collaboration with their peers and with their teachers. To begin to build a learning community, create an environment in which students feel secure and comfortable both physically and emotionally. First, get to know your students and help them to get to know one another. Set up a social context that encourages collaboration, in which asking questions and seeking help are appreciated. Empower your students rather than overpowering them with rules. In a learning community the teacher is required to hand over some of the control of the classroom to the students. But the good news is that if the students feel empowered and part of a club or community, they will be more likely to monitor themselves when it comes to both academic and social matters.

Hold a regular class community meeting. This is a wonderful way for the students to get to know each other better and to bond as a group. First, set aside about 20–30 minutes at the same time each week. Begin your first meeting by collaboratively establishing some ground rules for the year (for example, listening attentively, showing respect, avoiding side conversations, saying "pass" if you don't want to talk). You might also want to designate a gesture that can bring the group back in control if needed.

At each meeting announce a prompt for sharing. For example, go around the circle and take turns finishing sentences such as *One thing I like about our classroom is* _____ or *One good thing that happened to me recently is* _____ or *I'm bigger than a* _____. *I'm smaller than a* _____ (Gibbs, Rankin, & Ronzone, 2006). Your class meeting can also be a forum for conflict resolution. You might reflect on the previous week and ask students to check in as to how they are feeling about school or their lives outside school. They can feel welcome to bring up things that worked or didn't work (in terms of lessons or relating with one another). If there is a conflict between students, let the group hear multiple perspectives and try to come up with a resolution. Once students realize that their insights and opinions are valued, they will begin to feel part of something larger than themselves. This can have a powerful effect on motivation and learning.

▶ *Use dialogue as much as possible.*

Conversation and reflection are the pillars of critical thinking and cognition. They are at the foundation of empowered learning communities. Greek philosopher Socrates is said to have invented this form of exploratory intellectual discussion, in which questioning brings deeper levels of understanding and ideas become illuminated. As Freire has observed, "only through communication can human life hold meaning.... The teacher cannot think for his students, nor can he impose his thought on them" (1970, p. 63). Participants engaging in collective, supportive dialogue (including young children), learn to put aside their own thinking and listen to the thinking of others. This is a recipe for making them feel valued and heard. The power of shared insight via participation in dialogue is a palpable motivator for community joining.

Incorporate open-ended Socratic seminars into your daily teaching practice. Once your students are in the habit of listening, thinking, and discussing in groups, you can engage them in lively discussions on anything from science to art. The purpose of an open-ended seminar is for the students to deepen their understanding of a "text" (which can be a story, a nonfiction book, a film, or an experience). The outcome of the seminar must not be predetermined. Students may make discoveries as surprising to the teacher as to themselves. The goal is the inquiry process. The teacher should avoid "telling" the students and instead guide the class in the hard work of questioning, deliberating, and searching (Finkel, 2000).

First, find a compelling short text to share—for example, the classic fairytale *Cinderella*. You might begin with reading the text aloud or asking the students to read quietly on their own. They can then work in pairs to develop questions for discussion. Remind them that their questions should be supported with evidence from the text and also might be open to interpretation (an example might be *Why didn't the fairy godmother just change Cinderella's life?*). The children should be encouraged to write down their questions and to mark the parts of the text (with sticky notes) that lend support (Chorzempa & Lapidus, 2009). The next step is sharing the questions and deciding which one to open with. A go-around works well. You might also write questions on the board and decide together which are the most compelling. Then, sitting in a circle (either by moving their desks or on the floor), they can begin a dialogue on the questions and the text. Each child should be encouraged to share his or her opinions and to back them up with evidence. They should build on one another's statements, connecting them to their own experience and to previous lessons. The children will begin to compare their perspectives with those of their peers and of the authors. They will begin to feel that their opinions are important, all the while respecting the views of others, improving their reading comprehension and vocabularies, and learning how to evaluate evidence and make arguments. They will also feel the excitement and energy that go along with a tight-knit intellectual community, which in itself spurs motivation for learning.

▶ *Work within the child's zone of proximal development.*

Vygotsky wrote, "What the child is able to do in collaboration today he will be able to do independently tomorrow" (1934/1987, p. 211). Indeed, children learn best when encouraged to move just slightly beyond what's already comfortable for them. You can create this optimal learning situation by presenting ideas and concepts that are just above your students' current understanding, tasks that require a significant amount of help to complete. Then, by pairing them with peers of different skill levels or scaffolding their budding abilities yourself, encourage them to reach and challenge themselves.

Teach math concepts with board games. For example, to win at backgammon, a player must have an understanding of probability. After presenting the basic rules of the game to your class and letting them play a few times, break them into collaborative teams to figure out the odds of rolling particular numbers (Doolittle, 1995).

First, the students can calculate the probability of rolling a certain number by figuring out all possible outcomes in rolling two dice. Two students from each team can then be responsible for calculating the likelihood of each total using mathematical probability. In this pair, one child might be in charge of determining the number of possible ways that each sum can be rolled, while the other child records the information and calculates the actual probability percentage. The members of the team can be charged with figuring out the probability of each outcome by actually rolling the dice enough times and recording the results. One student in this dyad might roll the dice and sum the tallies, while the other is in charge generating the probability percentage. Then, the student team can come together to compare results and share them with the rest of the class. Finally, the team can play a series of games together, but this time announcing before they roll what sum they would like to get and what the probability is of actually rolling that number (Doolitle, 1995). You can create learning experiences at the top end of the children's zone of proximal development with other challenging games as well. Try cribbage, chess, or mancala next!

▶ *Focus curricula on relevance to students and on applicability to their lives outside school.*

In order to be motivated to learn from school activities, students must see them as meaningful and worthwhile. In other words, they must see a need for learning the material you present. Let children (as valued members of the learning community) bring their ideas and thoughts to bear on new topics. Learning is not something that is reserved for the classroom—children are constantly learning! They also come to the educational setting with a whole range of beliefs and experiences that have been relevant to their lives. If this real-world knowledge becomes the starting point for learning, rather than being treated as irrelevant, lessons will come alive and be better integrated. To connect children with real-world applications and value, be explicit about what they are learning, why they are learning it, and how new knowledge and skills can affect their lives. Being respected as an interesting, knowledgeable member of the community will spur their motivation for learning.

Find out what your students love and what they are excited to master, understand, or comprehend on their own in their lives. For example, if the children in your math class love to skateboard, design and build a half-pipe! In the words of a student whose teacher did just that, "When you're building a half-pipe, everything has to be precise, and you have to do the math to figure out where you need to cut the wood or where you need to put the angles, and there's a lot of math in it. But since we wanted to build the half-pipe, it was a lot easier to do the math for it" ("What Helps Us Learn," 2010, p. 68). Indeed, as developmental science shows, the best possible way to get and keep your students motivated in school is to capture the motivation that they already have, as humans, and as confident and playful children seeking novelty and community.

2

Understanding Children's Attention

at·ten·tion Take a deep breath and notice all of the hundreds of sights and sounds around you, the subtle smells and textures that come and go. Our world is filled with stimulation. We can't possibly take in all of this information all the time, because if we did, we would feel constantly overwhelmed. Attention is the mechanism we use to bring certain things to our conscious awareness and to quiet or ignore others. It is a selection tool and a filter that allows us to focus on what we need to see or hear. On the pathway to learning, after first being motivated, the next step is attention—the orienting of our minds and bodies toward the events and information that interest us. Children's ability to learn depends upon whether they can allocate and sustain focused attention. Traditional wisdom tells us that the longer we spend paying attention to a topic, the more mastery of it we will have. (James, 1890/1983)

It is no surprise then, that children's ability to stay on task, actively participate in learning activities, and pay attention are the most important predictors of their success in school (DiPerna, Lei, & Reid, 2007; Ladd, Birch, & Buhs, 1999). In fact, research has shown that a child's attention capabilities predict his or her developmental level and IQ, problem solving, and language skills (Bono & Stifter, 2003; Choudhury & Gorman, 2000; Lawson & Ruff, 2004).

Attention is a hot topic in the news today. At last count, the Centers for Disease Control and Prevention [CDC] estimated that 1 in 10 American children have been diagnosed with attention-deficit hyperactivity disorder and that more than half of them are regularly medicated (CDC, 2010). Children who were once seen as "fireballs" and "bundles of energy" are now labeled "distractible" and "impulsive." Rather than running around and kicking up their heels, these kids are monitored and medicated for dysfunctional behavior (Armstrong, 1997).

Non-Western cultures have very different requirements of children in terms of attention. Educator Terry Orlick (1982) writes, "If I take my daughter out to eat in North America, she is expected to sit quietly and wait (like an adult) even if there are all kinds of interesting objects and areas and people to explore... if I take her out to a village feast in Papua, New Guinea, none of these restrictions are placed on her. The villagers don't expect children to sit quietly and wait for an hour while orders are taken and adults chat. Children are free to do what is natural for them" (p. 128). It seems that the goals of school are not commensurate with where children are developmentally. Recall that the primary goal of our formal education system (which was set up during the Industrial Revolution and has changed very little since then) was obedience. We need new models of functioning in schools and a broader range of attention possibilities.

One hundred years ago, a group of townspeople would stand in the town square for three hours listening to a politician's platform. Fifty years ago, a nightly news program would feature the anchor sitting in a chair verbally presenting nuanced stories for a full hour. Today's television news programs consist of snippets under seven seconds, flashy graphics zooming in and out, dancing bars on the top and bottom of the screen with previews of upcoming shows, and they are up to 40 percent advertising. Children are besieged with information in a frantic, fast-paced community, which they are trying desperately to join. Our culture is sending them a mixed message: watch and be like us (filling every waking moment with activity and multitasking), but when you are at school, sit still in rows and quietly listen. When children have trouble reconciling these splintered directives, we are quick to anaes-thetize them with medications, shutting off their senses and putting them to sleep. Instead we should be waking them up to the excitement of learning and engagement that all humans have inside of themselves (Robinson, 2010).

To better understand attention and how we can approach it, let's take a step back and look at what we know about attention from a devel-opmental science perspective. Like learning, attention is rather difficult to define. It is the process of transition from sleepiness to alertness, or the change from a focus on a single object to general awareness of a whole scene. We say we are "paying attention" when we are privy to events going on or when we are motivated to achieve a goal (Posner & Rothbart, 2002). We garner attention to concentrate on some aspects of the flood of information that our sensory systems pick up. Attention occurs at varying levels of our beings, in our sensory systems (looking at something), our minds (caring about something), and our nervous systems (maintaining a calm, alert state).

A Developmental Science Approach to Attention

The story of attention begins very early in the individual child's develop-ment and is very much a whole body phenomenon. When we begin to examine how attention develops, we must look to the way that young infants respond to the world. Remember that newborn reflexes help helpless babies to survive—these reflexes are built into the species via natural selection. Reflexes set up ways that the organism functions in response to its environment, and they feed learning as they transform into cognitive processes. Of course we can never separate the body from the mind. At no time is this more apparent than with newborn infants.

One of the fundamental inborn reflexes is the orienting reflex. This response of the subcortical brain regions (those that have existed the longest in our species) allows us to avert danger. Called the "Shto eto takoi?" or "What is it?" response by Russian physiologist Ivan Pavlov, the orienting reflex is at the foundation of attention. As I type this, I am playing white noise for my sleeping daughter, Sonia, to drown out iso-lated sounds from outside her bedroom that might draw her attention. Compelled to orient, every time her brother pulls out a new toy to play with, she becomes aroused and gets further from the sleep she desperately needs. Infants reflexively orient their attention toward new things in their environment and will habituate to repeated presentations of the same objects or events. In a recent study, a group of physicians at a children's hospital in Houston, Texas, discovered that babies who had spent time in the neonatal intensive care unit (NICU) became used to the typical sounds that they heard during their time there. They remembered the sounds of beeping machines, of intercoms, and of the swish of curtain dividers, and they did not show an orienting response to them months later. A control group of infants who had not spent time in the NICU responded very differently to the same sounds, by orienting their attention when recordings of the sounds were presented to them (Barreto, Morris, Philbin, Gray, & Lasky, 2006). The orienting reflex allows young infants to scan their worlds and develops into more deliberate attention skills.

Processing visual information during infancy is one of the strongest predictors of learning in later childhood and adolescence (McCall & Carriger, 1993; Rose & Feldman, 1995; Rose & Wallace, 1985). In a series of studies from the laboratory of UCLA developmental scientist Marian Sigman, visual attention in newborns predicted cognitive development from 5 months of age to 18 years of age (Sigman, Cohen, Beckwith & Parmelee, 1986; Sigman, Cohen, & Beckwith, 1997). By the time a child enters preschool, he or she can choose what to attend to based on goals for action. This selective attention will set the stage for perceiving more and more subtleties.

Attention Propeller 1: Self-Regulation

As her turn grows closer, Nancy can feel her heart begin to race. She can barely pay attention to the words that the other children are spelling, and every sound in the room is suddenly like a buzzing in her ears. Then she remembers to take a deep breath, and she closes her eyes for a split second and feels the warm air release from her lungs. When Mr. Roche reads her word, she slows down and focuses on it. She can see the spelling as if it's on a piece of paper right in front of her. The letters "H-E-I-G-H-T" come from her mouth, and she advances in triumph to the next round.

When we think about attention we need to begin with the body. Paying attention is a prerequisite for all learning, and regulating our bodies—keeping physical arousal calm and stress levels even—propels attention. The autonomic nervous system takes care of states of arousal. In the course of a day we go through many states of arousal: sometimes our arousal is up, our hearts pounding, and other times we are calm, our breath slow and steady. When we are excited or upset, it is very difficult to concentrate. Throughout our lives we have learned (some of us better than others) how to regulate our arousal states by coming back down when we get too amped up and gearing up when we are feeling low. These skills develop slowly over childhood, and infants and children depend on caregivers to regulate their arousal for them before they themselves become able to do it.

Developing Self-Regulation

Last Friday evening we took our infant and toddler out to a lively pub for dinner. It was happy hour and the pub was filled with cheerful folks talking and laughing. We sat in a booth right in the middle of the action. It had been a while since we had gotten out of the house for a social event. Both kids were so well behaved that we were astounded. Alexei toddled from table to table saying hello to people and dancing to the jukebox. When our food arrived, he sat right up in his booster chair and ate every bite. Sonia practically slept through all of the commotion. After this fun and easy night out, we started to imagine ourselves as local socialites. But as soon as we arrived back home, both children had meltdowns, screaming and crying for over an hour. What happened to our little angels?

Infants and young children are adept at communicating their emotions but rely heavily on adults to regulate them. What looked like peaceful sleep at the pub for our baby might have been a response to overstimulation (Brackbill, 1973). Expecting our son to go from the excitement of lights, interaction, laughing, and dancing to the quiet of his bed was too much for his developing nervous system to handle. He needed us to slowly bring his arousal levels down, to decelerate. Also, because it was past his bedtime, his overtired body was likely in a stress response and had started producing adrenaline.

Caregivers often use speech, singing, rocking, and smiling to move their children into states of activity or rest depending on the situation. Evidence from the laboratory shows that emotion regulation from caregivers allows infants to focus their attention. The babies can use the biological information from the other person (e.g., heartbeat and breathing rate) to match with their own arousal states. Feeling soft skin and hearing whispered sounds also soothes infants. In fact, skin-to-skin contact improves attention in preterm infants and has long-term effects on their learning.

Preemies who have been held close to a caregiver's body throughout their early weeks show higher levels of exploratory behavior at 6 months and more advanced cognitive skills up to 2 years of age (Feldman, 2004; Feldman, Eidelman, Sirota, & Weller, 2002). In research studies, crying newborns who were held stopped crying, opened their eyes, and began to scan their environment. Held newborns also track moving objects more alertly compared to newborns not being held (Korner & Grobstein, 1966). With time, infants develop strategies for regulating their own arousal, such as sucking their thumbs and looking away when something is overstimulating (Cole, Michel, & O'Donnell-Teti, 1994). But even in toddlers, maternal emotional support during complex cognitive tasks results in higher levels of attention (Grolnick, Frodi, & Bridges, 1984).

Some infants and children have an easier time than others bringing themselves into the calm, alert state necessary for focusing their attention. A physiological measure called vagal tone is linked to individual differences in attention. The vagus nerve is a part of the peripheral nervous system, which regulates the organs of the body, gearing us up when we need to act quickly and calming us down when we need to rest. Newborn babies who display higher vagal tone also show more advanced cognitive development (Porges, 2003). On the flip side, preterm infants, who tend to be delayed in attention spans and ability to handle stress, also have undeveloped and immature vagal tones. Babies with higher vagal tones process visual information more efficiently and are less distracted during the presentation of visual stimuli, compared to infants with lower vagal tone (Richards, 1987). These babies also show more advanced cognitive skills, higher social competence, and fewer behavior problems as 6-year-olds (Feldman & Eidelman, 2003).

When children develop the ability to regulate their own arousal and emotions, they gain control over their attention, thinking, and learning (Bronson, 2000). By school age, children are expected to manage their emotions, focus on the task at hand, inhibit some behaviors while activating others, and sift through information coming from many sources in the environment (Smith-Donald, Raver, Hayes, & Richardson, 2007). For example, a teacher might say, "Get your papers, put them in your folder, and put your folder in your backpack." In this case the child needs to inhibit a dominant response (to keep working), focus on a new task (putting away work), and remember the directions (Rimm-Kaufman, Curby, Grimm, Nathanson, & Brock, 2009). The ability to self-regulate and pay attention is associated with positive adjustment to school, both socially (being able to follow classroom rules, to remember directives, and to participate in social situations) and cognitively (being able to solve problems and monitor, inhibit, and direct actions) (Blair & Razza, 2007). At-risk children who are skilled at regulating their arousal states and emotions are able to deal with adversity better than their peers without these skills (Buckner, Mezzacappa, & Beardslee, 2003). Self-regulation allows them to guide goal-directed activities over time and across challenging circumstances.

Meditation as Self-Regulation

We often go through our days on a sort of automatic pilot. Children, due to their often hectic lives, also fail to notice what they have passed on the way to destinations, what they have tasted at lunchtime, or what they have heard when talking with their friends. For thousands of years, people in Vedic, Buddhist, and Chinese traditions have sought to purposefully pay attention to the present moment by harnessing emotions and attention (Buddhaghosa, 1979).

Meditation is a state of mental silence characterized by the elimination of unnecessary thought, effortless attention on the present moment, and alert awareness (Srivastava, 1997). Meditation is metacognitive: it necessitates reflection on the functioning of one's own mind. In the practice of mediation, introspection is used to monitor quality of attention, recognize when attention has wandered, and guide it back to the chosen stimulus.

When meditating, we typically focus on one thing, such as the sensation of our breathing in and out (Wallace, 1999). To keep on task, we need to constantly monitor our attention. At first try, attention might seem like a puppy, jumping and running from thing to thing all over the room. When that happens, we recognize the wandering of the mind and try not to judge it. (How can we be mad at that puppy?) Then we try to restore our attention to breathing. If, for example, you were trying to focus on the sensations in your lungs when you breathed deeply, and suddenly you noticed that you had some pain in your back, you would release the distraction and return to your breath. Practicing this way cultivates attention on a single locus of stimulation, but it also develops other attention skills such as monitoring distractions, regulating emotions, and redirecting attention (Lutz, Slagter, Dunne, & Davidson, 2008).

Meditation and the Brain

Brain activity is altered due to the practice of meditation. Meditation increases regional blood flow in the key brain areas for attention and emotions. It also activates the neural structures involved in arousal and autonomic nervous system control. The brains of meditating yogis show increased alpha wave activity (which indicates relaxed alertness) both during quiet meditation and during distracted meditation (Anand, Chhina, & Singh, 1961). In a recent study, meditating Buddhist monks' brains produced much greater amounts of fast-moving, powerful gamma waves than did the brains of meditation novices. Some of the monks produced gamma waves more powerful than any ever recorded (Kaufman, 2005). In another study that used a brain scanner (fMRI) to measure the activity of specific brain regions, researchers compared the brains of Tibetan Buddhist monks with over 54,000 hours of meditation experience with same-aged adults interested in learning to meditate. The trained brains showed increased activation in the prefrontal cortex, a key brain area for attention control and regulation. But even more striking, as the most experienced meditators settled into their practice, their frontal activation decreased, indicating that for them the act became effortless. As experience increased, the impact of distracting sounds on the frontal brain regions decreased. For the most experienced monks, the sounds produced no effect at all (Brefczynski-Lewis, Lutz, Schaefer, Levinson, & Davidson, 2007).

Training Meditation

Anyone can learn to meditate. Research shows that meditation-based training enhances self-regulation. Meditators are better at stabilizing their arousal levels and emotions; they have more even and positive moods, and fewer negative feelings (Wallace, 1999). In a powerful study, the participants were divided in two groups. The first group received mindfulness meditation-based training, and the second received just relaxation training. After five hours of training per day for three months, the meditating group responded to environmental stress with a significantly lower physiological hormone response than their counterparts in the relaxation-only group (MacLean et al., 2010).

Meditation also directly enhances cognitive functioning. In a striking study, short-term meditation training led to large differences in attentional abilities. Specifically, 40 college students were given cognitive tests measuring orienting, alerting, and the ability to pay attention amid distractions. Then they were randomly split into two groups. One group received meditation training for 20 minutes a day for five days. The other just received relaxation training. The meditation group not only showed significantly greater improvement on all cognitive tests, but also had significantly less of the stress hormone cortisol present in their bloodstreams (Tang et al., 2007). In other experiments, students who participated in meditation training daily for one to three months showed improvements in visual discrimination, orienting, and focused attention (Jha, Krompinger, & Baime, 2007). Long-term meditation practitioners show superior sustained attention skills in comparison with average students (Brefczynski-Lewis et al., 2007).

Meditation is a proven attention-training tool for children. In a classic study, 3rd graders from a socioeconomically disadvantaged background were taught to meditate by focusing their minds and disregarding distractions. The children were also coached to ask themselves,

"Where am I (attentionally)?" and if the answer was not "here," to let go of their current focus and return to a target object in the present. This training taught the children how to relax and notice their feelings. It taught them to cope with anxiety during testing by voluntarily changing their arousal states. The children were able to shift their attention from sources of stress (e.g., fear of failing the test) to the flow of their ongoing mind and body experience. These children greatly benefitted from short-term meditation training; their attention and self-regulation improved significantly as determined by scores on measures of word knowledge and reading comprehension (Linden, 1973).

Other recent work has shown that children diagnosed with ADHD and their families can benefit from meditation training. In one study, families participated in a program of 90-minute guided meditation sessions twice a week, with parents attending one group and the children another. The meditation instructors directed both groups to become aware of calm states within themselves by becoming silent and focusing their attention inside. After several weeks, the children showed improvements in their distracted, hyperactive behavior. They also reported better self-esteem and relationship quality, better sleep, and less anxiety. The parents reported feeling happier, less stressed, and better able to manage their child's behavior (Harrison, Manocha, & Rubia, 2004). It was over a hundred years ago that William James (1890/1983) asked how we might educate attention. If we could figure that out, James said, we would have figured out the best education possible. A meditation regimen might just provide a key answer to James's question (Brefczynski-Lewis et al., 2007).

Remember:

▶ In order to focus attention, children must maintain a calm, alert physical state.
▶ The ability to regulate one's own arousal levels develops slowly over childhood with help from caregivers and teachers.
▶ Meditation changes our brains and nervous systems, activating areas that control alertness and calm states.
▶ Practicing meditation can teach children to harness attention and emotions.

How to Enhance Classroom Attention Using Self-Regulation

▶ *Raise emotional awareness and promote self-regulation by providing external supports for behavioral and emotional control.*

Children in elementary school are in the midst of the complex developmental process of becoming self-regulators. For some children, this transition from having others regulate their autonomic arousal to being able to do it on their own is one of the most challenging hurdles of their cognitive and emotional development. Because even subtle improvements in children's self-regulation can produce lasting improvements in their attention and subsequent cognitive achievement, teachers should organize their classrooms in ways that encourage children to know what state they are in and to be able to deliberately shift it if necessary (Howse, Lange, Farran, & Boyles, 2003).

Give children a context and a language for self-regulation. Model for them by saying, "I feel stressed," or "I have lots of energy right now." Ask your students, "Do you need a break right now?" Or, if they are clearly not relaxed, "How can you change your state?" Let them know that it is physically impossible to remain stressed after taking 10 huge, deep breaths. Also, set clear limits and expectations, provide feedback and consistent consequences, and teach other self-regulation strategies such as counting to 10 or progressive muscle relaxation (Goldberg, 2002). In his documentary *Raising Cain* (2006), developmental scientist Michael Thompson features 5th grade teacher Mr. Oteri, who works with Kevin, a charismatic student diagnosed with ADHD. When Mr. Oteri sees Kevin's attention shifting, he says, "Kevin, do you need a walk?" and sends him around the school building so that he can take a break, move around, and then return to his work. With time Kevin begins to understand his own state of arousal and can then tell Mr. Oteri, "I think I need a break."

The secret to raising emotional awareness is practice. Like building muscles in the gym, the more you flex your emotions, the more "emotional muscle" you will build (Helpguide, 2010). Children who practice will become able to change the way they feel, think and act. They will become able to harness their bodies toward better relationships and school performance. As their nervous systems mature, children will be more able to internalize self-regulation strategies.

Ask your class to do an emotion and arousal state assessment before and after an important assignment. You can use a simple tool such as the Self-Assessment Manikin (SAM) (see Figure 2.1) (Bradley & Lang, 1994). This is a chart that helps children directly pinpoint their states of pleasure, arousal, and dominance in response to a particular situation. You might try running a class experiment on the students' emotions throughout the day. Collect your data by asking students to anonymously fill out the SAM after recess, before lunch, or before a quiz. Then collect the sheets and graph the information. When did people feel the most stressed? The most relaxed? What were possible reasons for their arousal and emotional states? Ask the students to propose strategies for calming down when arousal is high or when emotions are low. Ask them to make links with their perceived attention during these times.

Figure 2.1 | **The Self-Assessment Manikin (SAM) Emotion Assessment Tool**

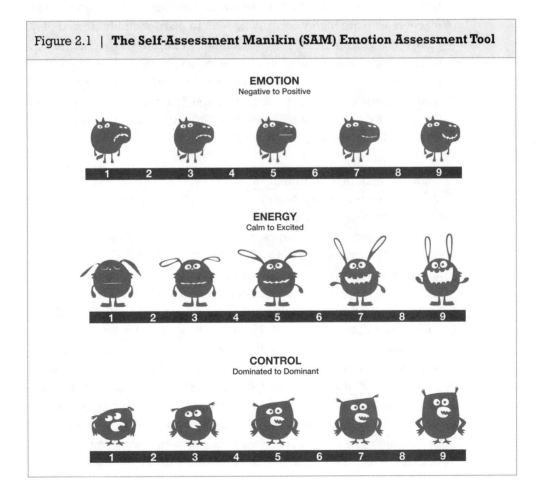

▶ *Be emotionally supportive of your students and avoid excessive micromanaging.*

Both positive affect and praise by adults during dyadic teaching and problem-solving interactions have been linked with persistence at tasks, self-praise, and performance on measures of selective attention in young children (Stipek, Recchia, & McClintic, 1992). Emotional support enhances children's willingness to explore and thus facilitates their engagement with the environment.

In contrast, toddlers of depressed mothers, who are less emotionally responsive and supportive, show depleted focused attention and task persistence (Redding, Harmon, & Morgan, 1990). Parents and teachers who are highly controlling tend to disrupt child-directed play, interfering with spontaneous engagement. Children who become accustomed to adult control of their actions are less able to follow their natural interest in engaging with the environment and, in turn, have more trouble initiating and sustaining attention (Calkins & Johnson, 1998). When adults constantly redirect children's attention, those children's attention levels decline (Bono & Stifter, 2003).

Maintain and build upon children's focus rather than redirecting their attention. Devote a school day to total openness in terms of time. You can take a lesson from preschool settings, and create stations with materials and prompts to facilitate self-directed learning. For example, for a unit on the Roaring 20s, you might have a literary station. Type up quotes and phrases from famous Lost Generation writers' works. Find beautiful lines from Ernest Hemingway, F. Scott Fitzgerald, and Gertrude Stein and put several copies of each out on a table in strips of paper. The students can select lines and juxtapose them into collage poetry. Place the books on the table, too, in case they want to find more lines. Let the children read their poems aloud.

You might also have an art station with images from Salvador Dalí and Pablo Picasso and easels and paints available. Finally, you could have an invention station with images of the technology that was developing in the 1920s and clay, Legos or other sculpting materials, so that the children can model the inventions they find most bizarre or interesting. If children become hooked into any one project, ask them how much time they would like to spend on it. If they seem to be finished, direct them to other possible attention-grabbing activities.

▶ *Guide children in mindfulness and meditation.*

Meditation enhances self-regulation and attention. Meditation also enables the child's mind to become free, to explore, and to bring their imagination to the fore. Once I heard a Japanese kindergarten teacher speaking about her classroom. I was shocked when she said that her 5-year-old students meditate for an hour a day! Her method involved asking the children to close their eyes and to imagine that they were "melting like ice cream" into the floor. After embedding meditation into the classroom, teachers report that children with difficulty concentrating begin to significantly improve (Garth, 1991).

Guide your class in the rainbow meditation (Garth, 1991). First, ask them to relax their bodies by tensing and relaxing each body part, starting with the toes and ending with the top of the head. Next, gather the children and have them close their eyes and begin deep breathing. You might say, "Breathe in to a count of three, hold the breath and breathe out to a count of three. As you breathe, you breathe in fresh energy, love, joy and peace. They are entering and spreading throughout your body. As you breathe out, imagine any negative feelings, sadness, boredom, anger or tiredness coming out through your nose and leaving your body and disappearing" (Garth, 1991, p. 76). With older children you might use counting with breathing: number one with inhale, and one with exhale, number two with inhale, two with exhale, and so on. Once the children's bodies, emotions, and minds are quiet, they are ready for the guided meditation. By using imagery, the children will learn to see themselves on a movie screen in their minds. You can then slowly and quietly begin the rainbow meditation:

Feel your body becoming lighter and lighter. See all the colors of the rainbow. Feel your body becoming all of the colors of the rainbow. Slowly, you are now giving out red color. Your whole body becomes red color. Feel yourself giving out energy and strength. You are now full of energy and strength.

Try doing an Internet search on "rainbow meditation" to find the full script. Finally, end the meditation session with some productive activity. Bring the children's attention to their bodies. Ask them to feel all of their parts—to slowly wriggle their fingers and toes, to rotate their heads. When they are ready, they should slowly open their eyes. You might then direct the children to channel this newly focused energy into the creativity of dance, art, writing, or music, or into the cognitive work of sharing, a class discussion, or an academic lesson.

Attention Propeller 2: Executive Control

Eli cracks jokes and makes faces with the timing of a seasoned comic. Sometimes he bursts out of his seat inappropriately in the middle of a lesson, unable to contain his excitement over a new game or a poster on the wall. He can barely sit still through an hour of math class, never mind focus during our quiet reading period. But when the class takes nature walks, Eli always leads the pack. He can find more hidden bugs, brilliant leaves, or oddly shaped sticks than anyone else, and he makes up elaborate stories with them, complete with silly names and rhyming songs.

Beyond maintaining a calm, alert state, in order to focus our attention we need to be in control of our thoughts and actions. This is the job of the executive system of the brain. Like a little CEO, the executive system integrates information from every part of the brain and body, making sure that all systems are functioning smoothly and efficiently together, and then decides how to respond (Goldberg, 2002; Holler & Greene, 2010). The executive system is sometimes considered the most important cognitive system in the brain. It is associated with the frontal cortex, the most recent brain area to evolve in our species and the area that takes the longest to develop. In fact, the frontal cortex is not completely developed until the third decade of life (Welsh & Pennington, 1988). Executive control enables us to consciously learn, focus, and study using our judgment and reason. It also supports the focus and maintenance of attention, planning, decision making, impulse control, and cognitive flexibility (Müller, Lieberman, Frye, & Zelazo, 2008).

Like many cognitive milestones, executive function develops in fits and starts. In fact, some of the most illuminating research on the development of executive control comes from observing children's "mistakes." For example, young children often overuse plans and rules, and perseverate on inappropriate strategies, even when they have been shown otherwise. In a classic hide-and-seek game called the A not B task, infants of about 8 to 10 months of age are shown an attractive toy being hidden in front of them. They successfully find the toy in the first location (location A). The next time, they watch as the toy is hidden in a new location (location B). Even though they saw the toy being moved to location B, the infants still search in location A, committing the A not B error (Marcovitch & Zelazo, 1999; Piaget, 1954). This response shows classic underdeveloped executive functioning. Although the infants saw the new hiding place, they were unable to shift their attention to it and to inhibit the response that was successful previously. Brain measures during the A not B task show activation of the frontal lobes, as measured by the electrical activity of firing neurons (called electroencephalography, or EEG) (Bell & Fox, 1992).

Executive control develops rapidly during the preschool period (Zelazo & Müller, 2002). Whereas most 2-year-olds perseverate on searching behaviors when looking for hidden toys (including searching where the item was previously hidden), 3-year-olds can reliably switch search locations (Sharon & DeLoache, 2003). Whereas 3-year-olds have difficulty understanding the difference between appearance and reality, 4-year-olds are twice as likely to have the cognitive flexibility to allow an object to look like one thing and be another (Flavell, Green, & Flavell, 1995). (Which is why the old "I got your nose" trick, with the thumb between your first two fingers, is so compelling early on.) Children whose frontal lobes are in an earlier stage of maturation also have great difficulty inhibiting attention to irrelevant information and focusing attention on relevant targets (Ridderinkhof & van der Molen, 1995). Older children improve their ability to deal with interference and to pay attention to two or more pieces of information, as their executive system and supporting brain structures develop (Bunge, Dudukovic, Thomason, Vaidya, & Gabrieli, 2002).

Entering formal school has a positive effect on children's executive control and contributes to the overall age-related changes that we see (McCrea, Mueller, & Parrila, 1999). The hallmarks of executive control in the classroom are clear—children are able to focus, sustain, and shift their attention appropriately to the task at hand; to inhibit competing urges; and to plan ahead and adjust to changes along the way. School gives children routines, helping them to organize and integrate multiple sources of information. The classroom also presents children with new and different situations, which they learn to respond to in appropriate ways, both emotionally and behaviorally. In one experiment, kindergarteners played a game called One of These Things Is Not Like the Others. They were asked to select an odd item from three things, but the test objects were set up in a way that they could not apply the same rule from one trial to the next. Sometimes the odd item would be a different color, other times a different size, and other times a different orientation. Children who did well on this executive function task also scored highest in measures of academic achievement. In this study, executive control predicted academic achievement above and beyond vocabulary level, social skills, and success in kindergarten (George & Greenfield, 2005). A child can have a strong vocabulary, score high on IQ tests, and have terrific social skills, but if that child cannot focus attention, generate solutions to everyday problems, or be flexible when old problem-solving strategies don't work, that child will struggle in school (Goldberg, 2002).

Training Executive Function

Whereas we tend to talk about attention spans as given endowments, bound by genetics or age, recent research indicates that human attention is malleable and responds exceedingly well to training. Practice focusing, sustaining, and dividing attention leads to improved attention skills that go above and beyond those specific tasks. Recently, some important studies have looked at the effects of experience on children's developing executive control and attention. One group of developmental scientists created a five-day attention training for 4- to 7-year-olds (who are in the midst of major development in the executive control brain centers). The children learned to use a joystick in a computer game to move a cat to the grass to avoid mud. Over time the grass shrank and the mud increased, requiring more careful control of the cat. As the task difficulty increased, the game required children to use both working memory and conflict resolution skills. After five days, the children who had practiced the game were compared to another group of 4- to 7-year-olds who had spent five days playing other interactive games. Not only did the children who had received training show superior attention skills, but they also showed significantly greater improvements on intelligence tests than the other children, evidence that the training generalized. But most interesting, the brains of children who had received attention and executive control training were changed as a result of the experience. The brain activation in attention networks and emotional control areas looked more like that in typical adults (Rueda, Rothbart, McCandliss, Saccomanno, & Posner, 2005). Attention training also helps dyslexic children with written composition and verbal fluency. Likewise, working memory training helps children and adults with ADHD (Klingberg, Forssberg, & Westerberg, 2002).

Far from being fixed, static organs, our brains can and do change in response to our experiences. If we change the way we do something, our brains will reorganize to reflect new patterns of behavior (Doidge, 2007). This is great news for attention training, because it means that children who struggle with learning due to attention difficulties can overcome their diagnoses and rewire their attention systems.

Speech and Language in Executive Control

Our ability to regulate our thoughts and actions emerges out of experience in interaction with others. Humans are social beings who use language to create meaning and to learn about culture. Language plays an important role in the development of executive function: it not only frees the child from the immediate perceptual experience, allowing him or her to plan actions, but also allows the child to master his or her own behavior for the first time. According to Russian developmental scientist Vygotsky, "the most significant moment in the course of intellectual development, which gives birth to the purely human forms of practical and abstract intelligence, occurs when speech and practical activity, two previously independent lines of development, converge" (1930/1966, p. 24).

Language directs attention to relevant dimensions of a problem, assisting children in forming hypotheses and plans of how to proceed, and helps maintain short-term memory (Meichenbaum, 1977). It is interesting to note that a child's socioeconomic status (a measure of both education and income) is a predictor of his or her language development. Parents of higher socioeconomic status talk more to their children and use speech to initiate conversation rather than to just direct behavior (Hoff, 2006). In one study, mothers who helped their 3-year-old children solve a problem by verbally explaining possible uses of an object had children with both more advanced language skills and better spatial reasoning at 4 years of age (Landry, Miller-Loncar, Smith, & Swank, 2002). This is the movement from the social to psychological plane that Vygotsky championed.

Private Speech

When my toddler son, Alexei, creates a new track with his wooden train set, he talks himself through the process: "I'm putting the bridge over here.... I need another curved track.... This one has to line up to go on here." Throughout childhood, children talk out loud to themselves to direct their own behavior and guide their attention. The inner voice that helps us to guide our actions takes time to become internalized—it goes through an intermediate step before becoming thought (Luria, 1961). Using private speech, children become capable of transforming social interaction into individual psychological organization. Private speech is a hallmark of developing executive function; children use private speech to identify internal states and external conditions and to plan and direct behavioral responses. In short, they use private speech to control the executive system (Diaz & Berk, 1992).

Private speech supports problem solving. In a now classic study, 3-year-old children were instructed to press a button when a red light came on and to refrain from pressing the button when a blue light came on. The task proved very difficult for the children. They were unable to inhibit the pressing most of the time. When they saw the light, their little arms reached out for the button almost automatically. Then they were instructed to say to themselves "press" or "don't press" when the light came on. Their performance skyrocketed (Luria, 1961).

We see a similar effect in the reverse: when researchers prevent children from using private speech during difficult tasks, their performance suffers. In an important experiment, one group of 7- to 10-year-olds were directed to complete the Tower of London task, which requires that children mentally preplan a sequence of moves to arrange and match a set of disks in a sample (see Figure 2.2) while also repeating the word "Monday" in time with the experimenter (therefore suppressing their ability to talk while planning). A second group completed the Tower of London task while also tapping their feet in time with the experimenter. The children who had their private speech disrupted (by having to repeat a word) performed significantly worse than those who only had to tap their feet. Those individuals who tended to use more private speech suffered more from articulatory suppression than their peers (Lidstone, Meins, & Fernyhough, 2010). Without talking themselves through this difficult task, they were unable to maintain planning and attention. In summary, task-related private speech is important for both task performance and future achievement.

Figure 2.2 | **The Tower of London Task**

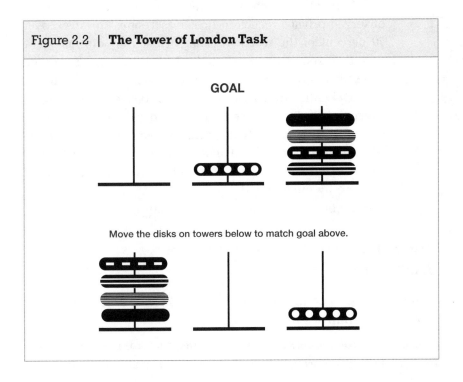

GOAL

Move the disks on towers below to match goal above.

Private speech has important implications for the classroom (an environment where children are often admonished for not being quiet, especially during evaluations and tests). Teachers' views of private speech are important, because research shows that teachers can actively support or hinder private speech based on their beliefs and practices (Deniz, 2009). In one study, children's use of private speech more than doubled as a result of adult encouragement (Lee, 1999). In another experiment, 40 children worked on solving difficult problems with or without their teacher's scaffolding. Children who talked to themselves while working on the problems were much more likely to get future items correct. Importantly, children were more likely to talk themselves through the problems if they had received adult scaffolding (Winsler, Diaz & Montero, 1997).

When regular and special education elementary teachers were interviewed about their experiences with and beliefs about private speech, all of the teachers reported having observed private speech in their classrooms. However, over 70 percent of the teachers claimed that they did not know how to respond to private speech in their classroom, and more than 57 percent of teachers reported that private speech negatively affected classroom learning (Oliver, Edmiaston & Fitzgerald, 2003). Because a volume of developmental science research now shows that private speech production boot-straps executive control, it should not be squelched in the service of maintaining a quiet classroom. Private speech propels learning by guiding and regulating attention. In an effective classroom, learning triumphs over control.

Remember:

▶ Executive control is the job of the frontal cortex, the last brain region to develop.

▶ Executive control is fundamental to cognitive skills required for attention, including planning, decision making, inhibition, and flexibility.

▶ Attention and executive control can be improved by training.

▶ Private speech helps children master their behavior and guide their attention.

How to Enhance Classroom Attention Using Executive Control

▶ *Devote class time to the training and practice of attention and executive control skills.*

Executive control is a term for many abilities that are governed by the frontal lobes of the brain. These abilities are critical for attention and learning, and develop discontinuously throughout childhood. When designing classroom lessons, adapt demands considering that the ability to initiate, organize, plan, problem solve, adapt, integrate, and self-monitor will come on line at varying ages (Goldberg, 2002). With preschool children, establish daily routines and encourage the use of narrative language to promote organization. Remind children almost as a mantra, "When we come into the classroom, we hang up our coats and put our backpacks in our cubbies." Use imagery and symbols to guide preschoolers through multistep tasks such as getting dressed, eating breakfast, combing hair, and brushing teeth in the morning. With elementary-school-aged children, teach strategies for identifying goals and planning steps to attain goals. Help children to create time lines for long-term projects; to carry a written log of activities, schedules, assignments, and due dates; and to monitor the effectiveness of organizational styles and tools.

Make planning part of the assignment. For example, 4th graders in California do a mission project. They research the architecture and design of one of the original 21 missions in their state and make an accurate scaled model including the church, quadrangle, mission buildings, and surrounding gardens. For a multistep assignment like this, begin with asking the students to come up with plans. They should list the steps that they will need to take, the time line for each step, the physical materials they will need, and the research materials that they should find. Help students to break down the steps and create a time line. In this case, the planning for the project is as instructional as the implementation. When they have created the final sculpture or model, part 2 will be a process report. Similar to a lab report, a process report is the "making of" the project. This can also be a multimedia, creative assignment. Students might photograph and document the steps they took to complete their mission model. There should also be a place for self-critique of the process. If there is an oral presentation component, ask the students to mention both the information about their mission and their process of creating and learning. Setting up a section entitled, "Things I would do differently next time" or "Revised time line" will help students reflect upon the role of executive control in attention.

▶ *Provide structure while fostering independence.*

Effective classroom learning is balanced between providing external structure and scaffolding to children and encouraging their independence during learning experiences. Whereas young children do not yet have the ability to plan and organize their behavior, older children will benefit from having external supports decreased gradually so that they can take responsibility for using the executive skills they are accumulating in their mental toolboxes. When children have opportunities for independence, they can test and refine their executive skills while still having an adult safety net (Goldberg, 2002). With preschool children, you might allow them to choose materials to use for an art project out of several appropriate options. With older children, you might let them choose the type of assignment they want, be it an oral report, creative story, or visual diorama.

Let your students teach the class. Playing school is how many of us spent our time before becoming real teachers, and we know how important play can be for learning. First, pick a topic that you have already introduced. Then, let your students know that they will not have to read the whole next section—they will have to only read one part. After they are done reading their part, they will have to find a creative way to teach that part to the class. Children love to perform, and they pay more careful attention to a text if they are preparing to present it to others. At the same time they are learning important executive function skills, such as planning, organizing, integrating, and self-monitoring.

Divide students into groups and assign each group one part of the section to read, research, and teach to the class. Elementary school teacher and Discovery Educator Tracie Belt (2008) recommends the following rules for students' teaching:

1. Everyone in the group must read the section they are assigned for homework and be prepared to discuss it the next day in class with their group.

2. Everyone must participate in planning the group's presentation. Assign a facilitator for each group whose job it is to make sure each group member is participating and contributing.
3. Choose one group member to find or make a visual aid for the group's presentation.
4. Choose another group member to find a magazine, web, or newspaper article about one part of their section. This article must be used in the presentation.
5. Choose a third group member to research three interesting facts about the topic that cannot be found by reading the textbook.
6. Choose a fourth group member to write a summary and three review questions to read to and ask the class at the end of the group presentation.

All presentations must have a skit, props, or something else creative to become memorable. The students should be given a day or two of class time to prepare their presentations. On the third day, each group presents their section to the class. The students can dress up if they wish. At the end of each presentation, when the group summarizes what the class should have learned and asks three review questions, students should copy those key points into their notebooks. That way, the entire class will have the notes they need to study for a possible quiz or test on the unit (Belt, 2008).

▶ *Encourage meta-attention.*

Understanding and reflecting on attention and its brain mechanisms helps children take control of their attention (Cardillo, 2009). Research on the training of attention indicates that attention is subject to deliberate control. A child's awareness of attention can affect his or her ability and propensity to pay attention. In an interesting study, kindergarteners, 2nd graders, and 6th graders were given meta-attention training and asked to complete difficult attention tasks while being distracted by music. The children were specifically taught about the nature of human attention, ways to assess task difficulty, how to determine types of attention needed, and ways that background music and other distractions make attention tasks more difficult. The children were also coached in private speech and encouraged to quietly talk themselves through the task as a means of guiding their own attention. Not surprisingly, the group who received meta-attention training far surpassed their peers on the attention tasks (Kaniel & Aram, 1993).

Institute a Self-Scan before attention-demanding classroom tasks, like tests or group discussions. Ask the children to focus on what they are bringing to the attention situation before them. They should ask, *Where am I? What is this situation? What are my goals for this situation? Are my goals different from my desires? How have I done in these situations in the past? How would I want to behave differently? How can I avoid actions that I don't want to repeat?* Next, encourage them to focus on the demands of the environment by asking, *What is my relationship to others in this situation? What kinds of attention does this require? What processes should I activate (e.g., remain calm, don't ask questions)? What processes should I inhibit? What distracters can I anticipate and what can I do when they arise?*

Repeating these or similar questions will create automatic habits in the children. Self-Scan questions can be answered in written form and saved for a portfolio, or they can be discussed with a partner as a paired-sharing exercise. The Self-Scan can also be done silently, as the teacher reads the questions and the student reflects quietly on his or her own experience. Self-Scans can be used as a meditative time or as a time to amp up with a bit of adrenaline. They are useful for a variety of types of attention that children may require throughout the day in the classroom.

Attention Propeller 3: Movement

"Fidgety Phil, He won't sit still, He wriggles, And giggles, And then, I declare, Swings backwards and forwards, And tilts up his chair..." (Hoffmann, 1845/ 1995).

Movement and action are often thought of as the opposite of attention. This is especially true when we imagine the industrial-era classroom model, with children quietly sitting in rows, facing front and obeying the rules by concentrating on the sage wisdom of the teacher. Moving around does have major consequences for the development and use of attention. When harnessed effectively, children's movements and actions can be powerful propellers of their attention.

Beginning in infancy, learning to control one's own movements is a heralded accomplishment. For my infant daughter Sonia, the job most worthy of her attention each day is her own effortful movement—marveling at her hands, getting them into her mouth, batting the toys hanging overhead in her baby gym, or the best of all, getting her hands around a toy and successfully shoving it into her mouth. When she begins to crawl and walk, she will go through an important transition of early development, and her skills of perception, cognition, and social and emotional development will skyrocket (Campos et al., 2000). To philosopher Mark Johnson (1987), our reality is shaped by our body movement patterns. Research indicates that moving by one's self (or "self-locomotion") changes the infant's experience of distance, compelling attention to objects and events that may not be right in front of them (Campos, Kermoian, & Zumbahlen, 1992). In one study, infants developed the ability to divide their attention (e.g., to look around the room, while also manipulating objects near them) only after they began crawling or walking (Freedman, 1992, cited in Campos et al., 2000). Infants who can self-locomote have an easier time focusing their attention. In cognitive "hide-and-seek" tasks like the A not B task, those who kept an eye on the correct hiding location were more apt to search correctly for a hidden object. To a mobile infant, knowing where objects are, even when they have disappeared from immediate view, is the coin of the realm for getting around (Acredolo, 1985).

Young children, too, devote most of their waking hours to movement. Running, jumping, rolling and playing, doing somersaults, and wrestling are what it means to be a kid. In fact, children's bodies, their metabolisms and bone structure, are designed to be active all day long (Oz, cited in Imus, 2008). Rather than trying to get children to sit still and stop fidgeting, we can embrace children's movement and action. New York University sociologist Barbara Katz Rothman recalls a telling moment when she moved with her children to the Netherlands, "We moved into an apartment building that was mostly filled with elderly people... [and] Victoria was a very active, bouncy five-year-old. I took her downstairs to the apartment immediately below mine and introduced myself to our neighbor. I told her I wasn't sure how much noise carried, so please tell me right away when she was bothered by Victoria's running or jumping. She looked confused, and I thought maybe it was a language problem so I explained again more slowly and carefully.... When she understood what I was saying to her, the old woman looked concerned, reached out to me and said, 'But dear, children have to run' " (2000, p. 12). Let's rethink movement as an asset to children's attention; to harness their natural energy and to welcome them wriggling, giggling, and bursting out of their chairs.

Movement and Self-Regulation

The first way that movement propels attention has to do with self-regulation. If children get out all of their pent-up energy by running and moving and playing vigorously, they can then focus their attention better. Recess is a wonderful tool for self-regulation. In the 1950s, three recess periods per school day was typical in the United States. Today more than 40 percent of school districts have eliminated recess or are considering eliminating it (Mulrine, 2000). Teachers and administrators are under intense pressure to provide more "academic" time, with legislation linking test scores to school funding. Teachers have also cited school violence as a reason to cancel recess. Giving up recess potentially reduces costs, too, because of less need for first aid and less risk of litigation over accidents and inappropriate behavior (Lindsay, 1994).

Of course, developmental science research reveals a very different set of priorities. Children should have more, not less, time for freely moving their bodies, and one key reason is attention. Some developmental scientists have suggested that the increased diagnosis of ADHD could be due to the fact that children no longer have enough opportunities to run around (Panksepp, 1998; Robinson, 2010). In fact, the rise in ADHD strongly correlates with both the rise in standardized testing and the fall of the amount of free time that children spend running and playing at recess.

In the 19th century, pioneering German memory researcher Hermann Ebbinghaus studied massed versus distributed practice and discovered that taking breaks during difficult tasks maximized learning (Ebbinghaus, 1885/1913). More recently, developmental science research has shown very clearly and consistently that recess enhances children's attention to lessons. Following recess, children of all ages focus more and fidget less. In one study, children's postrecess attention greatly increased regardless of the amount or type of physical activity that they did during recess (Ridgway, Northup, Pellegrin, LaRue, & Hightshoe, 2003). On the flip side, studies have shown that the longer time children were confined to class without a recess break, the less attentive they were (Pellegrini & Davis, 1993; Pellegrini, Huberty, & Jones, 1995; Pellegrini & Smith, 1993). Likewise, levels of inappropriate behavior among children with and without ADHD were significantly lower on days when the children had recess (Holmes et al., 2006). It is so important to take breaks; there are many rationales behind letting kids run and use their bodies, not least of which is that we are asking so much of them during class time.

Brain, Body, and Academic Achievement

Physical activity provides healthy stress for the brain. Just like exercising your muscles, physical movement followed by recovery promotes brain adaptation and growth, allowing the brain to respond to future challenges (Mattson, 2004). Scientists have recently discovered that participating in aerobic activity increases the ability of the heart to deliver oxygen to the brain, affecting cerebral structure, cerebral blood flow, the production of neurotransmitters, and the production of proteins responsible for growth and survival of developing neurons. Each of these enhancements is associated with improved cognitive performance (Chodzko-Zajko & Moore, 1994; Etnier, Nowell, Landers, & Sibley, 2006). Aerobic activity also stimulates the growth of new neurons in the hippocampus (a brain region primarily involved in learning and memory) (Hillman, Erickson, & Kramer, 2008). Movement provides physical, social, and intellectual challenges, creating opportunities for the brain to adapt and resulting in healthy cognitive development (Sattelmair & Ratey, 2009).

Aerobic fitness is related to improved cognitive functioning during childhood, the time of greatest brain development (Hillman, Buck, Themanson, Pontifex, & Castelli, 2009). When children are regularly involved in strenuous play, they show increased stimulation of the frontal lobes, less impulsiveness, and increased ability for executive control (Panksepp, 2007, 2008). Highly fit children who are in the habit of running around and playing show much greater success on attention tasks requiring executive control, and much better performance on mathematics and reading achievement tests (Castelli, Hillman, Buck, & Erwin, 2007). Indeed, a recent review of the child development literature found a strong relationship between children's exercise and perception, IQ, achievement in school, standardized math and verbal test scores, and school readiness (Sibley & Etnier, 2003). In one laboratory study, 7- to 12- year-old children with better aerobic fitness performed significantly better on executive control tasks. Their brains also showed increased attentional resources and cognitive speed (Buck, Hillman, & Castelli, 2008).

The cognitive benefits of physical movement far outweigh any losses that theoretically could incur from time away from academic areas (Taras, 2005). A study involving 8,000 school children found that their academic ratings and grades were significantly correlated with exercise levels and with performance on physical fitness tests (Dwyer, Sallis, Blizzard, Lazarus, & Dean, 2001). In 2004, the California Department of Education examined the standardized test scores of almost 1 million students in grades 5, 7, and 9. They discovered that overall fitness (assessed via aerobic capacity, muscular strength, muscular endurance, and flexibility) was strongly correlated with higher test scores (California Department of Education, 2005). Considering the obesity epidemic and these new findings showing that physical exercise improves cognitive development and academic performance, we might just want to embrace children's desire to jump out of their chairs.

Learning with Movement

Simply being in motion affects attention and learning because movement allows the brain an opportunity to "do the information" rather than see or hear it, providing additional data points for the learning mind. The more a child's whole body is involved in any learning experience, the more engrossed and focused he or she will be. Reaching, jumping, balancing, and hopping teach children how to understand and negotiate the world in a multimodal fashion. Movement also provides perceptual benefits. Taking a few running steps in the outfield, for instance, will help you be able to make more accurate judgments about your ability to catch a fly ball than just standing still will (Oudejans, Michaels, Bakker, & Dolne, 1996).

Biologists Brian Kreiser and Rosalina Hairston (2007) always struggled to get students to understand the mitosis and meiosis when they taught Mendelian inheritance, and year after year their students found the concepts confusing. That's when they came up with the idea of "Dance of the Chromosomes." In this interactive exercise, students were guided through the setup ("How many chromosomes are we going to need?" or "How is prophase 1 in mitosis different from prophase 1 in meiosis?") and then they each played a part in representing a part of the cell, learning the choreography, and physically reenacting the process. Students overwhelmingly characterized the experience as having a positive impact on their learning, and they remembered the nuances of the two types of cell division far better than the previous groups.

Movement and Attentional Flow

Have you ever been so caught up in something that the very act of it became effortless? Historians claim that while he was painting the ceiling of the Sistine Chapel, Michelangelo worked for days at a time, not even stopping to rest or eat, until he would pass out from exhaustion, only to wake up refreshed and become completely immersed again. This extreme form of attention during movement is sometimes called flow, and it is often accompanied by clarity, confidence, a loss of the sense of time, serenity, and strong feelings of motivation and satisfaction. Across a wide variety of actions (e.g., visual arts, sports, playing music, or playing chess), the feeling of a flow state is associated with objective measures of high performance (Csikszentmihalyi & Csikszentmihalyi, 1992). A person in a flow state may lose all awareness of other things, because all of his or her attention is focused, often effortlessly, on the task at hand (Csikszentmihalyi, 1997a). To experience intense focus and effortlessness at the same time seems like contradiction in terms, but this heightened, unforced concentration has a unique physiological pattern and seems to arise out of an interaction between positive affect and high attention (de Manzano, Theorell, Harmat, & Ullén, 2010).

When in a flow situation, worries, problems, and stress disappear for the simple reason that there is not enough attentional capacity for worries and also the actions at hand. According to ancient Japanese martial arts masters, a state of "no mind" (in which attention moves from one activity to another without the interference of thought) is the ideal. Indeed, when I am engrossed in complex sports like skiing or mountain biking, I find that as soon as I pay attention to the moguls or rocks on the trail, I will fall. Instead, if I just let my attention flow, I become one with the mountain.

How can we create such tremendous involvement, enjoyment, and excitement in school?

Fostering a sense of flow in the classroom first requires changing our relationship to time. When we stop watching the clock, we can let how we feel guide how our time is spent. Rather than having to switch topics during short blocks of time, children need to be able to become absorbed in their projects, their sports games, or their reading. We need to find a way to minimize distractions. The reason that children report the most flow experiences from extracurricular activities like drama, orchestra, sports, or working on the student paper is because these activities often follow a more natural rhythm, rather than a jerky exposure to information (Csikszentmihalyi, 1997a).

Another important prerequisite to creating flow is to match the children's abilities with the challenges of the lessons. If the challenge is much harder than the child's skills, he or she will feel anxiety. On the other hand, if the child's skills are not being adequately tapped, he or she will become bored. Finding the perfect level of difficulty is not an easy task in a classroom of 30 children at all different skill levels (Csikszentmihalyi, 1997a). But as the Montessori model has shown us, if the classroom environment and available materials are

Remember:

▶ Movement and action can powerfully propel attention.

▶ Movement gets out pent-up energy and helps children to regulate their arousal, so that they can pay attention.

▶ Taking breaks during difficult tasks maximizes learning.

▶ Aerobic activity directly enhances brain function.

▶ The more a child's whole body is involved in any learning experience, the more engrossed and focused he or she will be.

▶ Finding flow is the ideal for focusing and sustaining attention.

stimulating and varied, each child will find the right level of challenge. Like all people, children will seek out flow experiences in any way they can. If they can't find them in school, they will find them in video games, or if they are victims of unfortunate circumstances, by breaking into cars or burning things (Csikszentmihalyi, 1997a). It should be our goal as teachers to channel children's actions toward meaningful attention and experience.

How to Enhance Classroom Attention Using Movement

▶ *Schedule in time for children to let out their physical energy with aerobic exercise and strenuous play.*

Developmental scientists, physicians, and teachers alike advocate aerobically demanding activities for children on a daily basis. Physically strenuous play should be engaging, challenging, and enjoyable to children. Phil Lawler, the director of physical education at Madison Junior High School in Naperville, Illinois, has sparked a revolution in his school's approach to physical education (Viadero, 2008). His program, called "PE4life," encourages each individual student to progress toward his or her personal fitness goals. The students engage in physically strenuous play, both traditional and current, like climbing rock walls, dancing in video game platforms (like *Dance Dance Revolution*), and riding interactive, gaming stationary bikes. The children wear heart monitors to assess whether they are working in their optimal aerobic zones. PE4life is now setting up academies in schools around the country. So far, the group has trained over 1,000 educators and 350 schools to emulate their program. The results are staggering in both physical and intellectual realms. Whereas up to 30 percent of students are overweight in the state of California, less than 3 percent are overweight in California schools using PE4life. In Titusville, Pennsylvania (a PE4life school), test scores in reading and math have gone from below the state average to 18 percent above average. At Woodland Elementary School in Kansas City, Missouri, PE4life has coincided with improved literacy and also a 67 percent drop in suspensions and reduced academic probation (Sattelmair & Ratey, 2009).

Pair physical education with cognitive and other intellectual goals to get the benefits of both. You might ask students to race around on scooters to match words with their definitions on opposite sides of a gym floor (Viadero, 2008). Or you might ask your students to show the answers to arithmetic problems by jumping (Hruska & Clancy, 2008). Exercise and learning sessions should be enmeshed together, rather than just added on to existing lessons. Movement can be incorporated into your core curriculum if you work collaboratively across academic disciplines. Ask your students to keep track of their own progress and to help one another to reach both their academic and fitness goals.

▶ *Use creative movement to teach cognitive concepts.*

Kinesthetic experiences can make learning more accessible, expanding children's creativity and understanding of their own bodies. Once performed, the concept will stay with the children forever. After all, as choreographer and educator Susan Griss (1994) points out, they were rolling down hills, flailing their arms, banging on the floor in tantrums, and jumping for joy long before they began to express themselves with language. In a science lesson on sound waves, she lets children guess the medium through which sound moves the fastest, air, water, or solid. Then she lines them up in "molecule formations" (closest together being solid, furthest apart being air) and passes a "sound wave" (shoulder tap) through the line. When the solid group finishes first, they suddenly understand.

Devise math curriculum that uses dance and movement. Elementary teacher Katherine Wood (2008) noticed that her students were more engaged with ideas and learning if there was an element of movement involved. So she created a square dance activity in which the students could use counting and number sense in a specific, purposeful context. The activity was designed to highlight the concept of doubling numbers—for instance, doubling the number eight. Counting was emphasized during the dance and later discussion centered on how many counts it took to complete sections of the dance.

The children's understanding of the concept was not immediate, but the activity created a very useful reference point when the topic was discussed later. By placing the concept in a context, Katherine was able to scaffold the students' learning toward new ideas. They did not learn a square had four sides by saying it over and over again. They knew because they moved around a square and had to really think about a square and its attributes when doing so. This led to deeper understandings and longer-term retention of information (Wood, 2008).

▶ *Allow time and space for intense, effortless attention and flow experiences to emerge.*

We know from the research on flow that challenge plus relevance can lead to superior concentration, interest, and attention. We also know that giving children a measure of autonomy can lead to the intrinsic motivation that feeds attention. Classrooms need to integrate academic intensity and positive emotion (Shernoff, Csikszentmihalyi, Schneider, & Shernoff, 2003). Perhaps teachers could afford the time to create enjoyable challenges that also allow children to let go and be completely present.

Create a Flow Activities Center in your classroom or school. The Key School in Illinois made just such a space for challenging play. Building on the notion that achieving a flow state leads to high attention and motivation (which, of course, are the best for learning), the Key School Flow Center is a place that children can go for 40 minutes per day. It is stimulating, orderly, and unstructured in the hope that children might hook in with an activity that captures them. Create your space with puzzles, games, and manipulative objects. This way children will have complete control and awareness of their actions as well as a sense of freedom. If you can free the minds of your students in a relaxed atmosphere, the learning that takes place there will become enjoyable and effortless. Their learning will become infused with a halo of attention and intrinsic motivation (Whalen & Csikszentmihalyi, 1991).

3

Understanding Children's Memory

mem·o·ry All that we have learned in our lives, from multiplication tables to moral lessons, from sensory impressions to habits, is composed of memories. The hallmarks of cognition, including problem solving, decision making, and classifying are also based on remembering. In a sense, to learn anything is to remember.

Because the brain does not retain information that it deems irrelevant, much of what we take in is never stored in our memories. In terms of neural networks, such data is meaningless (Wolfe, 2001). Knowing how children learn requires understanding how and what they will remember (Cowan, 1998; Courage & Cowan, 2009).

Students of all ages, even those who excel in a course or lesson, often proceed to forget what they have "learned." In a now famous study, Schneps (1989) asked Harvard graduates the simple question at commencement "Why does the Earth have seasons?" and discovered that nearly everyone answered incorrectly. It was not that these students hadn't learned that the tilt of the Earth's axis causes seasons; most had probably learned that in the elementary school. It was simply that the information held no relevance or immediacy—nothing to make it stick in their memories.

A Developmental Science Approach to Memory

The term *memory* is a bit misleading. There is no file system in the brain or body that holds individual memories. Instead, what we call memory consists of many abilities corresponding to various brain structures and their interconnections (Cycowicz, 2000). Rather than speaking of memories as entities, developmental scientists speak of *remembering*, the action. For the brain, remembering is a process of organizing information in various networks in real time (Wolfe, 2006). Quite literally, when we remember something, we conjure it in the present, assembling details based on our experiences and expectations (Reeder, Martin, & Turner, 2008). Each time I remember a life event, my brain will trigger slightly different pathways of neurons. Because our brains always operate in the most efficient way possible, patterns of brain activation that correspond to each act of remembering will always be unique (Freeman, 1991).

The impressive memory capacities of adults emerge out of the memory abilities of very early life. In fact, remembering begins prenatally. Because fetuses cannot directly tell us what they remember, developmental scientists have had to devise clever tests to uncover their memories. Research studies have shown that fetuses can remember and recognize a vibrating sound up to 24 hours later (van Heteren, Focco Boekkooi, Jongsma, & Nijhuis, 2000). In one study, newborns who listened to a popular tune in the womb showed increased movement and heart rate when they heard the same song two to four days after birth (Hepper, 1991). In a similar experiment, mothers played a 30-minute music tape to their fetuses, both before getting up in the morning and before going to sleep at night, and then recorded any movements they felt. A second group of mothers simply recorded movements of their fetuses as they naturally occurred. The fetuses who heard the music showed specific patterns of movement that persisted even after being born (Hong, 1994). Third-trimester fetuses have short-term memories of up to 10 minutes and long-term memories of up to 4 weeks (Dirix, Nijhuis, Jongsma, & Hornstra, 2009). Early memory use during prenatal development will lay the foundation for the emergence of other cognitive skills. Fetuses who exhibit stronger memory skills in the womb also show later successes in childhood, including developing attachments to caregivers, recognizing caregivers' voices, establishing a healthy breastfeeding relationship, and developing language (Gagnon, Hunse, Carmichael, Fellows, & Patrick, 1987).

Just like fetuses, infants display an astounding ability to remember. Throughout their first year, infants build the most complex memory capacities of their lives (Gathercole & Alloway, 2008a). They begin by associating certain sights and sounds and smells with comfort—knowing, and remembering those people who care for them. In one study, researchers asked mothers to read a single nursery rhyme to their new babies once a day for two weeks. Three days later, the infants were brought into the lab and given special pacifiers, which could sense the rate of their sucking (a procedure known as *high-amplitude sucking*). For half of the infants, sucking vigorously triggered a recording of the familiar nursery rhyme, and sucking more slowly triggered the unfamiliar one. For the other half, sucking slowly played the familiar rhyme. By sucking the pacifiers in whichever way produced the familiar rhymes (fast or slow), the infants showed long-term memories for them (Spence, 1996).

Another clever way of assessing infant memory is a procedure called *deferred imitation*. Here infants watch an experimenter play with exciting, new toys in a way that they have never seen before. The infants are not allowed to touch the toys or to play with them, just to watch. Then, after a delay, they are given the toys to play with and compared with infants who did not see the original display. In one deferred imitation experiment, infants were shown a puppet with mittens on. The experimenter removed one mitten from the puppet's hand and shook it to reveal a jingle bell inside. She then replaced the mitten on the puppet's hand. Immediately after the demonstration, 6- and 12-month-olds were given the puppet to play with. Both groups of infants removed the mitten and shook it (in contrast to a group of 6- and 12-month-olds who had not seen the initial demonstration). They did the same after a 24-hour delay. But when given the puppet a week later, only the 12-month-olds remembered the bell inside the mitten (Barr & Hayne,

2000). Developmental scientists once believed that long-term memory was impossible before the development of language, but deferred imitation studies have demonstrated that preverbal infants can form long-term memories lasting up to a year (Bauer, 1997; Meltzoff, 1995b).

Carolyn Rovee-Collier and her colleagues at Rutgers University have created other innovative methods for studying long-term memory in very young infants. In these studies, the infant is placed in a crib with a mobile hanging above her head. A ribbon is tied to the infant's ankle, and she quickly learns that when she kicks, the mobile moves. After a delay, the infant is placed in the same crib, but this time the ribbon is not attached to the mobile. If the infant remembers the game, as soon as she sees the familiar mobile she will begin vigorously kicking! Using this mobile game (called a *conjugate reinforcement procedure*), infants as young as 2 months of age have shown us that they can store and retrieve long-term memories for up to two weeks (Sullivan, Rovee-Collier, & Tynes, 1979).

During the time that infants and children are just beginning to develop their memory systems, immediate context is powerful for both encoding (the taking in of the memory) and retrieval (the remembering). In one study, 6-month-olds learned the mobile game within a distinctive environment, a crib surrounded with either bold-colored stripes or polka dots. Later, when it came time to test their memories, half of the infants' environments were switched. Those infants whose surroundings changed from polka dots to stripes or vice versa did not remember as well as those whose surroundings stayed the same (Rovee-Collier et al., 1992). Changes in visual designs and changes in the foreground versus background also disrupted memory (Hayne, Greco, Early, Griesler, & Rovee-Collier, 1986). Across many experiments like this, a pattern has begun to emerge. When an infant's memory is developing, the experience of an event involves taking in individual components rather than responding to the situation as a whole. Infants and children do gradually become better at generalization (the ability to use a memory in a different situation than the one in which it was encoded), but this skill is slow to unfold over the first few years of life (Hayne & Simcock, 2009).

Whereas we usually think of crawling and walking as strictly motor milestones, moving around on one's own also jumpstarts major changes in perceptual, cognitive, and social development (Campos et al., 2000). Learning how to walk or crawl affects memory generalization, because infants must suddenly be able to recognize familiar objects in new places (Rovee-Collier, 1996). On average, infants begin to generalize remembering across context at about 9 months of age, which is also the average time to begin crawling. In one experiment, two groups of 9-month-olds (one crawling, one not) were presented with a deferred imitation task. They were shown how to press a hidden button on a toy cow or duck to make it "moo" or "quack." Twenty-four hours later, half of the infants were tested in the same context and half were tested in a new context to see whether they remembered how to get the animal to "talk." Both crawlers and noncrawlers pushed the button when tested in the original context, but only crawlers were able to imitate when tested in a new context (Herbert, Gross, & Hayne, 2007). The same results have been found with walking infants, with more complex deferred imitation tasks (Gross, Hayne, Perkins, & MacDonald, 2006).

Even after generalization becomes possible, context remains a powerful trigger for memory. That is why we become flooded with old memories when we visit the places of our youth. It seems that noting minute sensory details of a situation is an important part of our learning process (Glenberg, 1997; Smith & Vela, 2001). Later, when we are exposed to the familiar background scenes, our memories will be triggered. Throughout the life span, individuals show superior memory retention when the exact learning situation is re-created at test time (Smith & Vela, 2001; Tulving & Thomson, 1973). In a classic experiment, scuba divers were asked to learn word lists either on land or underwater. They were then tested for their memory of the words in the same or the opposite situation. Divers who were asked to recall the words in the original situation remembered significantly more words (Godden & Baddeley, 1975). Interestingly, familiar smells tend to stir up memories above and beyond the other senses. In recent studies, memories evoked by odors created a stronger feeling of being brought back in time than memories evoked by words (Herz & Schooler, 2002). At the level of the brain, smells are distinct from sights, sounds, tastes, and experiences of touch because they are the only sensation that does not need to traverse the thalamus on the way to the cerebral cortex. Odor-processing areas of the brain connect directly to higher-order areas, including the hippocampus, one key area of the brain for remembering (Cahill, Babinsky, Markowitsch, & McGaugh, 1995; Herz, Eliassen, Beland, & Souza, 2003; Shepherd, 2005).

Memory Propeller 1: Working Memory

Mr. Vargas reminded his second-grade class of the protocol after math lessons: "Put your manila sheets on the table, put your number cards in the packet, put your pencil away, and come sit on the carpet." Michael wandered from his desk a bit, and then sat down on the carpet with his manila sheet in hand. Exasperated, Mr. Vargas scolded him again, for the third time that week. "You need to follow directions, Michael!"

Whether we are setting out to tackle a complex cognitive problem, or just trying to keep track of the items on a mental grocery list, we need to hold some information for just a few minutes or seconds while doing other tasks. Working memory is like a sticky note for temporary storage in our minds, a system for storing information for very short periods of time to be used for further manipulation (Baddeley, 1986). For example, to divide 672 by 12 in my head, I need to hold the numbers in my mental workspace, remember how to do long division, store the partial solution, and integrate all of the sources of information into the answer. Other ways we use our working memories include remembering a phone number while trying to find a pen to write it down, or remembering someone's name after just having been introduced (Gathercole & Alloway, 2008a). Activities that require working memory are very common in the classroom. Children are asked throughout their days to do such things as follow complex, multilayered verbal directions, calculate arithmetic in their heads, or write from dictation (St. Clair-Thompson, Stevens, Hunt, & Bolder, 2010).

The content of working memory can easily be lost. I learned that lesson the hard way. Trying to impress customers when I worked as a waitress in college (and also trying to get good tips), I would remember the entire table's dinner orders without writing them down—that is, if I was able to get immediately to the computer to enter them in. If a coworker so much as asked me to grab the ketchup, the entire order would vanish, and I would have to sheepishly go back and take the order again. Once the data in our working memories has been lost to distraction, it is truly gone. The only possible way to regain it is to start over again.

Working memory does not function well with information overload. If we try to hold and manipulate too much, to multiply 6942 times 3867 in our heads, for example, we quickly run out of mental space (Gathercole & Alloway, 2008a). In the 1950s, Harvard psychologist George Miller (1956) discovered that most adults could hold in mind about seven bits of information at once, before becoming confused or forgetting. It was his research on this "magic number" that led to the creation of seven-digit phone numbers. Since then hundreds of studies have examined the working memory spans of children and adults. Two-year-olds can typically remember up to two unrelated bits of information, but as their understanding of the world expands (as they experience more things that they can link to meaning) so too does their working memory. For example, for a 5-year-old, the letters *F, B,* and *I* would be stored as three separate units. But a 10-year-old might know something about government agencies and might be able to store FBI as a single piece of information (Reeder et al., 2008).

Working Memory and Learning

Scientists evaluate working memory by asking children to do one remembering task while also focusing on something else. For example, children might listen to a series of sentences, decide whether each is true or false, and then be asked later to remember the last word of each sentence (Daneman & Carpenter, 1980). This research has shown that the working memory capacities of any group of children can vary quite a bit. In a class of thirty 7- and 8-year-olds, we could expect three to have the working memory skills of a 4-year-old and three others to have capacities close to those of an adult (Gathercole & Alloway, 2008b). Difficulty with working memory is not uncommon in childhood and can negatively impact children's learning. Those with poor working memory capacities often have difficulty remembering and following directions, often fail to complete assignments, act very shy in group settings, and show below-average abilities in both math and reading

(Gathercole & Alloway, 2008b). These children tend not to spontaneously catch up with their peers in the classroom.

Indeed, children who do poorly on tests of working memory struggle in other academic areas, such as literacy (Gathercole & Pickering, 2000; Swanson, Ashbaker, & Lee, 1996) and math (Geary, Hoard, Byrd-Craven, & DeSoto, 2004). In one study, researchers from the United Kingdom investigated the relationship between working memory and the National Curriculum assessment tests, given annually to children in 1st, 5th, and 8th grades. Across the board, working memory scores increased as achievement levels in English, math, and science went up (Gathercole, Pickering, Knight, & Stegmann, 2003). Further research indicated that children's working memory scores in kindergarten and 1st grade predicted their school achievement three years later (Alloway, Gathercole, Adams, & Willis, 2005; Gathercole, Brown, & Pickering, 2003). In other words, the more skilled a child was on working memory tasks, the better he or she performed in school in general.

Children who are deficient in working memory are often mistaken for those with attention issues. Teachers may think of these students as daydreamers or claim that instruction for them is "in one ear and out the other." Because they lose the information they need to complete the task at hand (the sequence of instructions they are trying to follow or the sentence they are trying to write, for instance), children with working memory issues are unable to stick with and complete their assignments (Gathercole, Durling, Evans, Jeffcock, & Stone, 2008). In an important observational study of young children, writing emerged as one of the most significant impediments for children with low memory spans (Gathercole, Lamont, & Alloway, 2006). Children frequently made errors, such as skipping or repeating letters and words, indicating that they had lost their place. When a child loses the information in his or her working memory due to distraction or overload, it cannot be recovered. That child must get the information all over again. Out of embarrassment, he or she may choose to guess or to simply give up. In this way, working memory issues account for missed learning opportunities and learning delays.

Remember:

▶ Working memory is a system of temporary storage for mental manipulation.

▶ The more skilled children are in working memory, the better they do academically across the board.

▶ Children with working memory deficits are often mistaken for children with attention problems.

How to Enhance Classroom Memory Using Working Memory

▶ *Reduce working memory loads.*

Set up your classroom in a way that prevents working memory over-load. In their guide for understanding working memory in the classroom, British developmental scientists Susan Gathercole and Tracy Alloway (2008a, 2008b) recommend lowering working memory expectations for children by reducing the amount of content material to be remembered, but also by increasing the meaningfulness of information for the students. Furthermore, they suggest simplifying linguistic structures of material, repeating important information like general classroom rules and task-specific instructions, breaking complex tasks into separate independent steps, and providing external memory aids in the classroom such as number lines and useful spellings.

You don't have to be the only one who lightens the memory load for students; you can let them share in the responsibility for breaking down complex instructions into manageable steps. Building on an old West African tradition, assign one student per week to be the class griot. The griot in traditional societies is the keeper of memories. He or she is responsible for remembering stories, keeping oral histories, and reporting them to the village. In the classroom, your griot can be responsible for reminding the class of routines, instructions, and assignments due. He or she can provide a structure for the day, keep track of what happened, and put it into context. You might ask the griot for that week, *Is there anything that we need to remember about quiet reading time before we begin?* The designated children will begin to delight in remembering details and be proud when they are able to lead their classmates. Their peers will also benefit from the reminders: the slowing-down of instructions and the reflection on where they are in the structure of an activity.

▶ *Put working memory training into your repertoire.*

Working memory training can improve performance across a variety of lessons and tasks. Skills like adding and multiplying in our heads, or remembering names, dates, and phone numbers are becoming lost arts with the advent of smart phones and other time-saving devices. Unfortunately, memory is more like a muscle than a repository and it requires practice. Research has shown that a working memory "workout" can have benefits beyond just those assignments that are obviously memory related. Working memory skills transfer to domains of reading, writing, math, and science, among others (Gathercole, Pickering, Knight, & Stegmann, 2003).

Combine a physical workout with a mental one, by running a Working Memory Relay. First, list each student's name and assign each person a word. It is more challenging if the words are unrelated. Next, give each student a piece of paper with his or her word on it. Depending on the level of your group, you can use more complex words or mix up parts of speech. Just like any relay race, the students should form two teams. Rather than passing the baton to the next runner, in this relay, runners have to pass their word. Upon arrival at the next runner, the child should whisper the word into the next person's ear. That person now has two words, runs to the end, and passes those two to the next runner, who now has three unrelated words to remember. In order to win the race, the runner at the finish must be able to list all of the words in the correct sequence.

For younger children, try the Snowman Memory Game. Ask students to bring in winter hats, earmuffs, scarves, gloves, mittens, and boots (if it is winter, they will probably already have these things with them). Designate one child to be the snowman. All of the other children will close their eyes, while this child will choose what he or she wants to put on as the snowman. The children in the class should be asked to open their eyes and look at the snowman for 30 seconds, then close their eyes again. The snowman will change one thing he or she is wearing and ask the others to point out what has changed. After a few rounds, the children will learn to carefully notice each detail and discover strategies for doing so (PreschoolPlanner101, 2007).

Memory Propeller 2:
Scripts, Schemas and Stories

Darren and Kim saved up for months in order to take their 3-year-old daughter, Lea, to Disney World. They planned each day of the trip carefully, so that they would be able to experience each theme park with its rides, parades, and fireworks, and still have enough hours of daylight to kick back and relax on the lazy river of the hotel pool. When Lea returned to preschool and Ms. Sloan asked about her family vacation, she gleefully recounted the bus ride to and from the airport.

Memory is not something we have but something we do (Fivush, 2000). That is to say that our memories are alive and active. Far from resembling video recordings, they are updated with new sources of information each time we conjure them up (Courage & Cowan, 2009). That is why our memories are notoriously inaccurate. Children are especially susceptible to confusing events and, for that reason, often prove to be unreliable as eyewitnesses in court (Ceci, Loftus, Leichtman, & Bruck, 1994; Deese, 1959; Roediger & McDermott, 1995). How does the ability to remember and make sense of events unfold?

Scripts

Remembering is linked to survival. It is a mechanism by which children learn to predict upcoming events by calculating their likelihood of occurrence in the past (Nelson, 1996). To understand and predict their world, young children create routines with scripts. They begin by noticing rules of how things typically unfold in a given scenario—at the grocery store or before naptime, for instance (Fivush, 1994; Nelson, 1993, 1996). To a child's mind, saying "When we do this, we always then do this" creates a structure on which to build a sense of meaning. In fact, research shows that young children fail to remember script-inconsistent information. In one study, when typical sequences of events were inverted (like blowing the candles on a birthday cake out before singing "Happy Birthday"), the children remembered them in the order they should have happened (Hudson & Nelson, 1986).

To the young child, when a certain sequence and set of steps is just "what we do," then joining the culture and community necessitates noticing, remembering, and following precise rules. For example, my toddler son will often "give me my lines" in the script we are playing together. When he is experimenting with taking things apart and putting them back together, I often have to remind him that some things cannot be put back together. The time he decided to cut the ball from the paddleball elastic, he exclaimed, scissors in hand, "I'm going to cut this off!" to which he replied (in my voice), "Then we won't have a paddleball game anymore!"

Schemas

Scripts are coordinated into larger theory-like structures in the child's mind, called schemas. A schema is an organization tool with rules that the child can remember and use to make inferences in new situations (Reeder, Martin, & Turner, 2008). Using schemas helps simplify the job of remembering. Information that is inconsistent with a child's schema is often not remembered or distorted. In a review of more than 40 developmental science memory studies, children remembered schema-consistent information significantly better than schema-inconsistent information. They also changed things to match their schemas, remembering a female physician as a nurse, for example (Signorella, Bigler, & Liben, 1997).

Remembering as a Social Endeavor

Parents and teachers play important roles in the development of remembering. Guided by adults, children learn to code their experiences as narratives using language (Bjorklund, 2005). A first grade teacher might ask, for example, "What did we see at the zoo?" or "Who went with us?" These questions let the child know what is important to attend to on a field trip: the who, what, when, and where of their experiences. Without this scaffolding, the child may not select the "right" things to remember. Young children pay attention to different aspects of events than adults do, because young children do not necessarily know the difference between what is considered culturally important versus what is considered trivial. To her parents' dismay, for Lea, the most memorable part of the Disney World vacation was the journey to the airport ("We could have taken a $20 bus ride and she would have been just as happy!" her mom lamented).

Parents and teachers tend to provide correct answers when a child can't remember, showing them how the conversation should go. They ask repeated questions, showcasing for the child how remembering is done. From a developmental perspective, everyday adult-child interaction facilitates the development of a personal past that can then be shared (Fivush, 2000). The research of developmental scientist Robin Fivush has shown that preschool children recall different information about a single event each time they recall it. In one study, children were asked questions about a special event from their past as determined from an interview with their mother (a trip to the circus or on a plane ride to visit grandparents, for example). The children were then asked about the same events six months, one year, and one and a half years later. Each time they tended to report almost entirely new information about the event (Fivush, 1994; Fivush, Hammond, Harsch, Singer, & Wolf, 1991; Fivush & Shukat, 1995). Perhaps the children were responding to the immediacy of the conversational context, and different conversational partners elicited different things. In other words, the goal of recalling certain things was different with different people. Indeed, the child's experience was re-created in real time.

Research shows that the more children talk about the events they experience, the better they remember them. In one study, experimenters recorded the number of times that mothers asked their children about past events, and then tested their memories for those events. Children of mothers who asked more questions showed better memory both immediately and a year later (Ratner, 1984). In another study, mothers who told elaborate stories when recounting events had children with superior memory for past events (Reese, Haden, & Fivush, 1993). Developmental scientist Catherine Haden and her colleagues (2001) created make-believe activities for mothers and their preschool children to carry out in their homes. For instance, in the camping event, the child and parent would load backpacks, hike to a pretend pond to fish, set up a campsite, and cook and eat their supper. The children were then tested for their memories of the events one day and three weeks later. The results overwhelmingly showed that children best remembered events that were both acted together and talked about together. If the mother and child had initially done the action together, but only the mother talked about it afterward, the child's memory was less reliable. Likewise, if only the mother did the action, talking about it together was not enough to cement the memory in the child's mind (Haden, Ornstein, Eckerman, & Didow, 2001).

Memories, like other forms of knowledge, emerge in social interaction. Understanding and representing our personal experiences are the ground from which all other knowledge grows (Fivush, 2000).

How to Enhance Classroom Memory Using Scripts, Schemas, and Stories

▶ *Use scripts and schemas in dramatic play.*

Dramatic play offers a wonderful opportunity to try out scenarios and can engender security and confidence. It contributes to the development of a sense of self in relationship with others, allowing children to plan and evaluate situations and stories, and to develop creativity and problem-solving skills (Piaget, 1962). Plus, young children love to try on roles and enact situations.

Use role-plays as a trial ground for understanding and resisting peer pressure. Organize your class into small groups and give them each a scenario to enact. The scenarios should include characters, a setting, and the action. For example, a rejection scene might look like this: A group of children are standing around talking about their favorite basketball team. They then call over to a new boy in school and ask him his favorite team. When the new boy answers with another city team, all the children laugh and turn away from him. One boy calls out, "I guess you won't be at our (team name) party this Sunday!" ("The Cool Spot," National Institute of Alcohol Abuse and Alcoholism, p. 4).

After a group has acted out the scene, the class should record the types of peer pressure that have been shown (e.g., rejection, put-down, reasoning), whether pressure was spoken or unspoken, and any

> **Remember:**
> ▶ Memories are updated with new information each time children conjure them up.
> ▶ Scripts and schemas help young children remember how to behave and to understand and predict their worlds.
> ▶ Parents and teachers inform children what is important to remember.
> ▶ The more that children talk about events, the better they remember them.

feelings that were evoked for the characters (e.g., coolness, impor-tance, fear, embarrassment, confusion, anger, loneliness, stupidity). Then lead your class in a discussion about the ways they may have used peer pressure against others and/or felt pressure from others. Conclude by asking your students to observe real-world peer pressure over the following week and report back on the events, noting tactics used and outcomes ("The Cool Spot," National Institute of Alcohol Abuse and Alcoholism, p. 8).

▶ *Frame upcoming events for children.*

Scripts and schemas help children to organize the world and make sense of uncertainty. They also help children to organize their memo-ries, often composing what is remembered. By using scripts in the classroom, you can provide children with a mechanism to understand and predict what is to come and at the same time foster remembering. Providing students with a set of guiding questions before a learning experience makes apparent the learning outcomes you hope for and shows them how to conceptualize and remember new information.

Set up your next field trip as an experience to remember. If you are planning to go to the aquarium with a group of 3rd through 6th graders, for example, create a scavenger hunt for your class to do there. You might ask students to "find three water animals that are not fish" or "list the Latin names of five fish that eat other fish." Children can collect the items on the hunt by writing them down, draw-ing them, or photographing them with disposable cameras. This will model for them some ways to represent their experience.

Ask the children to stand and watch a single species of fish for a full five minutes (with a chaperone or a friend timing them). During that time they should write down any and every detail that they can think of, using all of their senses to record the experience. Be creative; ask them to remember something they like, something purple, or something small, for example. Ask them to notice the space that the animals are in or the other people visiting the aquarium. Encourage the children to reflect on something they remember about that day that has nothing to do with the fish, or on one memory from after they left the building.

These observations and records can be turned into multimodal memory books to be created back in the classroom.

If the whole class has the chance to experience the same event (e.g., the dolphin show or the shark feeding), ask each child to write as detailed a story as possible about their experience when they return to school. Then have the children read their accounts aloud and notice how diverse memory can be.

► *Encourage children to open up their schemas and avoid generalizing to stereotypes.*

To young children, schemas are theories that help with understanding and predicting their worlds. Ironically, schemas are also at the root of stereotyping and prejudice. Research shows that children notice and remember examples that support their schemas, and overlook or forget those that do not correspond to their schemas (Hudson, 1988). Children must be shown how to use their frameworks in helpful ways, while also avoiding prejudging people and situations. A classic case of schema overgeneralization is gender-role stereotypes. Presenting diverse perspectives of gender in the classroom is a great way to help children widen their schemas.

Teach children about the nontraditional roles that men and women have played in the history of blues music. Listening to songs such as Muddy Waters's "Mannish Boy," B. B. King's "Three O'Clock Blues," and Shemekia Copeland's "The Other Woman" can be jumping-off points to discuss representations of men and women that support or challenge stereotypes. Listening to "Lost Your Head Blues" by Bessie Smith can highlight alternatives to traditional female gender roles. Learning about the biography of Bessie Smith (a woman who recorded some of the first blues albums and became a huge star, while embracing many masculine traits typical of the time) could also spark fruitful discussion.

Musical instruments are also typically labeled as appropriate for boys or girls, men or women. Ask your class to brainstorm instruments that men usually play and women usually play, and write them on the board (their answers will likely include trumpet, drums, and guitar for men, and piano, flute, or voice for women). Then go through and question why each instrument might be labeled that way. Ask whether the sound, shape, or weight of each instrument might be involved in their perceptions of them. Then consider exceptions to these rules by playing excerpts of the films *Warming by the Devil's Fire*, which includes footage of Memphis Minnie and Sister Rosetta Tharpe playing electric guitar, and *Red, White and Blues*, which discusses Tharpe and her guitar playing (Blues Classroom, 2003). Next, bring the discussion to women guitarists today. Encourage children to find images of men and women musicians defying stereotypes in magazines and on the Internet, and present collages of their newly developed schemas to the class.

▶ *Use storytelling as a way of preserving and creating memories.*

Because memories are constructed in real time, stories of what happened become what we remember. At the heart of learning is understanding and representing our personal experiences. All other knowledge grows from this (Fivush, 2000). Reminiscing with children is not simply reviewing an objective event or experience. Rather, when we tell stories of the past, we choose what to emphasize, informing children how to interpret these and other experiences. In a way, all remembering is storytelling, either to ourselves or to others.

Storytelling has a rich history for humans. It was once the activity of entire communities, regardless of age. The Native Americans told stories to welcome the changing of the seasons, to mourn, and to celebrate. Oral history traditions involved sharing memories and gleaning meaning from them. These stories became classics, they never grew tired, and as they were repeated, new insights would often arise.

Ask your students to re-create and present the story of one of their earliest memories. Novelist and cartoonist Lynda Barry (2008) says that we can use the imagery of our lives to summon memories. In one of her creative writing exercises, she asks students to make a list of the first 10 cars that come to mind from early in their lives (e.g., Uncle Raymond's station wagon), to choose one car image that is vivid, and to picture it in our mind's eye. She then asks a series of questions that encourage remembering the scene of a story in a visceral way. These questions include, *Where are you? What are you doing? Are you in the car or out of the car? Who else is there? What's in front of you? What's to your left? What's below your feet?* (Barry, 2008, pp. 144–147). Finally, Barry asks students to stay inside the image and write whatever stories come to them, for a full seven minutes. Prompts like these can help children organize their memories for experiences as stories, making them ripe for understanding and sharing.

Memory Propeller 3: Mnemonic Strategies

Lucinda bites the end of her pencil as she frantically tries to remember what she studied the night before. The first math problem on her test stares her in the face. Suddenly, she remembers the trick for order of operations that Mr. Andrews showed them in class: **Please Excuse My Dear Aunt Sally.** *She carefully begins by solving anything in parentheses, then she figures out the exponents, followed by multiplying and dividing, and finally she adds and subtracts. From then on, the rest of the math test is a piece of cake.*

Mnemonic strategies are any deliberate efforts we make to enhance performance on memory tasks. Studying memory strategies in children allows us to access one of the key themes in cognitive development, namely, how children come to have control over their learning (Schwenck, Bjorklund, & Schneider, 2009). Acquired through practice, these goal-oriented behaviors have a huge, positive effect on memory performance at all ages. Many tasks in school can only be done effectively with use of memory strategies (Bjorklund, Dukes, & Brown, 2009).

Throughout childhood, the number of strategies that children use increases, as does the efficiency with which they use them (Bjorklund et al., 2009). Children who use multiple strategies at the same time, by efficiently combining them, seem to remember more effectively (Schneider, Kron-Sperl, & Hünnerkopf, 2009). Toddlers and preschool children spontaneously use some simple memory strategies, like frequently looking at or talking about the things they are trying to remember (DeLoache, Cassidy, & Brown, 1985; Wellman, Ritter, & Flavell, 1975). Older children come to use rehearsal more effectively. In one study, kindergarteners were compared with 5th graders in their use of verbal rehearsal. Trained lip readers watched the lips of the children as they attempted to remember items they would later be asked to recall.

Whereas 85 percent of the 5th graders used some form of spontaneous rehearsal, only 10 percent of the kindergarteners did (Flavell, Beach, & Chinsky, 1966). Children who rehearsed showed better performance, even when they had to be reminded to rehearse.

A key mnemonic strategy for learning is organization. Grouping items into meaningful categories or clusters allows children to better remember large numbers of items, even when the items are presented randomly (Bjorklund et al., 2009). Spontaneous clustering increases throughout childhood and is linked to superior recall throughout the life span (Bower, 1970). In a classic study, 1st graders were given 16 cards with pictures on them. The pictures belonged to the categories of animals, clothes, tools, and toys. The experimenter showed the cards to the children, named them, mentioned which category they belonged to, and then placed them randomly on the table in front of the child. The children were then told that they would be asked to remember the pictures later and could organize them in any way they wanted. Only 27 percent of the children arranged the cards by category (Salatas & Flavell, 1976). Apparently, children need to be taught that organization will profoundly affect their ability to remember.

Elaboration is another very effective mnemonic strategy. In this case, images or words are used to create a representation of the concept to be remembered. I still use the little rhyme "Thirty days has September, April, June, and November…" when I am trying to figure out the date. Like other mnemonic strategies, elaborations must be told to us. Children do not spontaneously elaborate until adolescence (Pressley & Levin, 1977), and adults often need instructions to do so (Pressley & Hilden, 2006). Elaboration techniques are useful beyond just memorization. These strategies help with understanding and remembering complex ideas as well. The process of identifying, underlining, and summarizing concepts from text passages is a form of elaboration. Unfortunately, recent research indicates that textual elaboration techniques are not being taught in school effectively, if at all (Pressley, Wharton-McDonald, Mistretta-Hampston, & Echevarria, 1998).

The final mnemonic strategy has to do with self-awareness. Over the elementary school years, children become more skilled at planning and utilizing memory strategies and also become more aware of their own memory processes. Metamemory skills such as knowing the contents and processes of one's own memory are associated with superior memory performance (Schneider & Lockl, 2002). In an important study, 3rd grade children were taught to elaborate by creating meaningful sentences about items they needed to remember. Half of the children were given metamemory feedback concerning their performance (told, for example, "You did much better remembering these pictures when you made up more vivid sentences"). The children who received feedback were able to generalize the strategy to another task, while those who did not receive feedback were not (Ringel & Springer, 1980). Perhaps this is because children's awareness of their memory processes framed their own thinking, linking it to meaning, and helping it be better remembered itself.

Teaching and Learning Mnemonic Strategies

Because memory strategies require conscious effort, children must be motivated to use them. In an interesting experiment, 7- and 8-year-olds were asked to rehearse and remember two sets of words. The first set was called "10-cent words" because the children were promised a dime for each one they remembered. The second set was called "1-cent words" because the children would be given a penny for each. Results showed that the children were twice as likely to recall the 10-cent words (Kunzinger & Witryol, 1984). In related research, 4-year-old children were offered one of two rewards to complete a memory test: either a large, brilliantly colored crayon box or a single pencil. The preschoolers paid more attention to the task and used more sophisticated mnemonic strategies when they were expecting the crayons (O'Sullivan, 1993). Naturally, children who are interested in the task at hand don't need rewards or prizes to be motivated. Spending more time on memory tasks out of pure interest also leads to better memory performance (Renninger, Hidi, & Krapp, 1992).

For most children, learning to use memory strategies is not a gradual process, but rather a sudden jump corresponding to gains in other cognitive areas (Bjorklund, Periss, & Causey, 2009; DeMarie, Miller, Ferron, & Cunningham, 2004; Schneider et al., 2009). Just like working memory skills, use of mnemonic strategies varies widely in any group of children. In a 5th grade classroom, for example, we might expect some students to only use simple strategies typical of preschoolers and others to use the complex strategies of adults (Schneider et al., 2009). Understanding where a given student is in terms of memory strategy sophistication level is a key component of predicting his or her memory performance and classroom learning in general (Schneider et al., 2009).

Mnemonic strategies can be taught. Of course direct instruction on memory strategies improves performance on memory tasks. But it also improves performance on reading and math tasks (Palincsar & Brown, 1984; Swing, Stoiber, & Peterson, 1988). In one important series of studies, developmental scientists observed the teaching of memory strategies in elementary classrooms. They looked for the frequency of strategy suggestions, the providing of information on the usefulness of the strategy, and whether teachers explained how the strategy could be elaborated or generalized to other situations. Teachers' emphasis on strategies corresponded to age: teachers of older children were more likely to give rationales along with their suggestions for memory strategies, saying, for example, "This will help you with vocabulary words, too" (Moely et al., 1992). More importantly, when teachers offered strategy suggestions, they positively affected their students' task performance in comprehension and problem-solving tasks (Moely et al., 1992). In a related study, researchers discovered that first-grade teachers who emphasized strategy use and meta-memory (saying, for instance, "How did you study those words?" "If you make a picture in your mind, it will help you remember") had students who used memory strategies more often (Ornstein, Coffman, & McCall, 2005). In short, teachers who explained and modeled memory strategies had students who were more effective learners (Moely et al., 1992).

When children are "studying," what they are doing is trying to use mnemonic strategies for keeping the information in memory. One of the most common methods of studying is to read over the material. However, recent research suggests that reading has less influence on memory than we tend to think it does. In some studies, rereading material before a test was no more effective in improving learning than just reading the material the first time (Callender & McDaniel, 2009). On the contrary, effective methods of studying should include an active inquiry component. Elaboration, for instance, relates new information to what we already know, making it meaningful and memorable. By the same token, when children outline and take notes, they recode the information in their own words and improve retention. Turning information into vivid mental images can also improve children's remembering (McDaniel & Callendar, 2008).

Washington University cognitive scientist Henry Roediger has discovered that repeated retrieval is the key to long-term retention of material. In one study he asked students to study a brief passage from a textbook. He then divided them into three groups. The first group studied the passage three more times. The second group studied the passage two more times and took a test on it. The third group took three tests on the passage after reading it once. After one week, the students took a final exam on the material. The students who studied only once but were tested three times performed best on the exam, followed by the students who studied two times and were tested once (Roediger, Agarwal, & McDaniel, in press). The worst performance came from the students who studied the most!

A large body of research now shows that taking a test on new material provides a much greater benefit than not taking a test (Roediger & Karpicke, 2006). The effect of testing on memory seems to increase with the number of tests taken. Quizzes and tests are very effective learning tools because they allow practice retrieval and they help students become aware of what they do and do not already understand (McDaniel, Agarwal, Huelser, McDermott, & Roediger, in press). A wonderful technique for studying, then, is to test ourselves. Children should be encouraged to test themselves throughout the learning process. One powerful technique for doing this is called PQ4R, which stands for *Previewing, Questioning, Reading, Reflecting, Reciting,* and *Reviewing.* Using what we know about retention will help children to study and learn in the most effective ways possible. Mnemonic strategies are powerful tools to be able to access during the time when children are developing the habits of mind they will use throughout their education.

Remember:

▶ Using memory strategies greatly improves memory performance.

▶ The most effective memory strategies are organization, elaboration, and self-awareness.

▶ Children tend not to use memory strategies spontaneously. They must be taught to use them.

▶ To be effective, studying should involve repeated retrieval of the information.

How to Enhance Classroom Memory Using Mnemonic Strategies

▶ *Assess children's learning often, and provide feedback to help them understand their own memory processes.*

We tend to think of tests as tools for measuring and evaluating learning. But recent research shows that the act of preparing for and taking a test can impact students' long-term memory for the learned material. Assessments that involve recall (e.g., short-answer, fill-in-the-blank, or essay tests) are more effective memory enhancers than those purely tapping recognition (multiple-choice tests) (Butler & Roediger, 2007). Feedback is the key to enhancing memory via assessment. For instance, going over the correct answers after a test greatly enhances students' retention of themes from their lessons. This is especially true when the reasons behind correct answers are explained. We do not see the same enhancement on memory when answers are simply read aloud afterward and not explained (Kang, McDermott, & Roediger, 2007).

Design a posttest experience. Rather than the test marking the end of a lesson, make it the beginning of a metacognition and metamemory unit. After students receive a graded quiz or test, ask them to use their books and notes to find the answers to any questions that they had answered incorrectly. They can then write a sentence or two of reflection on why they answered the way they did, or what they think might have happened for them to forget or misunderstand the information. Ask children to think of strategies that might have worked better or might work next time. You might build in an opportunity to collaborate with other learners, and strive to create the feeling that the students are not in competition with one another, but rather part of a larger learning community. Perhaps ask students who got the answer correct to share how they studied or how they remembered. *What images or other elaboration strategies do they use? What study skills can they offer to their peers?* Understanding our own remembering is the first step to enhancing it.

► *Teach mnemonic devices.*

The strategies of rehearsal, organization, and elaboration can be very effectively taught, according to research. They also spill over into other areas of learning. The idea of mnemonic devices is to connect what is unfamiliar to what is familiar (Evans, 2007). The best mnemonics correspond to acrostic sentences (where the first letter of each word corresponds to the first letter of the word to be remembered), acronyms, rhymes, or wordplay (Evans, 2007). Many of us learned the Great Lakes by remembering HOMES—Huron, Ontario, Michigan, Erie, and Superior—and the musical scales with the line "every good boy deserves fudge." We should be in the habit of creating and disseminating such useful memory tools.

Invent a mnemonic for new classroom material, and teach it to the children. The more outrageous the trick, the better students will remember it (Evans, 2007). Try "My very eccentric mailman just showed up naked" for the planets, Mercury, Venus, Earth, Mars, Jupiter, Saturn, Uranus, and Neptune.

Next, ask your students to come up with mnemonics in teams, and present them to the class. This will be especially helpful for names that are difficult to remember. For instance, assign a song to remember the ages of geological time (Cambrian, Ordovician, Silurian, Devonian, Carboniferous, Permian, Triassic, Jurassic, Cretaceous, Paleocene, Eocene, Oligocene, Miocene, Pliocene, Pleistocene, and Recent). Creativity should be highly rewarded. When the groups get up to sing their silly songs, ask the class to vote on the best one, and then have the top group teach their song to the whole class. Not only will your students remember the song come evaluation time, but they might just remember it throughout their entire lives!

Memory Propeller 4: Knowledge and Expertise

Eric has seen all six of the Star Wars movies more than 10 times each. He has also read the books so many times that the pages are beginning to fall out. Not only can he name over a hundred characters, but he can report entire lineages from a variety of planets and galaxies. He recounts the stories in animated voices, never lacking even one important detail. With a memory like this, his parents can't figure out why he always brings home Bs and Cs on his vocabulary tests.

What children already know influences what they will learn. Recall and understanding hinge on connection, both among neurons in the brain and among ideas in the mind. That is because a key part of new learning is the brain's reliance on already forged neural pathways, sculpted by previous knowledge. When our sensory systems take in new information, our brains search their existing networks to find where new information "fits." If there is a match to concepts already there, the information seems to make sense or have meaning for us. On the other hand, when there is no clear match for new information, the brain must forge brand new networks to accommodate it (Wolfe, 2006). In terms of teaching, then, the best place to begin is to discover what the students already know to understand what they already have neural pathways for. Children's prior knowledge helps them understand new ideas and concepts. It is the teacher's job to link new skills and knowledge with existing ones.

In a classic study, John Bransford and his colleagues at the University of Washington demonstrated the benefits of knowledge for remembering. The researchers asked students to read and remember a string of 10 unrelated sentences, such as *Jim flew the kite. Bill picked up the egg. Jeff built the boat.* Most people could remember only two or three out of 10. But when the sentences contained information in our collective knowledge base (e.g., *Ben Franklin flew the kite. The Easter Bunny picked up the egg. Noah built the boat*) students had no problem remembering the entire list. The power of a memory strategy, like elaboration, was already built in (Bransford & Stein, 1984). The more knowledge we have, the more easily and efficiently we can encode and remember new material. Hallmarks of superior remembering, including speed and efficiency of processing and working memory span, are influenced by our knowledge bases (Bjorklund, Dukes, & Brown, 2009).

Because knowledge does not necessarily correspond to chronological age, it is as common to find adult novices as child experts

(Schneider, 1997). In one case study, a 4-year-old boy who had spent about three hours per week reading about and playing with dinosaurs was given new information about dinosaurs he already knew a lot about, versus dinosaurs he knew less about. His memory was significantly better for facts about those dinosaurs he knew more about already. Interestingly, a year later, he remembered much more about those dinosaurs he had already known a lot about as compared to the information about the less "linked" dinosaurs (Chi & Koeske, 1983). In another experiment, elementary school children were divided in two groups, expert and novice, based on their knowledge of and experience with soccer. Within these groups, they were also divided in high and low performing on general intelligence tests. All of the children were then read a story about soccer and asked to answer challenging questions that required remembering the story in detail, including being able to draw inferences from the text and to point out contradictions in it. At every age, the children's expertise in soccer predicted their ability to recall information about the stories and to detect the mistakes significantly better than their intelligence level. The same was true when the children were tested a year later (Schneider, 1997). In another classic example, the memory performance of college students was compared to that of 10-year-olds who played a lot of chess. When asked to remember strings of numbers, the college students outperformed the children, but when asked to remember parts of a chess game, it was the 10-year-olds who showed superior performance (Chi, 1978).

Why does this happen? For one thing, naturalistic learning propels memory performance, especially in young children. (Istomina, 1975; Piaget & Inhelder, 1973). Moreover, expertise lessens the amount of effort required in processing (Bransford et al., 2007). When individual items can be retrieved more quickly from long-term memory, the child has a more efficient system and a greater availability of mental resources (Bjorklund, Muir-Broaddus, & Schneider, 1990). Furthermore, experts notice things that novices might not notice. People with expert knowledge make more links between new information and already existing knowledge by organizing information into hierarchies in their minds (Bransford, Derry, Berliner, Hammerness, & Beckett, 2007).

Extraordinary Memory

Some people become experts at remembering regardless of the topic area. They show feats of memory nothing short of extraordinary. Often called memorists, these individuals do not seem to have any particular training to remember so well; they are just "naturals" (Neisser, 1982). For example, a man named Rajan Mahadevan was able to remember and recite the first 31,811 digits from the mathematical constant ∏ (called "pi"), by thinking of the digits in chunks and pairing the numbers with outside cues in his mind. Another famous memorist named Alexander Aitkin used the method of attaching new material to things he already knew. Using this method, he was able to remember 16 three-digit numbers (e.g., 397, 212, 958) after they were read to him. Two days later he was able to remember all but one of the numbers, and 25 years later, he could recall 12 of them. Perhaps the most famous memorist was A. V. Shereshevskii, who was studied for more than 30 years by Russian developmental scientist Alexander Luria. Shereshevskii had no idea that his memory was extraordinary until Luria began studying it, but Luria was unable to find a limit to his memory either in span or length of time. In one instance, without warning, Shereshevskii was able to recall a list of 50 random words that were read aloud to him 16 years later. His technique for remembering involved imagining detailed visual scenes to represent the information. He would "place" things to be remembered on a familiar street in his mind, for instance, and easily be able to imagine them there when he wanted them (Thompson, 2000).

Recent research on memory shows that ordinary people can gain expertise in memory with practice. One study showed that college students were capable of acquiring a level of memory skill that rivals that of the memorists by simply practicing (Higbee, 1997). Anyone can develop an exceptional memory if they learn to develop techniques consistent with their strengths and interests (Ericsson, Krampe, & Tesch-Romer, 1993).

Memorization

Memorization is a memory practice with a long history in the classroom. In the early 1920s, elementary school curriculum in the United States included memorizing Shakespeare, Longfellow, Dickenson, and Lincoln's "Gettysburg Address." Reciting the words of the great poets and thinkers of our culture goes back to the time of the Greeks, who founded their learning institutions on the notion that language could awaken the mind and shape morality. When students of antiquity learned the poetry of Homer by heart, they gained access to both the language and culture. Even Shakespeare himself was educated in a culture in which huge chunks of literary works were learned by heart (Wood, 2003).

From Dr. Seuss on up, children delight in the rhyme and rhythm of verse, and they come to understand sounds and then words in this context (Beran, 2004). Poetry teaches children about the abstract patterns and relationships that bind together the words of which it is composed. In fact, the melody and cadence of speech (in other words, its poetry) helps infants and children to understand and come to know its sounds. In an important series of experiments by Karzon (1985), 1- and 4-month-old infants were only able to discriminate embedded sounds "ra" and "la" in the nonsense words *malana* and *marana* when words were spoken with an exaggerated, poetic melody.

Memorizing poetry teaches children to articulate. It allows them to speak, write, and read language with ease. Developmental science research indicates that the complexity of a child's vocabulary is the number one predictor of his or her reading comprehension (Nagy, 1988). Learning poetry, verse, and songs "by heart" has to do with becoming an expert at language. It is clear that for children to become skilled at remembering, they need to hone their memory abilities and use them as often as possible.

Remember:

▶ Children's brains rely on already formed neural pathways to understand new information.
▶ The more knowledge or expertise a child already has on a subject, the better he or she can remember new information.
▶ Naturalistic learning makes for the best remembering.
▶ Memorization is a dying art that can aid children's memories and other cognitive skills.

How to Enhance Classroom Memory Using Knowledge and Expertise

▶ *Find out the expertise of your students, and then build your lessons and assignments from the bottom up.*

The learning that children do naturally, within the realm of their own interests and their participation in the world, leads to the highest levels of memory performance. Children come to the classroom with an entire history of experiences that are relevant for their learning. They may not think of it this way, but in terms of memory, they are experts at lots of things. If your students are interested in soccer or identifying dinosaurs, you can find a way to link their classroom learning to that expertise. Doing so will strengthen and build upon existing neural networks, enhancing memory and understanding.

Try designing a memory matching game from the child's area of expertise. Using photos or drawings, create sets of two cards that depict images that go together. For instance, you could do mothers and babies or tools and what materials they go with (hammers and nails). With older children you might match words to the language they are spoken in, plants with Latin names, or landmarks with international cities. Let the children see the project through from start to finish—tracing the cardboard cards and cutting them out, gluing the images on, and, finally, playing.

▶ *Allow children to exercise their memories and become experts at remembering.*

In one of his most famous dialogues, the philosopher Socrates told of the story of the invention of writing. When the Egyptian god Theuth showed his written characters to Ammon, Ammon was greatly dismayed. He said, "This discovery of yours will create forgetfulness in the learners' souls, because they will not use their memories; they will trust to the external written characters and not remember of themselves... they will be hearers of many things and will have learned nothing; they will appear to be omniscient and will generally know nothing" (Plato, 2008/370 BCE, p. 69). Before there was any writing, songs and stories were used to pass down knowledge from one generation to the next. It was the sound and structure of the language, the rhythms and repetitions, that allowed people to easily remember. When we memorize poetry and prose, we come to know it "by heart," meaning that we can hold it in our minds and delight in its words (Hollander, 1996). Let the children in your class use their memories and experience the pleasure of knowing.

Transform your students into passionate artists by staging a poetry slam! Slam poetry, a popular art form that blends literature and performance, is a wonderful way to get your class to exercise their memories. Coming out of hip-hop music and culture, a slam poetry movement is gaining momentum as a way of teaching children and adolescents literacy, creative writing, communication skills, and confidence (Rubenstein, 2009).

To get your class into slam poetry, start by helping them develop their ideas and put them into words and rhythms. Then coach them on standing in front of their peers and performing their original pieces, using gesture and intonation to breathe life into the words (Rubenstein, 2009). You might hold a workshop with critiques and conversation about creative expression and style, building up to a more public event, with other classes or in the community. You can use this as an opportunity for children to articulate and memorize their poetry, but also as a chance to express their emotions and drum up enthusiasm for powerful self-expression. The children's poetry should emphasize rich vocabulary words and figurative language, convey clear ideas, and capture human emotion and experience. Their delivery should involve body movements and gestures that enhance their ideas. After the poetry slam, give the children an opportunity to talk about the experience of performing personal work with their peers. Encourage them to remember their poems and to share them with other people in their lives.

4

Understanding Children's Cognition and Action

cog·ni·tion is the transformation of information that we most often call thinking. In many ways the word *cognition* is used synonymously with the word *learning*. When you imagine or daydream or divide in your head, when you talk or remember a birthday, when you laugh at a joke, mentally rehearse the steps you are about to take, or think about your list of things to do, you are engaging in cognition. When breaking learning down into its processes—first being motivated, then paying attention, then taking in information or experiences—cognition is the culminating process.

In the early 1900s, the scientific study of the mind was reduced to behavior, and all actions, thoughts, and feelings were studied only as they could be observed. By the 1960s, developmental scientists and psychologists began to think that the so-called "unknowable black box of the mind" was the most interesting part of being human. They began to realize that the mind could be studied empirically with a bit of creativity and technological savvy. The cognitive revolution was born.

A Developmental Science Approach
to Cognition and Action

Part of what makes human cognition unique is that we learn not only from direct experience but also from symbols like words, maps, and pictures that represent and communicate information (DeLoache, 2000; Tomasello, 1999). Whether we are learning directly (from our sensory experience) or indirectly (from symbols that stand for other things), we represent what we take in and make meaning from it. All of our communication and technology can be broken down to symbols for reading and computation. As you read this sentence, you are decoding squiggly lines known as letters into sounds that they symbolize, combining them, and mapping them onto meaning.

Beginning in infancy, we must adapt to and acquire an immense amount of knowledge that involves arbitrary and often nonobvious social belief systems and representational devices. Infants and children are surrounded by symbols from their earliest days. They see images and videos of themselves and those they love immediately on digital cameras, phones, and the Internet; they have toy models and stuffed animals in their nurseries; and they see drawings in picture books and on the walls. Coming to understand and respond appropriately to these symbols by recognizing familiar people in photographs, or understanding scale in storybook illustrations, for example, requires complex cognitive skills that emerge over the preschool years.

When my toddler son looks at his *Little Bear and Friends* book, he always asks why Emily's mommy and daddy are so small (in the illustration, Little Bear and Emily stand in the foreground, while her parents are way down the road, by the river). Research on children's understanding of maps has shown that the same problem exists for these external representations of space. In a series of studies, young school-aged children consistently misinterpreted the notational forms used in maps. They failed to interpret the markings as symbols and instead interpreted them literally as direct representations. For instance, children denied that the lines on a road map could indicate roads because they were too narrow for cars to drive on or because the road was not really red (Liben, 1999). It takes time for children to understand that maps are a notation, standing in for actual places and things. The early school years are almost entirely dedicated to teaching the symbolic systems of literacy and numeracy, conventional notations used to signify language and quantity.

From Cognition to Action

As we have seen, the path to learning is a complex one. It involves being motivated, paying attention, taking in new information or skills, remembering, and doing some mental manipulation. The final step in the process of learning is the integration of what has been experienced into action. The English philosopher Herbert Spencer said, "The great aim of education is not knowledge but action." In other words, learning is not just in our heads—it is both in our heads and in the world. If we are to consider the goal of learning to be knowing and doing in the world, we have to concern ourselves with knowledge grounded in the practical world of everyday life. We must take into account historical influences, social interactions, culture, and the environment, the context, cultural settings, and the situations in which actors find themselves (Norman, 1993).

Children commonly show a disconnect between formal learning and everyday contexts. Vocabulary learning is a prime example of this. In their seminal work on how children learn words, developmental scientists George Miller and Patricia Gildea (1987) compared methods for teaching vocabulary words in school (dictionary definitions and a few exemplary sentences) with how children learn vocabulary in their daily lives. From the time they begin learning language, children learn new words in the context of ordinary communication. Just this week, my toddler son watched as his dad untangled the strings of the blinds in our bedroom. "Hold on, I need some more slack." "Slack," whispered Alexei to himself. And then he used it appropriately the next day. This process is startlingly fast and successful; beginning from 18 months of age, children learn up to 10 new words per day, without explicit instruction. By the end of high school, the average child has learned vocabulary at a rate of 5,000 words per year (13 per day) for more than 16 years. In contrast, learning words from abstract definitions and sentences taken out of context, the way vocabulary has often been taught, is largely ineffective. At best there is time for teaching 100–200 words per year. Methods of learning that remove abstract concepts from authentic situations disregard the way that learning happens naturally throughout our lives. The way understanding is developed is through continued, situated use. All knowledge is inextricably a product of the activity and situations in which it is produced (Brown, Collins, & Duguid, 1989).

Participating in a new experience, solving a problem, engaging with a case study, or participating in a lab experiment creates new neural pathways, constructing knowledge. Just passively trying to absorb isolated information does not (it relies instead only on short term memory). If hands-on experience is not possible, the next best option is connecting to previous experience—that is, linking new ideas to those already understood using analogies, metaphors, and similes as a way of making meaning of them (Wolfe, 2006).

We should rethink classroom learning as authentic experience, in which the teacher confronts the students with strategies that can be used to solve everyday problems (e.g., everyday mathematical problems). Rather than simply knowing something, it is important that a student know where to find information and how to relate it to a broader body of knowledge (Palincsar, 1989). To accomplish this goal, teaching techniques such as modeling, coaching, scaffolding, fading, and articulation can be very effective (Hedegaard, 2003a).

Cognition and Action Propeller 1: Implicit Learning

Carmen spent most summer days with his grandmother in the garden. While she weeded and picked the day's harvest, he would run around the edges, pile up rocks, and play with the watering can, usually winding up watering his clothes as much as the flowers and vegetables. Noni would sing songs to him when he was little and tell stories about her life when he got a bit older. "How did you learn all of this?" his own son asked him years later during planting season. Thinking back, Carmen couldn't remember. It seemed that as long as he had been conscious, he had always just known how to plant, sow, weed, and water.

Much of our learning in life is done without trying, and often without our even being aware of it. It happens just by listening, observing, acting, and interacting. Such *implicit learning* is a fast-track way to adapt to the environment—new skills, information, and knowledge acquired this way are gleaned effortlessly (Smith, 1998). Often when my students are asked to describe how they solved a problem or succeeded at a new task, they have difficulty explaining their success.

Learning Without Awareness

Our brains constantly store and process new information without us being aware of it. As you read this paragraph, are you aware of decoding each squiggly black shape as a letter and blending their sounds into words that map to meaning? Likewise, when you were learning language at about 18 months old, did you consciously study and master 10–15 new words per day? In the lab as well as in life, we learn complex sets of rules and adhere to them strictly without being able to articulate what they are and without realizing that we are doing so. In a typical implicit learning experiment, the participant is shown a string of letters and told that their order is governed by a set of rules. For instance, the sequence F-J-L-L-O-F-J follows these rules: J always follows F; L is always repeated once and the second L is followed by a vowel; F follows vowels. Although participants are never told what the rules are, they begin to follow them. Specifically, participants anticipate appropriate letters with faster reaction times and react slower to letters that break the rules, even though they claim that they are guessing (Blakemore & Frith, 2005). Neuroscience research has confirmed that when participants respond to the implicit rules, blood flow increases to brain regions responsible for anticipation, motor control, and learning (Berns, Cohen, & Mintun, 1997).

In Sweden, early childhood education is based upon the idea that children will develop their own implicit understanding of the world when their inner lives are allowed to emerge through action (Pramling, 1998). The teacher's role is far from prescriptive; rather, it is to help children have as many experiences of the world as possible by taking them to visit places, telling them stories, creating stimulating environments, and asking them questions. Experiences in new situations are expected to inform behaviors and activities, which will make students capable of new thinking. Children, it is presumed, create their own knowledge. Developmental scientists hypothesize a synergy between implicit learning and that which is deliberately taught and learned. Perhaps those things we learn without trying can speed up and improve our learning when we *do try*, and implicit learning may facilitate the transfer of learned skills to new situations (Sun, Merrill, & Peterson; 2001; Sun, Slusarz, & Terry, 2005). If we can better understand the learning that happens naturally, our formal teaching will be enhanced. The most pervasive implicit learning throughout our lives is imitation of the tools, behaviors, rituals, and customs of our culture (Bransford et al., 2006).

For the most part, the skills, knowledge, and wisdom that we learn and use throughout our lives are not explicitly taught. The old view that learning occurs when we are imparted with information has been replaced with new thinking. In fact, implicit learning can account for some of the most complex skills in our repertoire, including the ability to use symbolic language, to walk and talk, and to function in a highly varied culture by following many subtle clues.

Remember:

▶ Much of children's learning happens without awareness or conscious effort.

▶ Children learn and follow complex rules without realizing they are doing so.

▶ Experience itself is powerful for thinking and learning.

How to Enhance Classroom Cognition and Action Using Implicit Learning

▶ *Provide students with individuals and groups that they can identify with.*

According to education scholar Frank Smith (1998), the basis of all permanent learning is identification with people more experienced in the things that we want to learn. We learn via relationships with people around us (with whom we identify); we can't help learning from them, and we learn without knowing we are learning. Research supports the notion of learning as an active process of construction and reconstruction by the learner with others (Moyles, 2005). Building relationships based on shared interests within the classroom (forming teams or interest groups for both academic and open-ended activities) is a wonderful first step toward engaging children with others they can learn from. You can also help students connect with role models in the local school community, including staff and older students.

Help each student pick a person from history, the arts, athletics, or politics and research the good and bad things about this person. Ask the children to decide why they chose their person and what personality traits they possess (or at least project to the world). Reflect on the attributes of the person that may have drawn them to their field. Then, pair the students up and ask them to pretend to be their character. They might even dress up for the part. They should stay in character and talk to their partner. Ask them to consider whether these two characters get along, what questions they might ask one another, what they might dislike about each other. After their meeting, ask each student to write a letter in character to the other character they met during the exercise. Ask them to be honest about whether they would like to meet again and give specific examples of why or why not (Vail, 1994).

▶ *Design lessons based on students' interests.*

Acknowledging, understanding, and supporting the learning that children do constantly (and implicitly) will feed the learning that you would like them to achieve. This means that you as the teacher must take an active interest in what *they* are interested in, even if you don't share their interests. When children are respected and valued as already experienced learners, they will grow in the self-esteem and self-efficacy that they need to engage in school. Furthermore, if children believe that something is important to their lives, they will learn about it. Our job as teachers is to help them see how new knowledge, understanding, and wisdom might matter to them.

We can begin by carefully observing the children in our classrooms and understanding their current knowledge and skills. No human is an empty vessel; every child comes to the classroom with valuable ideas, assumptions, and experiences. The best way for them to learn is if these are built upon. We know from neuroscience research that previously existing networks of neurons in the learner's brain are easily strengthened. If we can ascertain what the bases of those networks are, we can teach accordingly. For example, the students' glee and fear when a wandering spider gets trapped in the classroom can lead to anything from a science lesson on arachnids to an art project on making webs from yarn to the reading of *Charlotte's Web*.

Branch out! Identify an area that the children in your class already know something about and expand from there. Just as their neurons are making connections via dendritic branching, the children in your class are eager to reach out and make connections, increasing the reach and density of their knowledge (Vail, 1994). You could conduct a branching-out project to study the weather. Most children have lots of experience with weather patterns and know that some places have hot, cold, tropical, or desert climates. You might ask your class, "What are the elements that make up a place's weather?" and generate such answers as clouds, sun, humidity, precipitation, temperature, wind, and seasonal storms. This can lay the groundwork for exploring similarities and differences of different climates. You could divide the class into groups, each tackling a different continent. Then, agree on a common set of questions and explore the regions of the world. You might bring in math (probabilities or measurements), map making, graphing, mythology, and literature or poetry. You might encourage individual group members to make independent investigations; or if the entire class is interested in something, divide up that one region and look at it from an interdisciplinary perspective. Branching out lets children feel knowledgeable about their world and gives them the confidence to keep exploring and learning (Vail, 1994).

▶ *Deemphasize grades as the goal of school.*

It is very early on that children learn to master what my colleagues call "The Game of School." Once children shift from naturally exploring their world to pleasing their parents or teachers, they have lost much of the power of implicit learning. Nineteen-year-old Maria, like almost all of my students, remembers exactly when school became a chore. Rather than being about playing and creating, fourth grade was when she became overwhelmed with homework and exams, when she got labeled according to her grades and admonished for her high spirits.

One of the most important lessons that you can teach children is not to rely on you for feedback. If children can come to monitor their own performance, develop their own goals, and respond to their own feedback, they will be free of the system that administers rewards. Focusing the classroom activities too much on outcomes and external rewards communicates to the children, "This is not fun; this is not for enjoyment." As an example, thousands of kids with musical talent have been so driven by their parents or their teachers that they have come to hate music. It is our calling as teachers to bring learning alive moment by moment, not just in the service of future accomplishments (Csikszentmihalyi, 1997a).

Pedagogy that is designed on regurgitating facts for tests disregards what we know about implicit memory: that it is about lived experience, intrinsic motivation, and community, and that it is a seamless and efficient way to gain all kinds of complex knowledge. External controls (e.g., tests, grades, and competitiveness) *are* embedded in the education system, but a clever teacher can keep them from overtaking the spirit of the endeavor. We must take subtle and obvious steps to ensure that the classroom supports the wonder-filled, intricate learning that children are already undertaking themselves. This can be accomplished several ways, from using creative and group assignments to measure learning, to using narrative and self-evaluation tools to assess outcomes.

Ask each child to develop a chart of 20 ways to measure student learning and academic progress. Of course tests and quizzes are one way, but challenge your students to come up with 19 others. Educator and writer Priscilla Vail (1994) wrote about a particularly aggressive 6th-grader who seized this opportunity as a way of getting out of always being told what to do. He came up with audio-recorded descriptions, gallery-like exhibitions, portfolios, putting on a play, writing a newspaper, and letting kids write the test questions. You might even take it a step further and let the class vote on how they will be evaluated after the next unit or lesson. Or, elect students to present arguments to a "jury" of classmates and teachers on why certain assessment methods would be the most beneficial for the learning goals of the unit.

Cognition and Action Propeller 2: Imitation

"Stop copying me!" screamed Molly to her little sister Elsie. She had been following Molly around all morning and even trying to emulate Molly's new ballet steps, which she was obviously too young to do properly. "Imitation is the greatest form of flattery," said their mother as a means of stopping the bickering. Elsie kept her watchful eyes on Molly the rest of the day.

Imitation is a very efficient way for children to learn and is highly adaptive. It involves carefully observing and mimicking the actions and behaviors of others—no easy task. And yet, right from birth, infants will imitate the facial expressions of an adult (Meltzoff & Moore, 1977). For my newborn daughter, Sonia, to imitate me sticking out my tongue at her, for example, she had to perceive my face and tongue, and then somehow relate the action she saw to her corresponding body parts (she could not, of course, see her own face or tongue). Sonia then had to understand and remember which muscle movements controlled *her* tongue and coordinate them in real time.

Understanding why and how children imitate the behavior of others is critical to understanding their learning. Humans are unique in their ability to take advantage of the skills and knowledge of others (Tomasello, Kruger, & Ratner, 1993). Infants don't imitate in the service of learning per se; they simply wind up imitating to communicate shared understanding and mutuality with another person. Put another way, like so many other cognitive skills, imitation is first and foremost a survival skill for helpless infants, and they end up learning in the process. Faithfully copying others is a requirement for acquiring cultural skills (no matter how arbitrary) in order to embed oneself within one's cultural groups (Carpenter & Nielsen, 2008). Via observation and imitation, children quickly learn details about expected behaviors with objects and tools, interpersonal connectedness, mutual understanding, and identification with others. By the end of the first year, infants are complex perceivers of others' social cues (including participation in what developmental scientists call *referential triangles*, the sharing of interactions with others and objects). By the second year of life, toddlers more deliberately begin to learn functional, playful, symbolic, and other kinds of acts by emulating adults (Carpenter, Nagell, &

Tomasello, 1998; Casler & Kelemen, 2005; Gergely, Bekkering, & Király, 2002; Meltzoff, 1995a). Because children can achieve a whole host of skills by merely watching and emulating others, imitation research can be very helpful for teachers in designing lessons.

Young children will copy behaviors that are inefficient, irrelevant, and even ridiculous. This makes living with a 1-year-old fun, especially if you have an absurd sense of humor. At our house, when we put cups and bowls on our heads, make funny noises in echoing vessels, and bang on surfaces in different patterns, Sonia faithfully imitates in order to understand what it is that we humans do. Research on imitation has shown that sharing experience takes priority over functional goals (Carpenter, 2006; Nielsen, 2006). Children will always copy adults' techniques even when more efficient or more effective methods are available to them. Toddlers who are exposed to someone using a tool for a particular function *just once* will rapidly learn to use the object for that particular purpose themselves. They will return over time to use the object for *only* that function, even if other feasible purposes exist. They will also assume that others will do the same (Rakoczy, Warneken, & Tomasello, 2009). When imitating, infants and children are first and foremost trying to make sense of the world, to learn how things are done, and whom to trust and emulate. In other words, they are trying to understand how to join the culture or community. The first order of business when imitating is determining whom they can trust.

Studies have shown that when children were given the choice to imitate actions labeled either intentional or accidental (the actor saying "Whoops!" when the toy lit up versus saying "There!" when they toy lit up), they chose to imitate the intentional. On the other hand, when preschoolers observed an actor accidentally select the best tool for a task (a hammer to pound in a nail) and then intentionally reject it for one that was less suitable (a brick to pound in a nail), they ignored the actor and selected the optimally suited tool (Casler & Keleman, 2005). However, when the actor extolled the value of the brick, the preschoolers chose *it* over the hammer. In this case, the personal connection was the force behind imitation, rather than the tool's design or function. Two-year-olds believe that the best way to achieve a goal is to follow the actor, who clearly has the advantage of experience and may also have information that they don't have. In contrast, 4-year-olds are looking for the "right" way to do it. In related experiments by developmental scientists at the Max Planck Institute in Leipzig, Germany, 2- and 3-year-olds were shown how to play a simple game. During the demonstration, the experimenter performed two different actions. One action was explained as the part of the game and the other was called an accident. Later, when the children played the game, they imitated only the actions labeled as correct and criticized others who performed the accident actions (Rakoczy, 2008; Rakoczy et al., 2009).

Finding Role Models

Complex forms of imitation involve determining who and what to believe. In a set of interesting experiments, children watched two actors, one who correctly labeled familiar objects and one who incorrectly labeled them (e.g., calling a shoe a "ball"). They were then asked to choose between the two adults to help them label new objects. All of the 4-year-olds (and some of the 3-year-olds) preferred to learn from the reliable adult. The children were then shown an object they had never seen before, and each actor gave it a different unfamiliar nonsense name. When the children were asked what the object was called, 4-year-olds were significantly more likely to select the label used by the credible actor (Clément, Koenig, & Harris, 2004; Harris, 2007; Jaswal & Neely, 2006; Koenig & Harris, 2005a; Koenig, Clément, & Harris, 2004; Pasquini, Corriveau, Koenig, & Harris, 2007). Across similar studies, preschoolers have shown that they will trust and copy knowledgeable models over ignorant ones; confident models over uncertain ones; more experienced over less experienced ones; and more familiar ones (caregivers at their own daycare center) over less familiar ones (caregivers from other daycare centers) (Birch, Frampton, & Akmal, 2006; Corriveau, Pasquini, & Harris, 2006; Jaswal & Neely, 2006; Koenig & Harris, 2005b; Moore, Bryant, & Furrow, 1989; Sabbagh & Baldwin, 2001). Taken together, this body of empirical work shows that children's imitative learning is social and that rules for reasoning and critical thinking are also derived from social contexts. By watching, evaluating, and imitating, children are able to take others' perspectives within the subtle and sometimes arbitrary social patterns of our complex culture.

Guided Imitation

Caregivers assist their infants and young children in learning by imitation. They do this by directing attention to ongoing events that will expand the child's repertoire for action. Parents and teachers will often physically move the infant's or child's body to show how an action is done. When caregivers embody their infants in this way, the synchronous rhythms and tempos in the movements allow an infant or child to pick up proprioceptive cues about their bodies' capabilities. Caregivers often follow this physically guided experience by inviting the child to continue the action with scaffolding and fine-tuning, saying, "Now, you do it!" or "Let's do it." Providing such verbal and perceptual support can lead the child to new skills. Shared attention and assisted imitation are among the hallmarks of cognitive development (Zukow-Goldring & Arbib, 2007). These techniques naturally speed learning by reducing the child's trial and error time.

The Video Deficit

Research in developmental science has overwhelmingly shown that educational television is not an effective tool for imitative learning in young children. Because imitating what we observe is such a powerful vehicle for learning in real life, creators of educational television programs and DVDs for infants and children have assumed that the same should be true for virtual observation. However, young children have trouble using information presented on the television screen for cognitive tasks including solving problems, learning new words, recognizing themselves, and learning to imitate simple new skills (Barr & Hayne, 1999; Deocampo & Hudson, 2005; Hayne, Herbert, & Simcock, 2003; Kremar, Grela, & Lin, 2007; McCall, Parke, & Kavanaugh, 1977; Povinelli, Landau, & Perilloux, 1996; Schmitt & Anderson, 2002; Skouteris, Spataro, & Lazaridis, 2006; Suddendorf, 1999; Suddendorf, Simcock, & Nielsen, 2007; Troseth & DeLoache, 1998; Zelazo, Sommerville, & Nichols, 1999). The same tasks are incredibly easy for young children to learn from *direct* interaction. Termed the *video deficit*, several ideas have been offered as to why learning from video is by nature mismatched with our world. First, when interacting with a real person, young children undergo a constant process of checking in with him or her for information about shared experience (Baldwin & Moses, 1996). Actors on television (of course) cannot respond if the child wants to interact or communicate, and they do not share the child's environment or experience.

Sheer lack of information could account for the video deficit, video images being literally *flat* in comparison to experiences in three dimensions, which provide depth, texture, motion, edges, and patterned light. Research has only begun to identify all of the cues around us that aid in our understanding of the world (e.g., Barr, 2008; Barr & Hayne, 1999; Barr, Muentener, Garcia, Fujimoto, & Chavez, 2007). For young children, whose perceptual abilities are still developing, a lack of cues is especially detrimental. In one example, infants and toddlers from 12 to 30 months of age imitated simple actions significantly less often after watching a model on television complete them versus watching a live demonstration (Barr & Hayne, 1999; Hayne et al., 2003). Clearly, situated learning is higher-quality learning.

Imitation is perhaps the most efficient way of learning (Tomasello et al., 1993). It is distinctly human to be able to take advantage of the knowledge and skills of more experienced others, and children use this information right from birth. Via imitation, children come to communicate and identify with social partners and appreciate others' mental states. They also begin to enact complex series of behaviors from the first few years of life. Imitation can be a powerful and pervasive part of the child's learning repertoire in the classroom.

Remember:

▶ Imitation is an efficient way to take advantage of the skills and knowledge of others.

▶ Children actively seek role models to imitate and learn from.

▶ Sharing attention and assisting imitation can speed learning.

▶ Television is not an effective medium for imitative learning. Live experience is much more effective.

How to Enhance Classroom Cognition and Action Using Imitation

▶ *Become a consistent and reliable model of learning.*

Children look to reliable others to emulate. As the teacher, children will emulate you the most! You create and impart knowledge far beyond your lesson plan, including knowledge of cultural and social rules, however subtle. In fact, you will be looked up to as a model of learning. If you engage knowledge with enthusiasm and openness and are welcoming to different perspectives and styles, your students will glean that that is how to be in the world. The teachers whom students remember the most and those whom they learned the most from are individuals who enjoyed what they were doing, who loved teaching and learning, and who conveyed their enthusiasm. "Just enjoy" might be an appropriate mantra for teachers in training. Research on the chameleon effect has shown us that perception of others' ways of being is linked to later, unconscious behavior matching. Let the job of imitating be as straightforward as possible by making your assumptions about lessons and assignments, as well as your goals for learning, explicit.

Take the role of the student by participating in your own assignments and activities. Writing the poem or doing the art project yourself is not only fun but can remind you of the students' perspectives and your own love of learning. For instance, in a family history lesson in which the students will be interviewing someone from their family and reporting their discoveries of cultural roots, why not interview someone in your family and share your results? You can present before the students and model what you had in mind for the presentations. Or, you can present on the same day as your students and join in the camaraderie of having just gone through the process of inquiry. Of course, busy teachers aren't going to be able to plan and execute all projects, but now and then it can be refreshing to be a guide and a participant.

▶ *Avoid the use of video.*

Estimates indicate that average children in North America watch more than 28 hours of television per week, rivaling the time they spend in school (Kaiser Family Foundation, 2005). Even if these hours are spent watching so-called educational shows, developmental science research has revealed that children are not necessarily learning from them. Make your classroom a place of rich sensory and perceptual exploration in the three-dimensional, complex world. When you find a film or video that you think would work well with children, just show a clip, and then link it to other modes of more active learning. Likewise, encourage students to use their time outside school for engaging with others and being present in their world.

Encourage students to do a media fast. Begin with a class discussion on media and information, and how much we each process every day. You might point out to your class the recent research showing that by 3 years of age, children recognize hundreds of logos and brands of soda, fast food, candy and cookies, gender-stereotyped toys, and entertainment (Derscheid, Kwon, & Fang, 1996; Haynes, Burts, Dukes, & Cloud, 1993; McAlister & Cornwell, 2010). You might also discuss recent research on the lasting depressed feeling that young girls report after just minutes of reading fashion magazines or using social networking websites (Schurgin O'Keeffe, Clarke-Pearson, et al., 2011; Turner, Hamilton, Jacobs, Angood, & Dwyer, 1997). Then ask your class to speculate on the number of hours of their lives that have been spent processing information. As blogger Leo Babauta writes, "We are in the middle of a vast river of information, and it just flows by us constantly." Challenge your students to become more aware of the media they are taking in each day by fasting for one day. Perhaps they want to cut out all TV, Internet, DVDs, radio, and video games for the day, or perhaps they want to cut out one thing per day for a week. In either case, making students mindful about their habits is a wonderful practice. Ask them to set a goal to accomplish in the time they have freed up and to reflect upon and write about the experience. Instead of launching back into media and information habits, ask the children to use it more thoughtfully and to value real, palpable experiences, in addition to virtual ones.

Cognition and Action Propeller 3: Emotion

Macy hates math. The last time Mrs. Lin called on her, she gave the wrong answer and turned red in front of the whole class. Now Mrs. Lin is asking her to come up to the board and solve a problem involving fractions. Macy begins to sweat. She had trouble solving the fraction problems last night for homework and didn't finish them. The boy that she has a crush on is sitting in the front row, staring at her. She can't concentrate on the chalk numbers in front of her, her mind races, and her heart pounds. But she takes a deep breath and reminds herself that all of her friends said they also had trouble with last night's homework. She relaxes and remembers that she understood how to multiply fractions in class when Mrs. Lin showed them yesterday. Macy focuses and begins to multiply the fractions.

Thoughts and feelings work together in subtle and powerful ways, and both are fundamental to learning. Emotions affect knowledge by providing the energy that functions to organize, drive, amplify, or quiet all thinking and reasoning (Dodge, 1993; LeDoux, 1994). We humans feel and process emotions quickly, and only afterward interpret them using words, contexts, and reasons for our immediate responses. Our emotions determine whether or not we focus on and retain new information and influence our motivation, attention, and perception (Dweck, 1999). Student learning increases as stress and fear decrease, as students understand and use effective self-regulation strategies, and as exciting and engaging learning environments are created (Hinton, Miyamoto, & Della-Chiesa, 2008). Teachers can use the power of emotion to foster compelling learning situations.

The Development of Emotion

Infants quickly come to understand emotions of their caregivers. From as early as 7 months of age, babies can recognize and distinguish both facial and vocal expressions of fear, anger, sadness, and happiness (Kobiella, Grossman, Reid, & Striano, 2008; Walker-Andrews & Grolnick, 1983). When they start talking and walking, toddlers' social communicative skills deepen, and they begin to very reliably interpret even more subtle emotional signals. One strategy that infants and young children use for understanding emotions is social referencing—looking to a caregiver's emotional reaction to a situation as a gauge of one's own response to that situation (Campos, 1983). When caregivers respond to an unexpected event positively, infants and young children respond with positive emotions; when caregivers respond in fear, infants respond with negative emotions (Weinger & Anisfeld, 1998).

Children continue to improve in their ability to read and respond to emotional situations as they grow. Three-year-olds reliably identify the emotional expressions of happiness, sadness, fear, and anger and understand that certain situations typically elicit particular emotions in others—for example, that birthday parties usually make people happy (Denham, 1986). Preschoolers are also increasingly aware that other people may experience *different* emotions than they do in similar situations (Denham, 1986; Denham et al., 2003). Understanding facial expressions of emotions predicts social functioning and adjustment to school, popularity, and general social competence among children and adolescents (Boyatzis & Satyaprasad, 1994). Children with learning difficulties struggle to recognize and understand others' emotions, and the accuracy of recognizing facial emotions is related to degree of intellectual disability (Bloom & Heath, 2010).

Emotion and the Brain

Emotions help us adapt to our environment and survive. They are controlled by the amygdala, two almond-shaped structures deep within the brain. The role of the amygdala is to let the rest of the body know to react quickly in potentially dangerous or emotional situations. When danger is near, a response to flee the situation or fight off the perpetrator occurs within a fraction of a second. Such emotional signals are processed on brain "super-pathways," cueing a release of adrenaline, an increase in heart rate and sensory alertness, an increase of blood-clotting elements in the bloodstream, and a mobilization of all muscles and brain centers for movement. In an intense emotional response, our cortical memory systems prioritize information relevant to the emergency at hand, and our ability to access higher-order thinking and problem solving diminishes (Goswami, 2004; LeDoux, 1996; Wolfe, 2001).

When an event is mildly emotional or interesting, small amounts of adrenaline will be released, strengthening the quality of neural signaling in the brain. In fact, some amygdala activation during encoding and recall is correlated with greater memory for emotionally arousing material (Steidl, Razik, & Anderson, 2011). An emotional hook to a learning experience allows a child to notice something and speeds up the learning process. Up to a point, the more intense the physical or emotional arousal, the stronger the imprint a learning event can have. Children vividly remember those classroom activities that sparked their motivation or grabbed their attention.

In 1908, two Harvard psychologists, Robert Yerkes and John Dodson, wrote about the relationship between arousal and performance. These scientists noticed that as people became more emotionally aroused, their performance improved. But if arousal levels shot up too high, beyond a certain limit, performance would sharply decrease. The limit to what is now known as the "Yerkes-Dodson Law" is highly individual. During the 2011 NCAA tournament, University of Connecticut basketball player Kemba Walker seemed to have no upper limit to the amount of emotional arousal he could endure. The tougher the opposing team, the better he would play. When the pressure got too high, some of Kemba's teammates would reach their threshold and start missing easy shots (what is known in sports as "choking"). But apparently Kemba's range of optimal arousal was always broader than the competition. He almost single-handedly earned his team the conference and NCAA championship titles.

Emotions and the Experience of Learning

What children learn is influenced by expectancies, personal biases, prejudices, self-esteem, and other social-emotional needs (Caine & Caine, 1990). How children feel about school and their own learning depends a great deal on whether their needs are being met. Just like Macy, many children have come to associate fear with learning situations, and their high levels of stress disrupt learning (McEwen & Sapolsky, 1995). The worst moments of our lives are when we feel self-conscious: when we are judged by others or ourselves and begin to question how we measure up (Csikszentmihalyi, 1997b). Children cannot make connections if they have been made to feel shame or if they feel stupid for making mistakes or for not responding quickly enough. This happens in school a lot.

Second-grade teacher Michelle Schwartz recounts her experience with Tim, an 8-year-old who struggled with reading. In reading group when it was his turn to read, Tim clowned around and avoided the situation. When pressed, Tim yelled, "I can't read this—it's stupid. I hate this book and I hate you!" Tim's anger was a way out of the confusion and embarrassment he might experience when trying to decode all those letters on the page (Pitt & Rose, 2007). Children like Tim perceive many classroom situations such as meeting new classmates or teachers, imagining being laughed at, being called on when not prepared, timed testing, or a general fear of failure as stressful or threatening.

Because emotion is fundamental to learning, teachers must be responsive to the emotional needs of students and provide a secure learning environment (Zambo & Brem, 2004). If students' experiences in school are pleasurable, they will be more intrinsically motivated and take on more challenging problems (Linenbrink & Pintrich, 2003). Educators can decrease stress and enhance learning by creating a school culture focused on nurturing rather than judgment.

Being psychologically safe means feeling free enough to take risks. Learners cannot make connections if they have been or will be shamed or made to feel stupid for giving a wrong answer or not responding quickly enough. A positive learning environment creates the feeling of time, space, caring, and enough trust that learners in this type of environment feel free to try out even partly formed ideas (Daloz, 1999). The emotional security that allows students to construct meaning in open-ended learning situations is the hallmark of dialogue-based pedagogies (Feito, 2007).

British mathematician turned philosopher Alfred North Whitehead believed that romance is always present in any concrete or real learning experience. He wrote that learning begins with a feeling in the learner that there are "unexplored connections" between themselves and certain situations and subjects (Whitehead, 1932). In a recent exploratory study, researchers asked students to recount a learning experience that transformed their lives in some lasting way (Soini & Flynn, 2005). More than two-thirds of the students interviewed chose a learning experience with an emotional component, either as the information was presented to them or how they received it. Students commonly reported an intuition of relevance emanating from feelings of personal and emotional connectedness with some situation or subject matter. Feelings of connectedness with topics in school were described as personal and emotional. Students made comments like, "I love looking at the stars and was really excited to learn about astronomy. Even though science class was hard, I couldn't wait to get to class, and I learned an amazing amount." In this study, lasting learning seemed to be dominated by the wonder and joy that emanates from within the individual. In fact, emotional significance emerged as the single most important predictor of learning (Soini & Flynn, 2005).

How Emotion Affects Cognition

When children experience positive feelings and moods, they do better on memory tests and classification tasks and show more creative and flexible learning during problem solving (Nadler, Rabi, & Minda, 2010). In one study, 7th graders who were put in a good mood did better than those in a neutral mood on a reading task (Bryan, Mathur, & Sullivan, 1996). In another study, students in great moods could better distinguish between pleasant and unpleasant sentences and better remember both types, as opposed to their depressed counterparts (Hettena & Ballif, 1981). In terms of the brain, emotional reactions are more primary than cognitive ones and tend to come first (Zajonc, 1984). We must deal with our emotions before we can hope to be analytical thinkers. When children experience negative feelings and moods, they use less complex learning strategies and lower effort. This is because they spend some of their time thinking about things irrelevant to the work at hand, like the causes of their bad mood (Brand, Reimer, & Opwis, 2007).

Emotions seem to have an especially potent effect on memories. For example, in one study, students were asked to play a computer game called "Weather Prediction." During the learning phase of the game, images were presented that were either emotionally arousing or neutral. Students who saw the arousing images took longer to learn the game. But, two months later, the students who saw neutral images had forgotten a substantial amount of what they learned from the game, whereas students who saw arousing images showed no evidence of forgetting (Thomas & LaBar, 2008). In other words, emotional arousal during encoding determined the mnemonic fate of the skills learning in the game.

In a recent classroom study, American history curriculum was taught with or without emotionally provocative images. The students who viewed emotional images paired with the historical information recalled significantly more than their counterparts who just received the information (Berry, Schmied, & Schrock, 2008). In this case, emotional images set the stage for content, creating a strong association between images and related concepts from the text. The more links a piece of information has to other pieces of information in memory, the better the chances that the information will be accessible.

How to Enhance Classroom Cognition and Action Using Emotion

▶ *Create meaning through affective experience.*

Our environments are bombarded with information. If we paid attention even to half of it, we would be overloaded and overwhelmed. To deal effectively with this problem, our brains have evolved to immediately filter all unnecessary information and only encode that which is relevant to the current moment, in essence to disregard any information that does not fit into an existing network. Unfortunately, much of the information that children encounter in school fits into this category: isolated dates of events, definitions of terms that are not useful, and other data that will be discarded as irrelevant (Wolfe, 2001). To make meaning of your curriculum topics, draw upon the vividness of children's own experiences, which have been imbued with rich contextual information, connection, and emotion.

Remember:

▶ Emotions determine whether or not children focus on and remember new information.

▶ The ability to recognize emotional expressions is related to social competence and learning.

▶ Small amounts of adrenaline can spark performance and enhance motivation, attention, and memory.

▶ To learn well, children's emotional needs must first be met.

▶ Lasting learning experiences have emotional significance to the learner.

When your students have little or no previous experiential knowledge to draw on, using current concrete experience is still among the most effective approaches. Problem-based learning, case studies, and other experiential learning approaches have long been designed on that premise (Taylor, Marienau, & Fiddler, 2000). The Socratic method is very effective for increasing understanding through inquiry. Rather than giving information, teachers facilitate dialogue that draws upon the collective experience of the group. Students in seminar either come to the desired knowledge by answering each other's questions, or they become aware of the limits to their knowledge (Taylor, 2010). Engage your students' feelings with simulations, role-plays, and experiential activities. Raise the emotional and motivational stakes in your classroom by asking children to tackle real-life problems.

Conduct a classwide participatory action research project. Together, your class can make positive changes in your school and community by combining research, educational work, and social action, while at the same time becoming problem solvers and critical thinkers. Lessons that are meaningful to students in a real way will tap their emotional lives and leave a deep impression on them. Santa Ana, California, elementary teacher Emily Wolk (2008) began an action research project by asking, "What are the problems in our community?" Then, together with her elementary students, she began by walking around the local area with notebooks and Polaroid cameras. The children's notes and photos clearly showed that an intersection close to the school was dangerous for pedestrians. The class formed teams who counted cars traveling through the intersection and pedestrians trying to cross. Next, her class borrowed a radar gun from the local police station to see how fast cars were speeding through the intersection. This background research led to an awareness campaign for the community that ultimately resulted in the installation of a 4-way stoplight at the intersection. "When people form a group with a common purpose, investigate their situation, and make decisions to take actions that re-form power and create justice, their reality is transformed. In so doing, they also are transformed—losing fear, gaining confidence, self-esteem, and direction" (Smith, Willms, & Johnson, 1997, p. 6). Through participatory action research, students and their teachers both cause change in the world and become changed themselves. Participatory action research applies critical theory and social justice to real-life situations as defined by the people most affected—namely, the students, the teacher, and their fellow community members.

▶ *Add an emotional hook to learning content.*

Emotion and reason are strongly linked and share common brain processing areas (Caine & Caine, 1994). In order to establish links between emotion and memory in students, we must engage their curiosity. Educators can use the power of emotion to affect learning and retention positively. In fact, the more emotionally engaged a learner is, the more likely he or she is to learn. Try intensifying the student's emotional state. For example, asking, "Why did the pioneers settle where two rivers came together?" is a much more emotionally loaded question than "Where did the pioneers settle?" (Schuh & Rea, 2001).

For a history unit, visit and interview senior citizens about their experiences and memories of the Great Depression. *How did scarcity bring out sides of people that they had not seen before? How has knowing that our economy is volatile affected the way that they lived their lives, even in times of plenty?* For a science lesson on technology, ask people of different ages about the inventions that came about in their lifetimes. *What was life like before cell phones or Internet? Do parents remember a time before they could watch movies at home, and instead just had to hope their favorite movies would come on TV? Do grandparents remember playing records on record players or calling their friends by speaking to an operator?* Some great-grandparents or older folks in the community may have even grown up without cars or electricity.

For the children, interview techniques can be a part of the preparation for the project. Encourage your students to develop thoughtful questions, record the answers, and represent their discoveries. All of the information gathered can be used to create individual presentations or a collaborative classroom museum exhibit. If it is possible, you might invite some guest speakers to talk about their lives or take part in a discussion with the students. Hearing the information firsthand would create an emotional context that no text could supply.

▶ *Use emotions in classroom processes.*

Help your students to develop self-control over their emotions. You can do this by encouraging activities that involve talking about emotions and listening to the feelings of others. Lessons that emphasize social interaction and dialogue tend to provide the most effective emotional outlets and serve as affordances for using affect in the classroom. Instead of avoiding emotional topics and issues, bring them to the forefront and make them the topic of discussion.

Rather than simply assigning punishments when students break class rules, bring together the group and give all parties an opportunity to express their experiences and feelings. You might do a go-around during circle time to give all of the children a chance to explain their perspectives of an incident. Then you could ask the children to discuss what a fair set of consequences might be and follow through with their suggestions. This way you model conflict resolution as an alternative to anger while giving your students a language to talk about their complex emotions.

▶ *Incorporate humor into lessons.*

Humor benefits children's learning by creating a comfortable classroom atmosphere in which they can relax. Laughter decreases social distance (Cosner, 1959). It invites motivation, attracts attention, and provokes thought: children are excited to listen to stories that they think are funny, even though they may not realize that they are using higher-order thinking processes to comprehend the silly stories, jokes, poems and riddles. In addition, we know from the laboratory that positive mood has a strong effect on reading, information processing, problem solving, and recall (Brand et al., 2007; Bryan et al., 1996; Hettena & Ballif, 1981). Humor has been effectively used to correct reading problems, control behavioral disorders, build vocabulary, teach foreign languages, and integrate social studies (Cornett, 1986).

Build laughter into a phonics lesson. The Be a Sport game can be played with beginning or more advanced readers. Bring three containers into your classroom. For beginners, fill the first container with consonants or consonant blends typically found at word beginnings (e.g., *sp, st, tr, bl*). In the second container, put vowels or vowel pairs (*ai, ea, ee, oa*). Put single consonants or consonant pairs found at the end of words in the third container (e.g., *rd, rt, st, nd*). Ask the children to pick one piece of paper from each container and create a nonsense words from the sounds. This word will become the name of a sport. The child must then fill in from his or her imagination the details of this sport. How is it played—on teams or individually? Does it use a ball, a Frisbee, a boomerang? What age is it for? How are points scored? For more intermediate readers, fill the first container with syllables such as *lof, pib, juf,* or *zat,* the second with open syllables such as *go, li, va, nu, he,* and the third with suffixes such as *ment, less,* or *able.* Your students might come up with sports like "Lof-Li-Ment" or "Zat-va-ness." Entertaining silliness is always welcome, and original humor is the grist for the mill of critical thinking.

Cognition Action Propeller 4: Metacognition

Charlie knows that when he gets ahead of himself, his answers get all jumbled up. He just has to remember that when the time comes to define the vocabulary words for the quiz at school. While studying at the kitchen table at night with Dad, everything seems so much quieter and easier. But when the slips of yellow paper are handed out, the pencils are in hand, and it's time to recall what the words mean, Charlie needs to remind himself, "These are the ones I studied all week. I know them very well." And as he thinks about how he wrote out the words and definitions to study, he can hear his dad's voice in his head, "Slow down and think. One word at a time." Charlie won't get ahead of himself today.

Classroom instruction is a joint cognitive enterprise, with teachers and student both playing intentional roles in the learning process (Berieter & Scardamalia, 1989). The child's understanding of the learning situation guides his or her intentions and actions. The term *metacognition* is often referred to as *thinking about thinking* or *learning about learning* and refers to knowing about one's own cognitive strategies as well as applying this knowledge to tasks at hand. In order to effectively learn, children must develop cognizance of their own thinking and the thinking of others and of changes in their own behavior and the behavior of others. Research indicates that students comprehend and retain complex concepts much better when they are sensitive to the actual process of learning (Gardner, 2001; Light, 1990). Metacognition is ultimately about developing awareness and control over one's own learning. Understanding the mind is integral to the learning process. Children's knowledge of basic psychological states in themselves and others, including ideas about memory and learning, beliefs, desires, thoughts, and emotions, affects their ability to think critically and to reason (Wellman, 2002).

Theory of Mind

Theory and research on the development of metacognition began in the 1970s and focused on children's knowledge about their own perception and attention, reasoning, remembering, and problem solving. In the 1980s developmental scientists broadened this work and termed it *theory of mind*. Theory of mind research assesses how children understand thinking itself and how they come to know that their thoughts, knowledge, desires, and feelings are separate and different from that of other others (Flavell, 1999). Theory of mind research lets us see the beginning of understanding knowledge and how children come to acquire this understanding. Because tailoring our messages to the audience requires understanding their perspectives, theory of mind is at the foundation of almost every act of communication.

The best-known theory of mind laboratory measure is called a false-belief task and goes as follows: The experimenter shows a 5-year-old child a candy box and asks her what she thinks is in it. "Candy," she replies. She looks inside and to her surprise finds it filled with crayons. The experimenter then asks the child what another child (who has not yet seen the box) will expect to find inside. "Candy!" she exclaims, amused at the trick. The same procedure is done with a 3-year-old. Her response to the first question is identical, of course. But when asked what another child will think upon seeing the candy box, the 3-year-old replies, "Crayons." Upon further questioning, the 3-year-old will also claim to have known it was filled with crayons all along and even claim that she said "crayons" when first asked (Gopnik & Astington, 1988; Perner, Leekham, & Wimmer, 1987). For children, the ability to distinguish between what they themselves know and what others know, as well as the ability to understand where their knowledge came from and when it has changed, are complex metacognitive challenges. In one study, even 6-year-olds believed an infant (who could not yet walk or talk) would know the contents of a trick box if they were told (Miller, Hardin, & Montgomery, 2003).

Pioneer developmental psychologist Jean Piaget described children as rooted in their own position. Indeed, children begin by seeing all people as a collective, sharing experiences and minds. They also tend to give others (especially those who have shown themselves to be reliable) the benefit of the doubt in terms of knowledge and abilities. Young children may even believe that others have access to their minds and actively share their thoughts, feelings, and visceral experiences (as anyone who has ever played hide-and-seek with a 2-year-old—covering their eyes to hide—can attest!)

In another classic theory of mind procedure, the child is told about the character Suzy, who hides a ball under the pillow and then has to leave the room. While Suzy is gone, another character sneaks in and moves the ball into the drawer before the initial character returns to look for it. The child is then asked, "Where will Suzy look?" Some 4-year-olds understand that Suzy, who has no knowledge of the trick, will look under the pillow. But most 3-year-olds claim that Suzy will somehow know to look in the drawer (Dalke, 1995). Interestingly, when the very same task is emotionally charged (e.g., a search for the child's missing parent rather than a ball), children up to age 5 have difficulty solving this false-belief problem (Symons, McLaughlin, Moore, & Morine, 1997).

Only by 4 to 5 years of age do children begin to understand that others' beliefs or misbeliefs guide what they say and do, and that others may see and experience things differently than they do. By age 6 or 7, children can see the world from others' perspectives. In other words, they can understand that someone with a false belief will think that he or she knows the truth. Likewise, they will understand that they themselves may have held false beliefs and though they did not know the truth, will have thought that they did (Astington & Pelletier, 1998).

Strangely enough, preschoolers have a tendency to claim that they have always known what they just learned. One group of experimenters taught 4-year-olds new facts about familiar animals, new actions performed with familiar objects, new actions performed with unfamiliar objects, and new color words. Following the learning session, the children were asked in a variety of ways *when* they had learned the new information. The children were just as likely to claim that they have known a novel fact for a long time as to report that they had known a familiar fact for a long time (Taylor, Esbensen, & Bennett, 1994). The Latin root of the verb "to educate," *educere*, means to bring out or draw forth what is already there!

Theory of mind impacts children's awareness of teaching and learning and ability to actively participate in both (Frye & Wang, 2008). A child's complexity of theory of mind is related to his or her ability to learn via instruction and collaboration (Tomasello et al., 1993). Skills required for success in school, including the ability to effectively collaborate, to participate in discussions, to engage with teachers and peers, and to understand complex language, are all easier for children with knowledge of how the mind works (Binnie, 2005). Indeed, studies have also shown that success in false-belief tasks is positively related to social-emotional maturity, popularity with peers, perspective taking, pro-social behavior, and general school readiness, all of which have been shown to enhance learning (Dockett, 1997; Lalonde & Chandler, 1995; Watson, Nixon, Wilson, & Capage, 1999). Other school skills, such as interpreting the intentions of others and revising beliefs about the world, are easier for children whose theory of mind is well developed. Intelligence aside, metacognitive understanding predicts early school success and correlates with the child's experience in school (Astington & Pelletier, 1998).

Language and Metacognition

Language creates a window into children's minds. In a sense, all language reflects thought, because any act of speech expresses the speaker's mental state. When a child uses explicit words that reference mental states including beliefs, intentions desires, and emotions, we can assess how that child thinks. Metacognitive language can also guide children toward a more complex understanding of the mind. Teachers and children grow to use language to exchange ideas and share understanding, creating better reciprocity in teaching and learning. Ultimately, when a child and a teacher share a common language with which to discuss learning, their classroom interactions become much more satisfactory and successful (Astington & Pelletier, 1998).

Smith College campus schoolteacher Elizabeth Cooney uses words to invite her 5th grade students into new ways of understanding. Using the word *misogynistic* in a unit on the Salem witch trials, for example, gives the children a framework to link the historical events to events of today. Likewise, using the word *anthropocentric* to describe the way that botanists' classifications of plants were based on the plants' relationships to humans teaches children to think critically about the relationship among point of view, knowledge, and power. Children need help with what to say, how to behave, and how to think and frame their experiences and learning.

Knowing how powerfully language links with thought, and in an effort to enhance metacognition, teachers at the Smith College Campus School developed "guiding words" for their elementary school students. Guiding words help children understand how to behave civilly in school and include bravery, negotiation, tolerance, courage, trust, resilience, empathy, and respect. Two guiding words are used throughout the year in each grade, and the teachers are encouraged to both use the words themselves and link them with curricula and learning experiences whenever they can. For example, in the 5th grade one of the guiding words is *resilience*. Elizabeth Cooney finds times to insert the word daily: "Do you give up right away?" "What would resilience look like in this situation?" or "Would you describe Van Gogh as resilient?" Over time the children begin to use the words themselves in the classroom, lunchroom, and playground. They begin to think about their own and others' behavior differently. Their sense of the world and their understanding of their learning experiences shift toward the complex (E. Cooney, personal communication, March 22, 2011).

Subtle differences in words do change the way that we think, whether or not we are aware of it. This was demonstrated in a recent study by Stanford University researchers, in which preschoolers were given either generic praise (i.e., "You are a good artist") or specific praise (e.g., "You did a good drawing") following a pretend event. After the praise condition, the children were asked to pretend that they had made a mistake in a drawing and then were asked a series of questions about how they felt and what they would like to do next. As compared with children who received specific praise, those who had simply been told that they were good at drawing seemed to take their mistakes harder, as if they indicated a failure in themselves. Specifically, these children showed significantly more helpless behavior in the face of the mistakes—they were less likely to want to fix them, felt sadness, denigrated their artistic skills, and wanted to avoid future drawing

(Cimpian, Arce, Markman, & Dweck, 2007). The minute differences in the wording of the praise had a startling impact on the children's motivation. As Mark Twain once said, "The difference between the right word and the almost right word is the difference between lightning and the lightning bug" (1901/1976).

Teaching Others as a Metacognitive Tool

Lots of us have fond memories of playing school with our stuffed animals, amused grandparents, or obliging younger siblings. When children take the role of the teacher, they automatically rely on their metacognitive knowledge. Observation of children shows that spontaneous attempts at teaching peers begin at around 3½ years of age (Ashley & Tomasello, 1998). Some developmental scientists have claimed that teaching is a universal or "natural" cognition because it appears so early in life, is ubiquitous among human beings, and does not need to be taught itself. Moreover, teaching is extraordinarily complex in that it requires knowing when specific skills are missing, representing problems and their potential solutions, and inferring the learner's motivation, emotions, and worldview (Ackoff & Greenberg, 2008; Strauss, Ziv, & Stein, 2002).

Developmental scientists examine children playing teacher by showing them a new skill (e.g., how to build something or how to play a game) and then asking them to teach it to a peer. Consistent age differences emerge in these experiments. Three-year-olds tend to rely on direct demonstrations, whereas 4-year-olds use more verbal instructions. Seven-year-old "teachers" will ask learners whether or not they understand and adjust their teaching strategies based on mistakes made by their "students." One study showed that children who understood others' perspectives (and who succeeded in a false-belief task) were more likely to add verbal explanations to the basic teaching techniques of modeling and demonstration (Strauss et al., 2002). In another interesting study, 9-year-old Navajo and Euro-American children were asked to teach a complex maze game to their 7-year-olds peers. Techniques of teaching varied by culture. Navajo children provided a

Remember:

▶ Metacognitive awareness enhances children's learning.

▶ Theory of mind is the beginning of metacognition and reflects children's perspective taking, maturity, and school readiness.

▶ Using words that reference mental states helps children develop metacognition.

▶ Playing school also helps children learn to understand and switch perspectives.

greater proportion of specific task information and were more support-ive of their partners than their Euro-American counterparts, perhaps due to differences in cultural values of collective achievement (Ellis & Gauvain, 1992).

How to Enhance Classroom Cognition and Action Using Metacognition

▶ *Make lesson plans and classroom agendas clear.*

A first step toward helping children gain awareness of how they learn is to make the process a part of the educational discourse. Keep expecta-tions of both the students and yourself clear and visible. In particular, put children in the habit of reflecting on experiences in class and on the ways they were or were not effective. If your motives for the les-son (where students should focus, the purpose behind any manipula-tions, the ultimate learning goals) are kept from the students, class becomes like a guessing game, limited to finding what will satisfy you, the teacher (Minick, 1993). Instead, help children to see themselves as active co-constructors of their own learning journey. Let them know where lessons are headed before you have gone there, and then teach them how to assess where they have been.

Share the lesson plan with the class. Children often need to be told explicitly why they are learning something. Why not involve your students in the rationales behind what you will be doing in their classroom? You may be used to hearing questions such as "Why do we need to know this?" or "When will I use this in my life?" Your students may not know the purpose of square roots or grammar or the civil rights movement. In this day of imposed content, sometimes you might not know, either. Finding out and trying to communicate the rationale and meaning behind what you are teaching is the highest order of business for effective teachers (Csikszentmihalyi, 1997b).

Guiding the students through the learning outcomes and objec-tives will open up discussion about learning and get them in the habit of thinking metacognitively. They might be surprised to find out the reasoning behind certain assignments or activities and may even be able to offer feedback about the success of certain experiences for their learning. Try asking your class what could be done differently next year, what would have made the lesson more enjoyable or memorable, or what they would have done if they were the teacher. Even outrageous or unrealistic suggestions open up dialogue on the processes of teaching and learning.

▶ *Help children become self-aware and reflective of their active learning process.*

Children comprehend complex concepts much better and retain them much longer when they become actively involved in (and reflective of) the learning process (Gardner, 2001; Light, 1990). It is helpful for children to acknowledge their contribution to shared learning endeavors and to the classroom community. Other ways of encouraging reflection include self-assessments at the end of lessons (as opposed to exams or teacher assessments) and written reflections about themselves as a learner, thinker, or even a philosopher.

Frame your lessons with the K-W-L method. Developed by education scholar Donna Ogle (1986), KWL stands for "What we know," "What we want to know," and "What we learned." Before reading a text or exploring a topic, ask your class to reflect on the statement "What I know." This helps children probe their own knowledge and encourages goal-directed learning and inquiry for gaining new knowledge. If you brainstorm answers to the "What I know" category together, you can scaffold your students' thinking by asking, "Where did you learn that?" or "How could you prove that?" Another way to approach the question is to ask, "What do we think we know?" as a collective and then determine whether that information has been confirmed, and if so, by what source.

Next, ask the children to think about what they want to learn. This question puts children in charge of their own quest for learning. It also makes learning self-sustainable and engaging. Help students think about their plan for learning, and commit to it by generating questions about things they want to know. Help them make links between what they already know and what they want to know. Finally, when the lesson is complete, ask your students to respond to the question "What have I learned?" They should reflect on whether their questions have been answered and what they still want or need to learn. The entire K-W-L method can be done individually or as a class. Sometimes thinking about learning in the collective helps children to understand how divergent background information and perspectives affect knowledge.

▶ *Become aware of your own beliefs about teaching and learning.*

Research indicates that teachers' belief systems affect their teaching just as students' theories of mind affect their learning. Indeed, your background conceptions of knowledge acquisition, ignorance, intelligence, misconception, and belief will all demonstrably shape your pedagogical practices (Strauss, 2001). Ultimately, your metacognitive beliefs and understanding will feed those of your students.

Try to read and study as much as you can about learning. Research how teaching and learning have been approached in different time periods and different cultures; discover whether brand new styles and philosophies might be worth a shot. Make it your priority to be as explicit as possible to yourself and to others about your views on teaching and learning, and make time to nourish and inspire your own love of learning.

Write an honest and thoughtful philosophy of teaching. Perhaps you did this as part of your teacher training or your job search. Revisiting this process occasionally is wonderful fuel for your practice. Begin by reading the philosophies of teaching of famous educators, such a John Dewey's "My Pedagogic Creed" or parts of Jean-Jacques Rousseau's *Emile*. Then read more contemporary philosophies on the Internet. Perhaps you could create a group at your school that would be interested in exploring together. Discuss themes of teaching philosophy over brown-bag lunches, and compile those of your colleagues in a book or on the school website. You could even get your students involved in this project. Ask them what they think the point of school is or should be. This can be done with even the youngest children. They can draw pictures to accompany their musings and reflect on their experiences of school. Examining education from both the perspective of the teacher and the learner is a valuable practice and leads to the metacognitive awareness that drives learning.

Cognition and Action Propeller 5: Articulation

Two-year-old Georgie screams when an older boy comes near her, knowing that he is coming after the lawnmower toy that she has finally claimed, after waiting half the morning at daycare. But it's no use—he begins to reach for the handle, and a tug-of-war ensues. Their teacher, Mary Kate, calmly walks over to the scene. "Use your words, Georgie," she reminds the wailing toddler, who only then is able to take a breath. "MINE!" she screams. To which her smiling teacher replies. "Great job—next time, just use words to tell your friend that it is your turn with the lawnmower. There is no need for yelling." As Georgie slowly learns this lesson, she will not only become clearer on what she wants but will be more effective at gaining it.

Explaining your thoughts not only *communicates* your knowledge but also *increases* your knowledge. Sometimes children have the beginning of an understanding of new material or concepts but do not yet have the words to express it. Teachers can help them find the words and at the same time help them form knowledge by framing for them their fragile understanding. Vygotsky (1986) wrote that verbal explanation was powerfully connected to thinking. He claimed that reasoning and reflection emerge via sharing, especially during collaboration. Because working together requires providing explanations, asking questions, listening, responding to others' perspectives, and giving feedback, learners are compelled to reorganize their thinking in light of the interchange with a partner. Partners also are given the opportunity to explore differences in their own versus others' knowledge in ways that would not happen in individual work.

Asking students to articulate their steps while solving a problem betters their performance. Studies have shown that the best problem solvers can describe the rules that govern their actions. In one experiment, students who could explain the examples in a physics textbook were better able to solve new physics problems. And when children were asked to describe exactly how they went about solving problems, they solved them *faster* (Willingham, Nissen, & Bullemer, 1989). The same result has been shown with a variety of tests, including serial reaction time (which tests the ability to learn a repeating sequence), artificial grammar learning, and navigation (Sun, Merrill, & Peterson, 2001). Evidence from these studies indicated that children who gave verbal instructions to other children during their lessons attained a *higher level of performance* than those who did not verbalize. Requiring articulation of their understanding allowed the children to make their implicit knowledge explicit (Bower & King, 1967).

Something about communicating our knowledge acts to cement it in our minds. For example, children asked to gesture as they tried to recall lessons and experiences displayed superior memory skills to those who either spontaneously gestured or did not gesture at all (Stevanoni & Salmon, 2005). In a related study, researchers asked one group of children to gesture as they explained their solutions to difficult math problems, and they asked a second group to just verbally explain the solutions. Children who were unable to solve the problems, but were in the gesturing group, tended to add new and correct problem-solving strategies to their repertoires. But perhaps more striking, when children from the gesturing group attempted to solve difficult math problems later, they were significantly more likely to succeed than those in the nongesturing group (Broaders, Wagner Cook, Mitchell, & Goldin-Meadow, 2007). In other words, expressing implicit knowledge and ideas led to heightened receptivity to learn in the future.

Questioning

Asking questions is an important part of articulating and making your learning process explicit. Research shows that children who ask themselves questions while they read comprehend books better than those who do not (Rumelhart, 1991; Trabasso & Suh, 1993). Likewise, when students are asked to explain what they have read as they go along (rather than at some later point), depth of learning is increased. In one study, students in the habit of actively explaining science textbook passages as they studied better comprehended scientific principles than those who were not (Chi, Bassok, Lewis, Reimann, & Glaser, 1989). In another interesting study, parents who typically read with their preschool children were asked to pose questions and present new words as they went along. The preschoolers learned more words than their peers whose parents were not asked to change reading styles (Blewitt, Rump, Shealy, & Cook, 2009).

Explaining

The ability to explain the causes or consequences of others' behaviors is linked to learning. As we all know, young children ask questions a lot! Their questions lead to explanations, reasoning, and an understanding of causality. In an interesting exploratory study, mothers of preschoolers kept diaries of their child's causal questions (e.g., *Why?* or *How come?*). Not surprisingly, the young children asked many questions about events and phenomena happening all around them. By far the largest category of questions focused on the causes of human behavior, motivations, and actions (e.g., *Why did she do that?*) (Callanan & Oakes, 1992). Other studies have corroborated this evidence. One research group found that 2- to 4-year-olds requested to understand motives of human behavior in 70 percent of their questions (Hickling & Wellman, 2001). Providing rationales is the essence of articulation and a herald to learning.

When we explain something to a child, we help them gain complex reasoning skills by connecting what they experience to meaningful concepts or frameworks. Children learn perspective taking when we explain various points of view to them and when we ask them to explain their own and others' perspectives to us. To illustrate, one research team recorded 2 hours of everyday conversation between mothers and their 3-year-old children. They then assessed children's perspective taking seven months later. The results showed that children who were provided explanations about the causes of everyday actions and events had greater perspective-taking skills and knowledge about other minds over time. They also displayed deeper and more complex general cognitive skills (Dunn, Brown, Slomkowski, Tesla, & Youngblade, 1991).

Explaining other people's reasoning requires children to take a metacognitive stance, infer about their own mental states, and reason about their reasoning. In a telling study from the lab, experimenters gave children feedback on their answers to math problems and then asked the children to explain the reasoning behind their feedback. For example, if the child had answered incorrectly, the experimenter might say, "Actually, these two rows *are* the same. How do you think *I* knew that?" These children were compared with others who were not asked to explain others' perspectives. The results showed a striking difference: children who were instructed to explain the experimenter's reasoning had a 70 percent success rate on a subsequent challenging cognitive task, whereas children in other groups had a 40 percent success rate (Siegler, 1995). Clearly, encouraging children to reflect upon and explain someone else's rationale advances thinking and learning.

Articulating via writing also propels children's understanding and reasoning. Just like other forms of reflective expression, writing goes beyond communicating knowledge to forming it. The writing process is ideal for making implicit ideas explicit because it requires several complex cognitive skills including: choosing techniques for discourse and description, thinking through arguments and structuring ideas, ironing out discrepancies, and making clear thoughts that may have only been half-formed. Research indicates that writing enhances critical thinking, reasoning, and applying knowledge (all of which are considered the cornerstones of quality learning) (Hand & Prain, 2002; Keys, 1993; Klein, 1999; Rivard, 1994; Rosaen, 1990). In one study, biology students were divided into two groups—one that responded to hands-on experiences by writing and another that took quizzes. The two groups had the same scores on measures of critical thinking at the beginning of the term. By the end of the term, the writing group made significant gains in their critical thinking skills (including analysis and inference skills), while the nonwriting group did not (Quitadamo & Kurtz, 2007). Writing is recursive in that it encourages continuing discovery and reflection in school subjects as diverse as science and music. It also helps students use language constructively toward integrating new information with their already existing knowledge (Armbruster, McCarthy, & Cummins, 2005).

Articulating Goals

Children learn best when the goals and objectives of a teaching situation are clearly articulated to them. Because the frontal lobes of the brain (which are responsible for planning) are not fully functional until adolescence, it is helpful if teachers allow children access to the intended result of a lesson before going through the steps. One important developmental science study illustrated the benefit of spelling out teaching goals. Four-year-olds were brought into the lab and shown a box with colored buttons that lit up lights in sequence when pressed a certain way. They were all given directions by "teachers" but were given varying rationales as to why the teachers pushed which buttons. Some children were told that the teachers were showing them how to learn the sequence. Other children were told that the teachers were pushing the buttons just because they liked doing it. A third group of children received no explanation for the teachers' actions; they were merely asked to watch. The children's ability to learn the complex sequence varied depending on the rationale given to them. Children who were told that it was a learning event being modeled for them learned the actions more accurately than children who were shown the same action accompanied by an inappropriate rationale or accompanied by no explanation (Sobel & Sommerville, 2009). Hearing a rationale for what they see can alert children to what they will see next and let them know to engage more deeply. In the same way, having a partner who articulates his or her upcoming plans during a collaborative effort enhances children's ability to remember and learn from their partner's actions (Ratner, Foley, & Gimpart, 2002; Sommerville & Hammond, 2007).

Remember:

▶ Articulating helps children communicate, but also form their knowledge.

▶ For children, explaining how they solve a problem is more important for learning than actually solving it.

▶ Gesturing aids in understanding.

▶ Questioning, explaining, and writing all propel thinking and reasoning.

How to Enhance Classroom Cognition and Action Using Articulation

▶ *Create classroom activities and assignments that utilize articulation and explanation.*

Articulating thoughts is not merely about communicating. For children especially, the act of articulating, revising, and sharing is generative of thoughts and ideas. In other words, undeveloped ideas can evolve while the child is in the act of explaining. Providing opportunities for children to offer explanations of their own thinking and action, as well as that of others, is an important method for engendering meaningful learning (Wellman & Laguttata, 2004). To help children present their theories and ideas across domains, incorporate various opportunities for discourse.

In math class, assign your students a writing assignment about the process of solving a math problem. This might be a step-by-step set of instructions to help another student do the same problem or more of a narrative about their visceral experience. ("I started to get nervous when I saw the last problem on the test because long division is not my strong suit. But then I remembered that 2 goes into 8 four times and was on my way to a successful solution.") This kind of articulation helps children understand their learning process and take control of it. Other possibilities include visually representing what happened in a story, creating knowledge maps before doing science projects, or using only gestures to teach someone else.

▶ *Encourage questions and taking other perspectives.*

Young children certainly don't need our encouragement to ask questions, but we need to make sure that inquisitive exploration continues within the structure of the classroom. Creating a culture of questioning involves modeling the asking of questions during the students' thought processes. Research indicates that requiring students to answer questions about a story as they go along (as opposed to waiting until afterward) enhances comprehension and learning (Andre, Mueller, Womack, Smid, & Tuttle, 1980; Hamilton, 1985). Questions that ask for explanations of what has been read are often particularly effective. Studies of science learning have likewise demonstrated that students who actively explain textbook passages (even to themselves) show better comprehension of scientific principles (Chi et al., 1989). Teach learners how to deepen their questions and take them further and also how to challenge their own assumptions. Invite them to question the motives and causes of behavior, texts, and authorities. Questions can be lead-ins to discussion and articulation, and they can foster taking others' perspectives, all key metacognitive skills.

Ask your students to keep a question journal throughout the year and across the different subjects of learning, such as math, reading, science, history, and current events. After the introduction of a new unit, you might have them write questions about things that intrigue them about the topic. You might also have them write questions at the end of the unit on things that still stand unanswered for them after their learning experiences. For more advanced students, ask them to write questions from the point of view of another person. For instance, "How could you explain the civil rights movement to a child much younger than you?" or "What was your grandparents' experience of the civil rights movement?" In any case, ask the students to review their questions at the middle and end of the year. *Do they see any patterns? What do the types of questions reveal about their interests and thinking in general?* You could spend some time helping them to develop critical questioning skills or use their questions as an assessment tool. (For instance, *Is their thinking deepening throughout the year? Are most questions literal, or are some developing into those that tap into reasoning skills?*) This is also helpful for your lesson planning. (For example, *Did the students' questions reveal a deep understanding of ideas that you explained?*) Just being in the habit of articulating questions, even if it seems forced at first, helps get students to formulate their thoughts concretely.

Cognition and Action Propeller 6: Collaboration

All morning at the beach, Sylvia and her cousins have been working on a sandcastle. They have filled buckets upon buckets of water and carried them sloshing up the hill from the shoreline. They dug moats and tunnels, built stairways and multilayered towers, and even put reed flags on the tops of each. When Grandpa walks down from the cottage and sees the castle, the bigger kids have gone swimming. Only little Sylvia remains behind, admiring the sandy kingdom. "Who made this?" Grandpa asks. "I made it!" shouts Sylvia. "Wow! All by yourself?" asks Grandpa in disbelief. "Yes—I did it!" she replies, glowing.

Collaboration catapults learning. Working with peers provides opportunities for guiding, structuring, and scaffolding children's knowledge. As mentioned above, this is partly due to making implicit learning explicit via articulation. In addition, working with someone else effectively requires such complex skills as coordinating various conceptions of the problem, making one's own thinking transparent, and understanding a partner's thinking. Simply put, collaboration invites high-level reasoning and critical thinking.

Collaboration in the Zone of Proximal Development

Developmental scientists in the sociocultural tradition view the whole of human development as a process of gaining mastery of cultural symbols and tools with others, in an effort toward joining one's community. According to Vygotsky (1987), children can always do more in collaboration than they can do independently. When one child is more experienced than his or her learning partners, that child can bootstrap the less experienced partners into understanding what they need to learn. Vygotsky labeled the difference between what a child can achieve on his or her own and what he or she can accomplish with the help of a more advanced peer *the zone of proximal development.* Instruction, therefore, is only useful when it moves ahead of development. Researchers in the Vygotskian tradition have shown that cognitive development is propelled when partners with different initial skill levels work collaboratively to arrive at a shared understanding. My husband Rob experienced this firsthand, growing up in a neighborhood where all the kids were four or five years older than him. From an early age (way too little to be using saws and hammers on his own), he was intricately involved in building tree houses and forts under the guidance of the older boys. The older boys supported his emerging construction skills while modeling the more advanced techniques. This allowed Rob, the budding carpentry enthusiast, to boldly attempt much more than he ever would have on his own and even to do things (like put up walls) before he actually knew *how* to do them.

Collaboration and Learning

There is a great abundance of evidence that working collaboratively with social partners enhances learning. When collaborating with peers, children achieve more across many domains, including planning skills, block-sorting abilities, prediction of physical movement, strategy use, causal attribution, and recall. In a series of studies, children worked alone or with a same-age peer on challenging assignments. Those kids who worked collaboratively showed higher engagement and enjoyment while performing the task. But they also showed improved performance (Perlmutter, Behrend, Kuo, & Muller, 1989; Samaha & De Lisi, 2000; Underwood, Underwood, & Wood, 2000). In a related study, children worked either in pairs or as individuals on a computer-based problem-solving task. Children working in pairs outperformed children working individually. Likewise, researchers discovered that complex strategies for solving problems were more readily achieved in collaborative settings than in individual ones. After participating in collaborative sessions, children abandoned their naïve reasoning methods in favor of more complex styles (Moshman & Geil, 1998).

Collaboration also enhances future solo performance, even on completely unrelated tasks. In one study, 3- and 5-year-olds who collaborated with their mothers on a difficult sorting task were much more successful later when doing a different independent task, as opposed to children who did not collaborate for the initial sorting task (even though the group who worked alone received corrective feedback from an experimenter) (Freund, 1990). In the same vein, developmental scientists asked 7th graders to take a break from difficult nonverbal reasoning problems and work collaboratively for an interim period. Those who had the peer-collaboration time in between scored significantly higher than students who worked alone the entire time (Samaha & De Lisi, 2000). Furthermore, when 7- and 8-year-olds were given training sessions for a logic game in pairs, they did significantly better on *individual* logic tasks later (Light & Glachan, 1985).

Paired work seems to bring about mastery of complex cognitive skills such as making proposals, drawing inferences, and countering partner's proposals. These skills stay with children and help them when it comes time to do individual cognitive problems. In a striking set of experiments, 5-year-olds were asked to build a replica of an intricate Lego model. Children were divided into two groups (expert or novice) depending on their skills at building the initial replica. They were then assigned to build Lego models in one of three ways: alone, with a matched skill-level partner, or with a partner of the opposite skill level. The results strongly indicated that collaboration led to greater learning than individual work. For novices, learning was maximized when they worked with an expert partner on Lego building and also when doing future solo building tasks (Azmitia, 1988). Taken together, this volume of evidence lends clear and compelling support to Vygotsky's notion of learning with others.

Why does collaboration enhance individual learning? Researchers have hypothesized that working with someone else provides opportunities for *internalization*, the process of transforming shared understanding into one's own repertoire. When we internalize, we are simultaneously the actor and the observer. During collaboration, students are working toward a shared goal, so they have to constantly switch from inside to outside their own minds, imagining and anticipating the other's actions as well as their own (Lawrence & Valsiner, 1993; Tomasello et al., 1993; Vygotsky, 1978).

The "I Did It!" Bias

An interesting side effect of collaborative learning in young children is the tendency to overinflate their contribution to the joint effort. When children are asked to remember who did what in a shared activity, they may claim to have done things that were in fact done by their partner. Sometimes called the *"I did it!" bias*, research shows that children who overestimated their contribution to a joint learning effort (e.g., building novel toys out of available parts) actually *outperformed* children who attributed more to their partners in this complex task (Foley Passalacqua, & Ratner, 1993; Foley & Ratner, 1998; Foley, Ratner, & House, 2002; Ratner, Foley, & Gimpert, 2002). Even more striking, children who showed the "I did it!" bias not only did better immediately rebuilding the toys; they also showed superior performance rebuilding them 4 months later! The strength of the child's bias also predicted his or her accuracy in rebuilding the toys alone (Sommerville & Hammond, 2007). These researchers hypothesized that the "I did it" bias is part of the process of effective learning from others. It seems to enhance children's tendency to adopt others' actions, a process that supports the hypothesis of learning via internalization.

Human brain mapping studies corroborate the "I did it" bias. Our brains have overlapping neural circuits for actions that are performed and actions that are perceived (Chao & Martin, 2000; Grafton, Arbib, Fadiga, & Rizzolatti, 1996; Grèzes & Decety, 2001; Hamzei et al., 2003; Hari et al., 1998). This was first documented within the motor centers (the parts of the brain involved in movement of the body) of macaque monkeys. In the initial studies, scientists discovered that certain neurons fired both when the monkey watched an experimenter perform an action and when the monkey executed the action. A similar system was subsequently found in human adults, infants, and children (Bertenthal & Longo, 2008; Falck-Ytter, Gredeback, & von Hofsten, 2006; Fecteau et al., 2004; Hauf & Prinz, 2005; Longo & Bertenthal, 2006; Sommerville, Woodward, & Needham, 2005). With so-called *mirror neurons*, the observation of someone else's action directly maps onto the motor representation of that action. The mirror system is activated when you are asked to watch someone's actions with the intention of doing the same actions yourself. It is also activated when you learn new skills by imitating others.

To your brain, watching someone else perform an action is the same as doing it yourself. That means that if you are collaborating, you can learn from your own actions as well as the actions of your partner. The mirror neuron system privileges collaborative learning by giving us the experience of doing while we internalize the insights and actions of others. When it comes to neurons, there is no concept of the individual self. My mirror neurons will adopt your point of view in a kind of virtual reality simulation as I watch you in the world. Mirror neurons may underlie all learning and perhaps our entire human civilization. University of California neuroscientist V. S. Ramachandran (2009) speculates that mirror neurons are responsible for the sudden emergence sometime in the last 100,000 years of skills unique to humans, such as the use of fire and tools, and, of course, language.

According to the sociocultural perspective of developmental science, true learning happens via collaboration (Rogoff, 1990; Vygotsky, 1978). Classrooms can no longer be

Remember:

▶ Children can do more collaboratively than they can do independently.

▶ Cognitive development is greatly enhanced when partners of different skill levels work collaboratively.

▶ Collaboration enhances performance on future solo tasks, even unrelated ones.

▶ Children transform shared knowledge into individual knowledge.

▶ Watching someone else perform an action has the same value for learning as performing the action yourself, both in subjective experience and literally, in the brain.

viewed as places where knowledge is transferred from teachers to students, since taking part in collaborative exchanges and working toward a shared goal (versus working alone) greatly enhances cognitive performance. Multiage classrooms provide fertile ground for co-creating knowledge. Collaboration provides opportunities for more experienced partners to guide, structure, and scaffold other children's learning. Working together with peers of different ages also exposes children to new problem-solving strategies and forces them to see solutions from different perspectives, as well as allowing them to assess their own knowledge. Ironically, the best model of this kind of learning may be from the one-room schoolhouse of the past.

How to Enhance Classroom Cognition and Action Using Collaboration

▶ *Convert solo work into opportunities for collaborative learning.*

True collaboration can be thought of as wrestling in real time to solve problems jointly. Giving children opportunities to share participation on traditionally high-stakes assignments (e.g., writing assignments and tests) can be powerful for learning. By thinking out loud, children learn more rapidly and deeply than by working quietly. Working together creates a cycle of articulating and learning, which continuously feed off of each other. Collaborative lessons can also serve to deemphasize grades and measuring up, and allow the process of learning itself to emerge. We need to open our own minds to possibilities other than individualism and competition.

Give quizzes, tests, and exams in pairs. Famous Stanford psychologist Philip Zimbardo and his colleagues recently tried this in their introductory psychology college courses. In two sections, he taught the material using the same curriculum and pedagogy—the only difference was that one group took the exams in pairs. The results were astonishing and called into question our dogmas about assessing learning. The students who took tests in pairs performed significantly better on all exams, and their scores were more consistent. They also reported a host of positive attitudes: reduced test anxiety, elevated confidence, and the irrelevance of cheating. The students who collaborated also reported lasting effects in their learning, including increased enjoyment of the course and the subject matter in general. This was true for students who chose their own partners and for students whose partners were assigned to them (Zimbardo, Butler, & Wolfe, 2003).

Of course, we would expect the same positive effects of paired testing in children. Your students might approach in-class exercises together in preparation for the test, study together, and come to understand each other's strengths. On test day they might quietly whisper strategies to each other or work silently on problems and then review the steps together. In terms of both understanding and enhancing their learning processes (not to mention minimizing their anxiety around tests), this strategy promises to be a great success.

▶ *Allow children to work within their zone of proximal development.*

Children's first attempts at new ways of thinking and acting can be supported by others and transformed into new strategies. That is why developmental scientists say that children begin to do things before they actually know *how* to do them. Vygotsky believed that children learn best by working with more experienced peers in the zone of proximal development. Pairing children with partners of different skill levels will help them find their zones. Whether one is the more or less experienced child in the pair, learning is still enhanced: the more advanced student must discern how to explain and articulate, and how to tailor the task to the needs of the less advanced student; the less advanced student will be pushed to the limits of his or her experience and then beyond. Both will be surprised at the learning they can accomplish.

Make learning pals of older and younger children at your school. You might team up children from your class with those in a colleague's class. Let them share and compare, either live or via handwritten letter or e-mail. The older children could help the younger ones with homework during free-time blocks or attempt to teach them some of the concepts that will be coming up in future grades. (I still recall how readily my 1st grade sister was able to learn

6th grade math when I taught it to her. Our games of school often consisted of my sharing what I had learned that day, and she was as eager to understand it as I was to help her). Your learning pals can also share the joys and struggles of the process of learning. Get them to talk to one another and ask about the topics they are studying. *What do they enjoy most? Least? If they could design the curriculum, what would stay in and what would go? Why?* These questions are just starters. Being a mentor to other students can be a tremendous confidence booster for the older child, and getting attention from older children fosters curiosity in younger ones. Learning pals can ask each other questions and then reflect with the larger group before they respond. Working together is how we have evolved to learn. It will propel children's learning to new planes above all else.

Conclusion

Science has much to offer to education. At its heart is the scientific method—a practice of approaching the unknown with carefully posed questions, which are then compared with previous discoveries. Scientists design clever ways of entering into the complexity and testing their ideas. Nothing could be more exciting than to notice, unearth, or pinpoint the mechanisms of the mind at work. Careful and systematic observation of student learning, put into the context of the research literature, leads us to ask deeper, better questions and to further refine and develop our pedagogies.

Developmental science as a field of inquiry is ripe with findings that can enhance the practice of teaching, some of which are quite counterintuitive and surprising. Learning is one of the most complex and nuanced of human proclivities, requiring motivation and attention, relying deeply on connection and memory, and culminating in cognition and action. This is an unusual time, as new knowledge about the human mind is coming to light at an astounding rate. We have been given access to examine learning as it happens, to understand what might open children up and what could shut them down. Those facets of the developing mind that guide or propel learning are the focus of this book, including habituation, confidence, community joining, self-regulation, executive control, imitation, emotion, metacognition, and collaboration. It is our job as educators to wed our own observations with the discoveries of others and to harness them to strengthen the learning of the individual students we work with regularly.

What we now know about young children's learning is that it emerges without their realizing it and without trying. Infants and children are the most efficient and successful learners of all—picking up new information and ideas is as natural to them as breathing. They do not need us to show them how to do it. They have been learning and developing with great success since before being born. As the child's experiential repertoire increases, his or her best learning will come from being interested, with noticing and choosing and focusing within the vast array of stimulation available at any given moment. Children take in their worlds by being present with experiences.

Learning is social. It works best when children work together, help each other, and remain reflective about what they are doing. It is about knowing and communing with their people, spending time together, and finding others to admire and emulate. Learning is also guided by emotions, a state of being that has to do with the child's overall feelings of wellness and support. The best learning involves self-expression, creativity, and effective communication. Most of all, learning is about being playful. Children need to be invigorated and experimental, to take risks and explore, to generate movement physically and mentally, and to enjoy themselves within the intellectual playgrounds of their lives, including the classroom.

But to truly understand how young children learn, I believe that we need to blur the division between teaching and learning. As teachers, we have the opportunity to be learners first and foremost, and our students have just as much to teach us as we have to teach them. If we can explore together and co-create a culture of inquiry, we can re-create the conditions in which human learning has emerged effortlessly and seamlessly for tens of thousands of years.

References

Abbott, J. S. C. (1839). *The school-boy or a guide for youth to truth and duty.* Boston: Crocker and Brewster.

Ackoff, R. L., & Greenberg, D. (2008). *Turning learning right side up: Putting education back on track.* Philadelphia: Wharton School Publishing.

Acredolo, L. P. (1985). Coordinating perspectives on infant spatial orientation. In R. Cohen (Ed.), *The development of spatial cognition* (pp. 115–140). Hillsdale, NJ: Erlbaum.

Alaimo, K., Olson, C. M., & Frongillo, E. A. (2001). Food insufficiency and American school-aged children's cognitive, academic, and psychosocial development. *Pediatrics, 108,* 44–53.

Alloway, T. P., Gathercole, S. E., Adams, A. M., & Willis, C. S. (2005). Working memory and other cognitive skills as predictors of progress towards early learning goals at school entry. *British Journal of Developmental Psychology, 33,* 1–11.

Amabile, T. M., & Hennessey, B. A. (1992). The motivation for creativity in children. In T. Pittman & A. Boggiano (Eds.), *Achievement and motivation: A social developmental perspective* (pp. 54–74). New York: Cambridge University Press.

Anand, B. K., Chhina, G. S., & Singh, B. (1961). Some aspects of electroencephalographic studies in yogis. *Electroencephalography Clinical Neurophysiology, 13,* 452–456.

Andre, T., Mueller, C., Womack, S., Smid, K., & Tuttle, M. (1980). Adjunct questions facilitate later application, or do they? *Journal of Educational Psychology, 72,* 533–543.

Armbruster, B. B., McCarthey, S. J., & Cummins, S. (2005). Writing to learn in elementary classrooms. In R. Indrisano & J. R. Paratore (Eds.), *Learning to write, writing to learn: Theory and research in practice* (pp. 71–96). Newark, DE: International Reading Association.

Armstrong, T. (1997). *The myth of the A.D.D. child: 50 ways to improve your child's behavior and attention span without drugs, labels, or coercion.* New York: Plume.

Armstrong, T. (2009). *Multiple intelligences in the classroom* (3rd ed.). Alexandria, VA: ASCD.

Ashley, J., & Tomasello, M. (1998). Cooperative problem solving and teaching in preschoolers. *Social Development, 7,* 143–163.

Astington, J. W., & Pelletier, J. (1998). The language of mind: Its role in teaching and learning. In D. R. Olson & N. Torrance (Eds.), *The handbook of education and human development* (pp. 593–620). Malden, MA: Blackwell.

Ayres, J., & Hopf, T. S. (1990). Visualization: Is it more than extra-attention? *Communication Education, 38,* 1–5.

Azmitia, M. (1988). Peer interaction and problem-solving: When are two heads better than one? *Child Development, 59,* 87–96.

Baddeley, A.D. (1986). *Working memory.* Oxford: Oxford University Press.

Bakhtin, M. M. (1965). *Rabelais and his world* (H. Iswolsky, Trans.). Bloomington: Indiana University Press. (Original work published 1941)

Bakhtin, M. M. (1984). *Problems of Dostoevsky's poetics.* (C. Emerson, Ed. and Trans.). Minneapolis: University of Minnesota Press.

Baldwin, D. A., & Moses, L. J. (1996). The ontogeny of social information gathering. *Child Development, 67,* 1915–1939.

Barnett, L. A. (1984). Research note: Young children's resolution of distress through play. *Journal of Child Psychology and Psychiatry, 25*(3), 477–483.

Barnett, L. A., & Storm, B. (1981). Play, pleasure, and pain: The reduction of anxiety through play. *Leisure Sciences, 4*(2), 161–175.

Barr, R. (2008). Attention and learning from media during infancy and early childhood. In S. L. Calvert & B. J. Wilson (Eds.), *Blackwell handbook of child development and the media.* Oxford: Blackwell.

Barr, R., & Hayne, H. (1999). Developmental changes in imitation from television during infancy. *Child Development, 70,* 1067–1081.

Barr, R., & Hayne, H. (2000). Age-related changes in imitation: Implications for memory development. In C. Rovee-Collier, L. Lipsitt, & H. Hayne (Eds.), *Progress in infancy research* (Vol. 1, pp. 21–67). Mahwah, NJ: Erlbaum.

Barr, R., & Hayne, H. (2003). It's not what you know, it's who you know: Older siblings facilitate imitation during infancy. *International Journal of Early Years Education, 11*(1), 7–21.

Barr, R., Muentener, P., Garcia, A., Fujimoto, M., & Chavez, V. (2007). The effect of repetition on imitation from television during infancy. *Developmental Psychobiology, 49,* 196–207.

Barreto, E. D., Morris, B. H., Philbin, M. K., Gray, L. C., & Lasky, R .E. (2006). Do former preterm infants remember and respond to neonatal intensive care unit noise? *Early Human Development, 82*(11), 703–707.

Barry, Lynda. (2008). *What It Is.* Montreal, Canada: Drawn & Quarterly

Bartzokis, G., Lu, P. H., Tingus, K., Mendez, M. F., Richard, A., Peters, D. G., Oluwadara, B., Barrall, K. A., Finn, J. P., Villablanca, P., Thompson, P. M., & Mintz, J. (2010). Lifespan trajectory of myelin integrity and maximum motor speed. *Neurobiology of Aging, 31*(9), 1554–1562.

Bauer, P. J. (1997). Development of memory in early childhood. In N. Cowan (Ed.), *The development of memory in childhood* (pp. 83–113). Hove, UK: Psychology Press.

Beghetto, R.A. (2008). Correlates of intellectual risk taking in elementary school science. *Journal of Research in Science Teaching, 46*(2), 210–223.

Bell, M. A., & Fox, N. A. (1992). The relations between frontal brain electrical activity and cognitive development during infancy. *Child Development, 63,* 1142–1163.

Bellflower, J. B. (2008). A case study on the perceived benefits of multiple intelligence instruction: Examining its impact on student learning. *Dissertation Abstracts International, 69*(3-A), 878.

Belt, T. (2008, January 21). Let the students teach. In *Tracie Belt's Blog.* Retrieved October 10, 2010, from: http://blog.discoveryeducation.com/traciebelt/2008/01/

Beran, M. K. (2004). In defense of memorization. *City Journal.* Retrieved November 20, 2010, from: http://www.city-journal.org/html/14_3_defense_memorization.html

Bereiter, C., & Scardamalia, M. (1989). Intentional learning as a goal of instruction. In L. B. Resnick (Ed.), *Knowing, learning, and instruction: Essays in honor of Robert Glaser* (pp. 361–392). Hillsdale, NJ: Erlbaum.

Berger, S. (2006, June). *Older siblings influence their younger siblings' motor development.* Paper presented at the annual meeting of the XVth Biennial International Conference on Infant Studies, Westin Miyako, Kyoto, Japan.

Berlyne, D. E. (1960). *Conflict, arousal, and curiosity.* New York: McGraw-Hill.

Berns, G. S., Cohen, J. D., & Mintun, M. A. (1997). Brain regions responsive to novelty in the absence of awareness. *Science, 276,* 1272–1275.

Berry, C., Schmied, L. A., & Schrock, J. C. (2008). The role of emotion in teaching and learning history: A scholarship of teaching exploration. *The History Teacher, 41*(4), 437–452.

Bertenthal, B. I., & Longo, M. R. (2008). Motor knowledge and action understanding: A development perspective. In R. Klatzky, M. Behrmann, & B. MacWhinney (Eds.), *The Carnegie Symposium on Cognition*, Vol. 34: *Embodiment, ego space, action.* New York: Psychology Press.

Binnie, L. M. (2005). TOM goes to school: Theory of mind understanding and its link to schooling. *Educational and Child Psychology, 22*(4), 81–93.

Birch, S. A. J., Frampton, K. L., & Akmal, N. (2006, June). The medium is the message: How infants' sensitivity to nonverbal cues influences what they learn from others. Paper presented by S. A. J. Birch at the International Conference on Infant Studies (ICIS) in Kyoto, Japan.

Bjorklund, D. F. (2005). *Children's thinking: Cognitive development and individual differences* (4th ed.). Belmont, CA: Wadsworth.

Bjorklund, D. F. (2007). *Why youth is not wasted on the young: Immaturity in human development.* Malden, MA: Wiley-Blackwell.

Bjorklund, D. F. (in press). Cognitive development: An overview. In P. D. Zelazo (Ed.), *Oxford handbook of developmental psychology.* Oxford: Oxford University Press.

Bjorklund, D. F., Dukes, C., & Brown, R. D. (2009). The development of memory strategies. In M. L. Courage & N. Cowan (Eds.), *The development of memory in infancy and childhood* (pp. 145–175). Hove, UK: Psychology Press.

Bjorklund, D. F., Gaultney, J. F., & Green, B. L. (1993). "I watch, therefore I can do": The development of meta-imitation over the preschool years and the advantage of optimism in one's imitative skills. In M. L. Howe & R. Pasnak (Eds.), *Emerging themes in cognitive development* (Vol. 2, pp. 79–102). New York: Springer.

Bjorklund, D. F., & Harnishfeger, K. K. (1987). Developmental differences in the mental effort requirements for the use of an organizational strategy in free recall. *Journal of Experimental Child Psychology, 44,* 109–125.

Bjorklund, D. F., Muir-Broaddus, J. E., & Schneider, W. (1990). The role of knowledge in the development of strategies. In D. F. Bjorklund (Ed.), *Children's strategies: Contemporary views of cognitive development.* Hillsdale, NJ: Erlbaum.

Bjorklund, D. F., Periss, V., & Causey, K. (2009). The benefits of youth. *European Journal of Developmental Psychology, 6*(1), 120–137.

Blair, C., & Razza, R. A. (2007). Relating effortful control, executive function, and false belief understanding to emerging math and literacy ability in kindergarten. *Child Development, 78,* 647–663.

Blakemore, S. J., & Frith, C. D. (2005). *The learning brain: Lessons for education.* Malden, MA: Blackwell.

Blewitt, P., Rump, K. M., Shealy, S. E., & Cook, S. A. (2009). Shared book reading: When and how questions affect young children's word learning. *Journal of Educational Psychology, 101*(2), 294–304.

Bloom, E., & Heath, N. (2010). Recognition, expression, and understanding facial expressions of emotion in adolescents with nonverbal and general learning disabilities. *Journal of Learning Disabilities, 43*(2), 180–192.

Blues Classroom. (2003). The Blues Teacher's Guide: Men, woman and the blues. Vulcan Productions, Inc. Retrieved November 3, 2011, from http://www.pbs.org/theblues/classroom/intmenwomen.html

Bono, M., & Stifter, C. (2003). Maternal attention-directing strategies and infant focused attention during problem solving. *Infancy, 4,* 235–250.

Bornstein, M. H., DiPietro, J. A., Hahn, C., Painter, K., Haynes, O. M., & Costigan, K. A. (2002). Prenatal cardiac function and postnatal cognitive development: An exploratory study. *Infancy, 3*(4), 475–494.

Bower, A., & King, W. (1967). The effect of number of irrelevant stimulus dimensions, verbalization, and sex on learning biconditional classification rules. *Psychonomic Science, 8,* 453–454.

Bower, G. H. (1970). Imagery as a relational organizer in associative learning. *Journal of Verbal Learning and Verbal Behavior, 9,* 529–533.

Boyatzis, C., & Satyaprasad, C. (1994). Children's facial and gestural decoding and encoding: Relations between skills and with popularity. *Journal of Nonverbal Behavior, 18,* 37–55.

Brackbill, Y. (1973). Continuous stimulation reduces arousal level stability of the effect over time. *Child Development, 44,* 43–46.

Bradley, M. M., & Lang, P. J. (1994). Measuring emotion: The self-assessment manikin and the semantic differential. *Journal of Behavioral Therapy and Experimental Psychiatry, 25*(1), 49–59.

Brand, S., Reimer, T., & Opwis, K. (2007). How do we learn in a negative mood? Effects of a negative mood on transfer and learning. *Learning and Instruction, 17,* 1–16.

Bransford, J., Derry, S., Berliner, D., Hammerness, K., & Beckett, K.L. (2007). Theories of learning and their roles in teaching. In L. Darling-Hammond & J. Bransford (Eds.), *Preparing teachers for a changing world: What teachers should learn and be able to do.* San Francisco: Jossey-Bass.

Bransford, J. D., Barron, B., Pea, R. D., Meltzoff, A., Kuhl, P., Bell, P., Stevens, R., Schwartz, D. L., Vye, N., Reeves, B., Roschelle, J., & Sabelli, N. H. (2006). Foundations and opportunities for an interdisciplinary science of learning. In R. K. Sawyer (Ed.), *The Cambridge handbook of the learning sciences* (pp. 19–34). Cambridge: Cambridge University Press.

Bransford, J. D., & Stein, B. S. (1984). *The IDEAL problem solver.* New York: Freeman.

Brefczynski-Lewis, J. A., Lutz, A., Schaefer, H. S., Levinson, D. B., & Davidson, R. J. (2007). Neural correlates of attentional expertise in long-term meditation practitioners. *Proceedings of the National Academy of Sciences, 104*(27), 11483–11488.

Broaders, S. C., Wagner Cook, S., Mitchell, Z., & Goldin-Meadow, S. (2007). Making children gesture brings out implicit knowledge and leads to learning. *Journal of Experimental Psychology: General, 136*(4), 539–550.

Bronson, M. B. (2000). *Self-regulation in early childhood.* New York: Guilford Press.

Brown, J. S., Collins, A., & Duguid, P. (1989). Situated cognition and the culture of learning. *Educational Researcher, 18*(1), 32–42.

Bruce, T. (2005). *Early childhood education.* London: Hodder Education.

Bryan, T., Mathur, S., & Sullivan, K. (1996). The impact of positive mood on learning. *Learning Disability Quarterly, 19,* 153–162.

Buck, S. M., Hillman, C. H., & Castelli, D. M. (2008). The relation of aerobic fitness to Stroop Task performance in preadolescent children. *Medicine & Science in Sports & Exercise, 40,* 166–172.

Buckner, J. C., Mezzacappa, E., & Beardslee, W. R. (2003). Characteristics of resilient youths living in poverty: The role of self-regulatory processes. *Development and Psychopathology, 15,* 139–162.

Buddhaghosa. (1979). *The path of purification* (B. Nanamoli, Trans.). Kandy, Sri Lanka: Buddhist Publication Society.

Bunge, S. A., Dudukovic, N. M., Thomason, M. E., Vaidya, C. J., & Gabrieli, J. D. E. (2002). Immature frontal lobe contributions to cognitive control in children: Evidence from fMRI. *Neuron, 33,* 301–311.

Burdette, H. L., & Whitaker, R. C. (2005). Resurrecting free play in young children: Looking beyond fitness and fatness to attention, affiliation, and affect. *Archives of Pediatric & Adolescent Medicine, 159,* 46–50.

Butler, A. C., & Roediger, H. L. (2007). Testing improves long-term retention in a simulated classroom setting. *European Journal of Cognitive Psychology, 19,* 514–527.

Cahill, L., Babinsky, R., Markowitsch, H. J., & McGaugh, J. L. (1995). The amygdala and emotional memory. *Nature, 377*(6547), 295–296.

Caine, R., & Caine, G. (1990). Understanding a brain-based approach to learning and teaching. *Educational Leadership, 48*(2), 66–70.

Caine, R., & Caine, G. (1994). *Making connections: Teaching and the human brain.* Menlo Park, CA: Addison-Wesley.

California Department of Education. (2005, April). California physical fitness test: A study of the relationship between physical fitness and academic achievement in California using 2004 test results. Retrieved April 6, 2011, from www.cde.ca.gov/ta/tg/pf/documents/2004pftresults.doc

Calkins, S. D., & Johnson, M. C. (1998). Toddler regulation of distress to frustrating events: Temperamental and maternal correlates. *Infant Behavior and Development, 21,* 379–395.

Callanan, M. A., & Oakes, L. M. (1992). Preschoolers' questions and parents' explanations: Causal thinking in everyday activity. *Cognitive Development, 7,* 213–233.

Callender A. A., & McDaniel, M. A. (2009). The limited benefits of rereading educational texts. *Contemporary Educational Psychology, 34,* 30–41.

Campos, J. J. (1983). The importance of affective communication in social referencing: A commentary on Feinman. *Merrill-Palmer Quarterly, 29,* 83–87.

Campos, J. J., Anderson, D. I., Barbu-Roth, M. A., Hubbard, E. M., Hertenstein, M. J., & Witherington, D. (2000). Travel broadens the mind. *Infancy, 1*(2), 149–219.

Campos, J. J., Kermoian, R., & Zumbahlen, M. R. (1992). Socioemotional transformations in the family system following infant crawling onset. In N. Eisenberg & R. A. Fabes (Eds.), *Emotion and its regulation in early development* (pp. 25–40). San Francisco: Jossey-Bass.

Cardillo, J. (2009). *Can I have your attention? How to think fast, find your focus, and sharpen your concentration.* Pompton Plains, NJ: Career Press.

Carpenter, M. (2006). Instrumental, social, and shared goals and intentions in imitation. In S. J. Rogers & J. H. G. Williams (Eds.), *Imitation and the social mind: Autism and typical development* (pp. 48–70). New York: Guilford Press.

Carpenter, M., Nagell, K., & Tomasello, M. (1998). Social cognition, joint attention, and communicative competence from 9 to 15 months of age. *Monographs of the Society for Research in Child Development, 63*(4), 176.

Carpenter, M., & Nielsen, M. (2008). Tools, TV, and trust: Introduction to the special issue on imitation in typically-developing children. *Journal of Experimental Child Psychology, 101*, 225–227.

Casler, K., & Kelemen, D. (2005). Young children's rapid learning about artifact functions. *Developmental Science, 8*(6), 472–480.

Castelli, D. M., Hillman, C. H., Buck, S. M., & Erwin, H. E. (2007). Physical fitness and academic achievement in third- and fifth-grade students. *Journal of Sport and Exercise Psychology, 29*, 239–252.

Ceci, S. J., Loftus, E. F., Leichtman, M. D., & Bruck, M. (1994). The possible role of source misattribution in the creation of false beliefs among preschoolers. *International Journal of Clinical and Experimental Hypnosis, 42*, 304–320.

Centers for Disease Control and Prevention, FastStats: Attention deficit hyperactivity disorder (ADHD). (2010). Retrieved December 20, 2010, from http://www.cdc.gov/nchs/fastats/adhd.htm

Chao, L., L., & Martin, A. (2000). Representation of manipulable manmade objects in the dorsal stream. *NeuroImage, 12*, 478–484.

Cheyne, J. A., & Rubin, K. H. (1983). Playful precursors of problem solving in preschoolers. *Developmental Psychology, 19*(4), 577–584.

Chi, M., Bassok, M., Lewis, M., Reimann, P., & Glaser, P. (1989). Self-explanation: How students study and use examples in learning to solve problems. *Cognitive Science, 13*, 145–182.

Chi, M. T. H. (1978). Knowledge structure and memory development. In R. Siegler (Ed.), *Children's thinking: What develops?* (pp. 73–96). Hillsdale, NJ: Erlbaum.

Chi, M. T. H., & Koeske, R. D. (1983). Network representation of a child's dinosaur knowledge. *Developmental Psychology, 19*, 29–39.

Chodzko-Zajko, W. J., & Moore, K. A. (1994). Physical fitness and cognitive functioning in aging. *Exercise and Sport Sciences Reviews, 22*, 195–220.

Chorzempa, B. F., & Lapidus, L. (2009). To find yourself, think for yourself. *Teaching Exceptional Children, 41*(3), 54–59.

Choudhury, N., & Gorman K. (2000). The relationship between attention and problem solving in 17–24 month old children. *Infancy and Child Development, 9*, 127–146.

Christakis, D. A., Zimmerman, F. J., & Garrison, M. M. (2007). Effect of block play on language acquisition and attention in toddlers: A pilot randomized controlled trial. *Archives of Pediatric & Adolescent Medicine, 161*(10), 967–971.

Cimpian, A., Arce, H. M., Markman, E. M., & Dweck, C. S. (2007). Subtle linguistic cues affect children's motivation. *Psychological Science, 18*(4), 314-316.

Clément, F., Koenig, M., & Harris, P. (2004). The ontogenesis of trust. *Mind & Language, 19*(4), 360–379.

Cole, P. M., Michel, M., & O'Donnell-Teti, L. (1994). The development of emotion regulation and dysregulation: A clinical perspective. In N. A. Fox (Ed.), The development of emotion regulation. *Monographs of the Society for Research in Child Development, 59*, 73–100.

Colombo, J., Mitchell, D. W., Dodd, J., Coldren, J. T., & Horowitz, F. D. (1989). Longitudinal correlates of infant attention in the paired comparison paradigm. *Intelligence, 13,* 33–42.

Cooper, R. P., & Aslin, R. N. (1990). Preference for infant-directed speech in the first month after birth. *Child Development, 61,* 1584–1595.

Cornett, C. E. (1986). *Learning through laughter: Humor in the classroom.* Bloomington, IN: Phi Delta Kappa Educational Foundation.

Corriveau, K. H., Pasquini, E. S., & Harris, P. L. (2006, May). Preschoolers use past accuracy and familiarity in deciding whom to trust as an informant. Presentation at the Annual Meeting of the Association for Psychological Science, New York, NY.

Cosner, R. L. (1959). Some social functions of laughter: A study of humor in a hospital setting. *Human Relations, 12*(2), 171–182.

Courage, M. L., & Cowan, N. (Eds.). (2009). *The development of memory in infancy and childhood.* Hove, UK: Psychology Press.

Courchesne, E., & Pierce, K. (2005). Brain overgrowth in autism during a critical time in development: Implications for frontal pyramidal neuron and interneuron development and connectivity. *International Journal of Developmental Neuroscience, 23,* 153–170.

Cowan, N. (Ed.). (1998). *The development of memory in childhood.* Hove, UK: Psychology Press.

Csikszentmihalyi, M. (1997a). *Creativity: Flow and the psychology of discovery and invention.* New York: HarperPerennial.

Csikszentmihalyi, M. (1997b). Flow and education. *The NAMTA Journal, 22*(2), 2–35.

Csikszentmihalyi, M., & Csikszentmihalyi, I. (1992). *Optimal experience: Psychological studies of flow in consciousness.* Cambridge: Cambridge University Press.

Cycowicz, Y. M. (2000). Memory development and event-related brain potentials in children. *Biological Psychology, 54,* 145–174.

Czajka, C. W. (2004). Elementary lesson plan 1: Criminal or hero. In *Slavery and the making of America.* Retrieved February 15, 2010, from http://www.pbs.org/wnet/slavery/teachers/lesson1.html

Dalke, D. E. (1995). Explaining young children's difficulty on the false belief task: Representational deficits or context-sensitive knowledge? *British Journal of Developmental Psychology, 13,* 209–222.

Daloz, L. A. (1999). *Mentor.* San Francisco: Jossey-Bass.

Daneman, M., & Carpenter, P. A. (1980). Individual differences in working memory and reading. *Journal of Verbal Learning and Verbal Behavior, 19*(4), 450–466.

Dansky, J. L., & Silverman, I. W. (1973). Effects of play on associative fluency in preschool-aged children. *Developmental Psychology, 9*(1), 38–43.

Deci, E. (1972). Intrinsic motivation, extrinsic reinforcement, and inequity. *Journal of Personality and Social Psychology, 22*(1), 113–120.

Deese, J. (1959). Influence of interitem associative strength upon immediate free recall. *Psychological Reports, 5,* 235–241.

DeLoache, J. S. (2000). Dual representation and young children's use of scale models. *Child Development, 71,* 329–338.

DeLoache, J. S., Cassidy, D. J., & Brown, A. L. (1985). Precursors of mnemonic strategies in very young children's memory. *Child Development, 56*(1), 125–137.

de Manzano, Ö., Theorell, T., Harmat, L., & Ullén, F. (2010). The psychophysiology of flow during piano playing. *Emotion, 10*(3), 301–311.

DeMarie, D., Miller, P. H., Ferron, J., & Cunningham, W. R. (2004). Path analysis tests of theoretical models of children's memory performance. *Journal of Cognition and Development, 5,* 461–492.

Denham, S. A. (1986), Social cognition, prosocial behavior, and emotion in preschoolers: Contextual validation. *Child Development, 57,* 194–201.

Denham, S. A., Blair, K. A., DeMulder, E., Levitas, J., Sawyer, K., Auerbach-Major, S., & Queenan, P. (2003). Preschool emotional competence: Pathway to social competence. *Child Development, 74,* 238–256.

Deniz, H. (2009, April). *Examination of changes in prospective elementary teachers' epistemological beliefs in science and exploration of factors mediating the change.* Paper presented at the Annual Meeting of American Educational Research Association, San Diego, CA.

Deocampo, J. A., & Hudson, J. A. (2005). When seeing is not believing: Two-year-olds' use of video representations to find a hidden toy. *Journal of Cognition and Development, 6,* 229–258.

Derscheid, L. E., Kwon, Y.-H., & Fang, S.-R. (1996). Preschoolers' socialization as consumers of clothing and recognition of symbolism. *Perceptual and Motor Skills, 82,* 1171–1181.

Diamond, A. (1995). Evidence of robust recognition memory early in life even when assessed by reaching behavior. *Journal of Experimental Child Psychology. Special issue: Early Memory, 59*(3), 419–456.

Díaz, R. M., & Berk, L. E. (1992). *Private speech: From social interaction to self-regulation.* Hillsdale, NJ: Erlbaum.

DiPerna, J. C., Lei, P., & Reid, E. L. (2007). Kindergarten predictors of mathematical growth in the primary grades: An investigation using the early childhood longitudinal study—kindergarten cohort. *Journal of Educational Psychology, 99,* 369–379.

Dirix, C. E. H., Nijhuis, J. G., Jongsma, H. W., & Hornstra, G. (2009). Aspects of fetal learning and memory. *Child Development, 80*(4), 1251–1258.

Dixon, W. E., & Smith, P. H. (2008). Attentional focus moderates habituation-language relationships: Slow habituation may be a good thing. *Infant and Child Development, 17*(2), 95–108.

Dockett, K. A. (1997, April). *Young children's peer popularity and theories of mind.* Paper presented at the biennial meeting of the Society for Research in Child Development, Washington, DC.

Dodge, K. A. (1993). Social-cognitive mechanisms in the development of conduct disorder and depression. *Annual Review of Psychology, 44,* 559–584.

Doidge, N. (2007). *The brain that changes itself: Stories of personal triumph from the frontiers of brain science.* New York: Viking.

Doolittle, P. E. (1995, June). *Understanding cooperative learning through Vygotsky's zone of proximal development.* Paper presented at the Lilly National Conference on Excellence in College Teaching, Columbia, SC.

Douglas, O., Burton, K. S., & Reese-Durham, N. (2008). The effects of the multiple intelligence teaching strategy on the academic achievement of eighth grade math students. *Journal of Instructional Psychology, 35*(2), 182–187.

Drake, K. N., & Long, D. (2009). Rebecca's in the dark: A comparative study of problem-based learning and direct instruction/experiential learning in two 4th-grade classrooms. *Journal of Elementary Science Education, 21*(1), 1–16.

Dugatkin, L. A., & Rodrigues, S. (2008, Spring). Games animals play: Animal play is serious business, say scientists. *Greater Good Magazine, 4*(4). Retrieved May 30, 2009, from http://greatergood.berkeley.edu/article/item/games_animals.play/

Dunn, J., Brown, J., Slomkowski, C., Tesla, C., & Youngblade, L. (1991). Young children's understanding of other people's feelings and beliefs: Individual differences and their antecedents. *Child Development, 62,* 1352–1366.

Dweck, C. S. (1999). *Self-theories.* Philadelphia: Psychology Press.

Dwyer, T., Sallis, J. F., Blizzard, L., Lazarus, R., & Dean, K. (2001). Relation of academic performance to physical activity and fitness in children. *Pediatric Exercise Science, 13,* 225–237.

Ebbinghaus, H. (1913). *Memory: A contribution to experimental psychology* (H. A. Ruger & C. E. Bussenius, Trans.). New York: Teachers College Press, Columbia University. (Original work published 1885)

Egertson, H. (2003). *The shifting kindergarten curriculum.* ERIC Clearinghouse on Elementary and Early Childhood Education, 1–4.

Einon, D. F., & Morgan, M. J. (1977). A critical period for social isolation in the rat. *Developmental Psychobiology, 10,* 123–132.

Einon, D. F., Morgan, M. J., & Kibbler, C. C. (1978). Brief periods of socialization and later behavior in the rat. *Developmental Psychobiology, 11,* 213–225.

Ellis, S., & Gauvain, M. (1992). Cultural influences on children's collaborative interactions. In L. T. Winegar & J. Valsiner (Eds.), *Children's development within social context.* Hillsdale, NJ: Erlbaum.

Ericsson, K. A., Krampe, R. T., & Tesch-Romer, C. (1993). The role of deliberate practice in the acquisition of expert performance. *Psychological Review, 100,* 363–406.

Erlaur, L. (2003). *The brain compatible classroom: Using what we know about learning to improve teaching.* Alexandria, VA: ASCD.

Etnier, J. L., Nowell, P. M., Landers, D. M., & Sibley, B. A. (2006). A meta-regression to examine the relationship between aerobic fitness and cognitive performance. *Brain Research Reviews, 52,* 119–130.

Evans, R.L. (2007). *Every good boy deserves fudge: The book of mnemonic devices.* New York: Penguin.

Fagan, J. F., & Knevel, C. (1989, April). *The prediction of above-average intelligence from infancy.* Paper presented at the meeting of the Society for Research on Child Development, Kansas City, MO.

Falck-Ytter, T., Gredeback, G., & von Hofsten, C. (2006). Infants predict other people's action goals. *Nature Neuroscience, 9,* 878–879.

Fecteau, S., Carmant, L., Tremblay, C., Robert, M., Bouthillier, A., & Theoret, H. (2004). A motor resonance mechanism in children? Evidence from subdural electrodes in a 36-month-old child. *NeuroReport, 15,* 2625–2627.

Feito, J. (2007). Allowing not knowing in a dialogic discussion. *International Journal for the Scholarship of Teaching and Learning, 1*(1). Retrieved August 8, 2009, from http://academics.georgiasouthern.edu/ijsotl/v1n1/feito/ij_feito.htm

Feldman, R. (2004). Mother-infant skin-to-skin contact and the development of emotion regulation. *Advances in Psychology Research, 27,* 113–131.

Feldman, R., & Eidelman, A. I. (2003). Skin-to-skin contact (Kangaroo Care) accelerates autonomic and neurobehavioural maturation in preterm infants. *Developmental Medicine Child Neurology, 45*(4), 274–281.

Feldman, R., Eidelman, A. I., Sirota, L., & Weller, A., (2002). Comparison of skin-to-skin (*kangaroo*) and traditional *care*: parenting outcomes and preterm infant development. *Pediatrics, 110*(1), 16.

Fernald, A. (1989). Intonation and communicative intent in mothers' speech to infants: Is the melody the message? *Child Development, 60,* 1497–1510.

Fernald, A., & Kuhl, P. (1987). Acoustic determinants of infant preference for motherese speech. *Infant Behavior and Development, 10*, 279–293.

Fiese, B. H. (1990). Playful relationships: A contextual analysis of mother-toddler interaction and symbolic play. *Child Development, 61*(5), 1648–1656.

Fifer, W. P., & Moon, C. M. (1995). The effects of fetal experience with sound. In J. P Lecanuet, W. P. Fifer, N. A. Krasnegor, & W. P. Smotherman (Eds.), *Fetal development: A psychobiological perspective* (pp. 351–366). Hillsdale, NJ: Erlbaum.

Finkel, D. L. (2000). *Teaching with your mouth shut.* Portsmouth, NH: Boynton/Cook.

Fivush, R. (1994). Constructing narrative, emotion and self in parent-child conversations about the past. In U. Neisser & R. Fivush (Eds.), *The remembering self: Construction and accuracy in the self-narrative* (pp. 136–157). New York: Cambridge University Press.

Fivush, R. (2000). Accuracy, authorship and voice: Feminist approaches to autobiographical memory. In P. Miller & E. Scholnick (Eds.), *Towards a feminist developmental psychology* (pp. 85–106). New York: Cambridge University Press.

Fivush, R., Hammond, N. R., Harsch, N. Singer, N., & Wolf, A. (1991). Content and consistency in early autobiographical recall. *Discourse Processes, 14*, 373–388.

Fivush, R., & Shukat, J. (1995). Content, consistency, and coherence of early autobiographical recall. In M. S. Zaragoza, J. R. Graham, G. C. N. Hall, R. Hirschman, & Y. S. Ben-Porath (Eds.), *Memory and testimony in the child witness* (pp. 5–23). Thousand Oaks, CA: Sage.

Flavell, J. H. (1999). Cognitive development: Children's knowledge about the mind. *Annual Review of Psychology, 50*, 21–45.

Flavell, J. H., Beach, D. R., & Chinsky, J. M. (1966). Spontaneous verbal rehearsal in a memory task as a function of age. *Child Development, 37*, 283–299.

Flavell, J. H., Green, F. L., & Flavell, E. R. (1995). Young children's knowledge about thinking. *Monographs of the Society for Research in Child Development, 60*(1, Series No. 243).

Foley, M. A., Passalacqua, C., & Ratner, H. H. (1993). Appropriating the actions of another: Implications for children's learning and memory. *Cognitive Development, 8*, 373–401.

Foley, M. A., & Ratner, H. H. (1998). Children's recoding in memory for collaboration: A way of learning from others. *Cognitive Development, 13*, 91–108.

Foley, M. A., Ratner, H. H., & House, A. T. (2002). Anticipation and source-monitoring errors: Children's memory for collaborative activity. *Journal of Cognition and Development, 3*, 385–414.

Freeman, W. J. (1991). The physiology of perception. *Scientific American, 264*(2), 78–85.

Freire, P. (1970). *Pedagogy of the oppressed* (M. B. Ramos, Trans.). New York: Continuum.

Freund, L. S. (1990). Maternal regulation of children's problem-solving behavior and its impact on children's performance. *Child Development, 61*, 113–126.

Frye, D., & Wang, Z. (2008). Theory of mind, understanding teaching and early childhood education. In S. K. Thurman & C. A. Fiorello (Eds.), *Applied cognitive research in K–3 classrooms* (pp. 41–83). New York: Routledge.

Gagnon, R., Hunse, C., Carmichael, L., Fellows, F., & Patrick, J. (1987). Human fetal responses to vibratory acoustic stimulation from 26 weeks to term. *American Journal of Obstetrics and Gynecology, 157*, 1375–1381.

Gardner, F. (2001). Social work students and self-awareness: How does it happen? *Reflective Practice, 2*(1), 27–40.

Gardner, H. (1993). *Multiple intelligences: The theory in practice.* New York: Basic Books.

Garth, M. (1991). *Starbright: A book of meditations for children.* New York: HarperOne.

Gathercole, S. E., & Alloway, T. P. (2008a). Working memory and classroom learning. In S. K. Thurman & C. A. Fiorello (Eds.), *Applied cognitive research in K–3 classrooms* (pp. 17–40). New York: Routledge.

Gathercole, S. E., & Alloway, T. P. (2008b). *Working memory and learning: A practical guide.* London: Sage.

Gathercole, S. E., Durling, E., Evans, M., Jeffcock, S., & Stone, S. (2008). Working memory abilities and children's performance in laboratory analogues of classroom activities. *Applied Cognitive Psychology, 22*, 1019–1037.

Gathercole, S. E., Lamont, E., & Alloway, T. P. (2006). Working memory in the classroom. In S. Pickering (Ed.), *Working memory and education* (pp. 219–240). Atlanta: Elsevier Press.

Gathercole, S. M., Brown, L., & Pickering, S. J. (2003). Working memory assessments at school entry as longitudinal predictors of National Curriculum attainment levels. *Educational and Child Psychology, 20*, 109–122.

Gathercole, S. M., & Pickering, S. J. (2000). Working memory deficits in children with low achievements in the National Curriculum at 7 years of age. *British Journal of Educational Psychology, 70*, 177–194.

Gathercole, S. M., Pickering, S. J., Knight, C., & Stegmann, Z. (2003). Working memory skills and educational attainment: Evidence from National Curriculum assessments at 7 and 14 years of age. *Applied Cognitive Psychology, 17*, 1–16.

Geary, D. C., Hoard, M. K., Byrd-Craven, J., & DeSoto, M. C. (2004). Strategy choices in simple and complex addition: Contributions of working memory and counting knowledge for children with mathematical disability. *Journal of Experimental Child Psychology, 88*, 121–151.

Gellevij, M., van der Meij, H., de Jong, T., & Pieters, J. (2002). Multimodal versus unimodal instruction in a complex learning context. *Journal of Experimental Education, 70*(3), 215–239.

George, J., & Greenfield, D. B. (2005). Examination of a structured problem-solving flexibility task for assessing approaches to learning in young children: Relation to teacher ratings and children's achievement. *Applied Developmental Psychology, 26*(1), 69–84.

Gergely, G., Bekkering, H., & Király, I. (2002). Rational imitation of goal-directed actions. *Nature, 415*, 755.

Gergely, G., Egyed, K., & Kiraly, I. (2007). On pedagogy. *Developmental Science, 10*, 139–146.

Gerner, M. (1981). The brain and behavior: Casting light into the "black-box." *Psychological Reports, 49*, 511–518.

Gibbs, J., Rankin, C., & Ronzone, P. (2006). *Reaching all by creating tribes learning communities.* Windsor, CA: CenterSource Systems.

Ginsburg, K. R., & The Committee on Communications and The Committee on Psychosocial Aspects of Child and Family Health Guidance for the Clinician in Rendering Pediatric Care. (2007). *American Academy of Pediatrics clinical report: The importance of play in promoting healthy child development and maintaining strong parent-child bonds.* Retrieved February 21, 2012, from http://www2.aap.org/pressroom/playfinal.pdf

Glenberg, A. M. (1997). What memory is for. *Behavioral and Brain Sciences, 20*, 1–55.

Godden, D. R., & Baddeley, A. D. (1975). Context-dependent memory in two natural environments: On land and under water. *British Journal of Psychology, 66*(3), 325–331.

Goldberg, E. (2002). *The executive brain: Frontal lobes and the civilized mind.* New York: Oxford University Press.

Goldish, M. (2006). *Memory-boosting mnemonic songs for content area learning.* New York: Scholastic.

Gopnik, A., & Astington, J. W. (1988). Children's understanding of representational change and its relation to the understanding of false belief and the appearance-reality distinction. *Child Development, 59*, 26–37.

Gopnik, A., Meltzoff, A., & Kuhl, P. (1999). *The scientist in the crib: What early learning tells us about the mind.* New York: Harper.

Gordon, P. R., Rogers, A. M., Comfort, M., Gavula, N., & McGee, B. P. (2001). A taste of problem-based learning increases achievement of urban minority middle school students. *Educational Horizons, 79*(4), 171–175.

Goswami, U. (2004). *Blackwell handbook of childhood cognitive development.* Oxford: Blackwell.

Grafton, S. T., Arbib, M. A., Fadiga, L., & Rizzolatti, G. (1996). Localization of grasp representations in humans by positron emission tomography. *Experimental Brain Research, 112*, 103–111.

Gray, P. (2009, January 1). The value of play IV: Play is nature's way of teaching us new skills. In *Freedom to learn: The roles of play and curiosity as foundations for learning.* Psychology Today Blog. Retrieved May 30, 2009, from http://www.psychologytoday.com/blog/freedom-learn/200901/the-value-play-iv-play-is-nature-s-way-teaching-us-new-skills

Gredlein, J. M., & Bjorklund, D. F. (2005). Sex differences in young children's use of tools in a problem-solving task: The role of object-oriented play. *Human Nature, 16*, 97–118.

Grèzes, J., & Decety, J. (2001). Functional anatomy of execution, mental simulation, observation, and verb generation of actions: A meta-analysis. *Human Brain Mapping, 12*, 1–19.

Griss, S. (1994). Creative movement: A physical language for learning. *Educational Leadership, 51*, 78–80.

Grolnick, W., Frodi, A., & Bridges, L. (1984). Maternal control style and the mastery motivation of 1-year-olds. *Infant Mental Health Journal, 5*, 72–82.

Gross, J., Hayne, H., Perkins, N., & McDonald, B. (2006). *Amount of crawling and walking experience has varying effects on cognitive development during infancy.* Paper presented at the annual meeting of the XVth Biennial International Conference on Infant Studies, Westin Miyako, Kyoto, Japan. Retrieved March 14, 2011, from http://www.allacademic.com/meta/p94676_index.html

Haden, C. A., Ornstein, P. A., Eckerman, C. O., & Didow, S. M. (2001). Mother-child conversational interactions as events unfold: Linkages to subsequent remembering. *Child Development, 72*, 1016–1031.

Hamilton, R. J. (1985). A framework for the evaluation of the effectiveness of adjunct questions and objectives. *Review of Educational Research, 55*, 47–85.

Hamzei, F., Rijntjes, M., Dettmers, C., Glauche, V., Weiller, C., & Buchel, C. (2003). The human action recognition system and its relationship to Broca's area: An fMRI study. *NeuroImage, 19*, 637–644.

Hand, B., & Prain, V. (2002). Teachers implementing writing-to-learn strategies in junior secondary science: A case study. *Science Education, 86*(6), 737–755.

Hari, R., Forss, N., Avikainen, S. Kirveskari, E., Salenius, S., & Rizzolatti, G. (1998). Activation of human primary motor cortex during action observation: A neuromagnetic study. *Proceedings of the National Academy of Sciences, 95*, 15061–15065.

Harris, P. L. (2007). Trust. *Developmental Science, 10*, 135–138.

Harrison, L. J., Manocha, R., & Rubia, K. (2004). Sahaja yoga meditation as a family treatment programme for children with attention deficit-hyperactivity disorder. *Clinical Child Psychology and Psychiatry, 9*(4), 479–497.

Hauf, P., & Prinz, W. (2005). The understanding of own and others' actions during infancy: "You-like-me" or "Me-like-you." *Interaction Studies, 6*, 429–445.

Hayne, H., Greco, C., Earley, L.,Griesler, P., & Rovee-Collier, C. (1986). Ontogeny of early event memory: Encoding and retrieval by 2- and 3-month-olds. *Infant Behavior and Development, 9*, 461–472.

Hayne, H., Herbert, J., & Simcock, G. (2003). Imitation from television by 24- and 30-month-olds. *Developmental Science, 6*, 254–261.

Hayne, H., & Simcock, G. (2009). Memory development in toddlers. In M. L. Courage & N. Cowan (Eds.), *The development of memory in infancy and childhood*. New York: Psychology Press.

Haynes, J., Burts, D. C., Dukes, A., & Cloud, R. (1993). Consumer socialization of pre-schoolers and kindergartners as related to clothing consumption. *Psychology & Marketing, 10*, 151–166.

Hedegaard, M. (2003a). Children's learning through participation in institutional practice: A model from the perspective of cultural-historical psychology. In B. Van Oers, E. Elbers, W. Wardekker, & R. Van Der Veer (Eds.), *The transformation of learning: Advances in cultural-historical activity theory* (pp. 294–318). New York: Cambridge University Press.

Hedegaard, M. (2003b). Cultural minority children's learning within culturally sensitive classroom teaching. *Pedagogy, Culture and Society, 11*(1), 133–151.

Helpguide. (2010). Developing emotional awareness: Recognizing and harnessing the power of your emotions. Retrieved April 24, 2010, from http://www.helpguide.org/toolkit/developing_emotional_awareness.htm

Hepper, P. G. (1991). An examination of fetal learning before and after birth. *Irish Journal of Psychology, 12*, 95–107.

Herbert, J., Gross, J., & Hayne, H. (2007). Crawling is associated with more flexible memory retrieval by 9-month-old infants. *Developmental Science, 10*(2), 183–189.

Herz, R. S., Eliassen, J. C., Beland, S. L., & T. Souza. (2003). Neuroimaging evidence for the emotional potency of odor-evoked memory. *Neuropsychologia, 42*, 371–378

Herz, R. S., & Schooler, J. W. (2002). A naturalistic study of autobiographical memories evoked by olfactory and visual cues: Testing the Proustian hypothesis. *American Journal of Psychology, 115*, 21–32.

Hettena, C. M., & Ballif, B. L. (1981). Effect of mood on learning. *Journal of Educational Psychology, 73*(4), 505–508.

Hickling, A. K., & Wellman, H. M. (2001). The emergence of children's causal explanations and theories: Evidence from everyday conversation. *Developmental Psychology, 37*, 668–683.

Higbee, K. L. (1997). Novices, apprentices, and mnemonists: Acquiring expertise with the phonetic mnemonic. *Applied Cognitive Psychology, 11*, 147–161.

Hillman, C. H., Buck, S. M., Themanson, J. R., Pontifex, M. B., & Castelli, D. M. (2009). Aerobic fitness and cognitive development: Event-related brain potential and task performance indices of executive control in preadolescent children. *Developmental Psychology, 45*(1), 114–129.

Hillman, C. H., Erickson, K. I., & Kramer, A. F. (2008). Be smart, exercise your heart: Exercise effects on brain and cognition. *Nature Reviews Neuroscience, 9*, 58–64.

Hinton, C., Miyamoto, K., & Della-Chiesa, B. (2008). Brain research, learning and emotions: Implications for education research, policy and practice. *European Journal of Education, 43*(1), 87–103.

Hirsh-Pasek, K., & Golinkoff, R. M. (2003). *Einstein never used flash cards: How our children really learn and why they need to play more and memorize less.* New York: Rodale.

Hoff, E. (2006). How social contexts support and shape language development. *Developmental Review, 26*, 55–88.

Hoffmann, H. (1995). *Struwwelpeter in English translation.* Mineola, NY: Dover. (Original work published 1845)

Hollander, J. (1996). *Committed to memory: 100 best poems to memorize.* New York: Turtle Point Press.

Holler, K. A., & Greene, S. M. (2010). Developmental changes in children's executive functioning. In E. Hollister Sandberg & B. L. Spritz (Eds.), *A clinician's guide to normal cognitive development in childhood* (pp. 215–238). New York: Routledge.

Holmes, R. M., Pellegrini, A. D., & Schmidt, S. L. (2006). The effects of different recess timing regimens on preschoolers' classroom attention. *Early Child Development and Care, 176*(7), 735–743.

Hong, L. (1994). Experimental study on the affection of fetal music on the fetus. *Acta Psychologica Sinica, 26,* 51–58.

Howse, R. B., Lange, G., Farran, D. C., & Boyles, C. D. (2003). Motivation and self-regulation as predictors of achievement in economically disadvantaged young children. *Journal of Experimental Education, 71,* 151–174.

Hruska, B., & Clancy, M. E. (2008). Integrating movement and learning in elementary and middle school. *Strategies: A Journal for Physical and Sport Educators, 21*(5), 13–20.

Hudson, J. A. (1988). Children's memory for atypical actions in script-based stories: Evidence for a disruption effect. *Journal of Experimental Child Psychology, 46,* 159–173.

Hudson, J. A., & Nelson, K. (1986). Repeated encounters of a similar kind: Effects of familiarity on children's autobiographic memory. *Cognitive Development, 1,* 253–271.

Huizinga, J. (1971). *Homo ludens.* Boston: Beacon Press. (Original work published 1938)

Hyson, M. C., Hirsh-Pasek, K., & Rescorla, L. (1989). *Academic environments in early childhood: Challenge or pressure?* Summary report to The Spencer Foundation, Chicago.

Imus, D. (2008). *Growing up green: Baby and child care.* New York: Simon & Schuster.

Istomina, Z. M. (1975). The development of voluntary memory in preschool-age children. *Soviet Psychology, 13,* 5–64.

James, W. (1983). *The principles of psychology.* Boston: Holt. (Original work published 1890)

Jaswal, V. K., & Neely, L. A. (2006). Adults don't always know best: Preschoolers use past reliability over age when learning new words. *Psychological Science, 17*(9), 757–758.

Jha, A. P., Krompinger, J., & Baime, M. J. (2007). Mindfulness training modifies subsystems of attention. *Cognitive Affective and Behavioral Neuroscience, 7,* 109–119.

Johnson, M. (1987). *The body in the mind: The bodily basis of meaning, imagination, and reason.* Chicago: The University of Chicago Press.

Kaiser Family Foundation. (2005, March). Generation M: Media in the lives of 8 to 18 year olds. Retrieved August 23, 2009, from http://www.kff.org/entmedia/entmedia030905pkg.cfm

Kamins, M. L., & Dweck, C. S. (1999). Person versus process praise and criticism: Implications for contingent self-worth and coping. *Developmental Psychology, 35*(3), 835–837.

Kang, S. H. K., McDermott, K. B., & Roediger, H. L. (2007). Test format and corrective feedback modulate the effect of testing on memory retention. *European Journal of Cognitive Psychology, 19,* 528–558.

Kaniel, S., & Aram, D. (1993). Developmental impacts of meta-attention instructions. *International Journal of Cognitive Education and Mediated Learning, 3*(2), 110–121.

Karzon, R. G. (1985). Discrimination of polysyllabic sequences by one- to four-month-old infants. *Journal of Experimental Child Psychology, 39*(2), 326–42.

Katz Rothman, B. (2000). *Recreating motherhood.* New Brunswick, NJ: Rutgers University Press.

Kaufman, M. (2005, January 3). Meditation gives brain a charge, study finds. *Washington Post*. Retrieved August 9, 2010, from, http://www.washingtonpost.com/wp-dyn/articles/A43006–2005Jan2.html

Keys, C.W. (1993). Revitalizing instruction in scientific genres: Connecting knowledge production with writing to learn in science. *Science Education, 83*(2), 115–130.

Kierkegaard, S. (1985). *Either/or: A fragment of life*. New York: Penguin Classics. (Original work published 1843)

King, N.R. (1979). Play: The kindergartners' perspective. *Elementary School Journal, 80*(2), 80–87.

Kitamura, C., Thanavishuth, C., Burnham, D., & Luksaneeyanawin, S. (2002). Universality and specificity in infant-directed speech: Pitch modifications as a function of infant age and sex in a tonal and non-tonal language. *Infant Behavior and Development, 24*, 372–392.

Klein, P. (1999). Reopening inquiry into cognitive processes in writing-to-learn. *Educational Psychology Review, 11*(3), 203–270.

Klingberg, T., Forssberg, H., & Westerberg, H. (2002). Training of working memory in children with ADHD. *Journal of Clinical and Experimental Neuropsychology, 24*(6), 781–791.

Kobiella, A., Grossmann, T., Reid, V. M., & Striano, T. (2008). The discrimination of angry and fearful facial expressions in 7-month-old infants: An event-related potential study. *Cognition and Emotion, 22*, 134–146.

Koenig, M. A., Clément, F., & Harris, P. L. (2004). Trust in testimony: Children's use of true and false statements. *Psychological Science, 15*(10), 694–698.

Koenig, M. A., & Harris, P. L. (2005a). Preschoolers mistrust ignorant and inaccurate speakers. *Child Development, 76*, 1261–1277.

Koenig, M. A., & Harris, P. L. (2005b). The role of social cognition in early trust. *Trends in Cognitive Sciences, 9*(10), 457–459.

Korner, A. F., & Grobstein, R. (1966). Visual alertness as related to soothing in neonates: implications for maternal stimulation and early deprivation. *Child Development, 37*, 867–876.

Kreiser, B., & Hairston, R. (2007). Dance of the chromosomes: A kinetic learning approach to mitosis and meiosis. *Bioscene, 33*(1), 6–10.

Kremar, M., Grela, B., & Lin, K. (2007). Can toddlers learn vocabulary from television? An experimental approach. *Media Psychology, 10*, 41–63.

Kuenz, J., Willis, S., & Waldrep, S. (1995). *Inside the mouse: Work and play at Disney World, The project on Disney*. Durham, NC: Duke University Press.

Kunzinger, E. L., & Witryol, S. L. (1984). The effects of differential incentives on second-grade rehearsal and free recall. *Journal of Genetic Psychology: Research and Theory on Human Development, 144*(1), 19–30.

Lalonde, C. E., & Chandler, M. J. (1995). False belief understanding goes to school: On the social-emotional consequences of coming early or late to a first theory of mind. *Cognition & Emotion, 9*, 167–185.

Landry, S. H., Miller-Loncar, C. L., Smith, K. E., & Swank, P. R. (2002). The role of early parenting in children's development of executive processes. *Developmental Neuropsychology, 21*(1), 15–21.

Lawrence, J. A., & Valsiner, J. (1993). Conceptual roots of internalization: From transmission to transformation. *Human Development, 36*, 150–167.

Lawson, K. R., & Ruff, H. A. (2004). Early attention and negative emotionality predict later cognitive and behavioral function. *International Journal of Behavioral Development, 28*, 157–165.

LeDoux, J. E. (1994). Emotion, memory, and the brain. *Scientific American, 270,* 50–57.

LeDoux, J. E. (Ed.) (1996). *The emotional brain.* New York: Simon & Schuster.

Lee, H. (1960). *To kill a mockingbird.* New York: Harper.

Lee, J. (1999). The effects of 5-year-old preschoolers' use of private speech on performance and attention for two kinds of problems-solving tasks. *Dissertation Abstracts International Section A: Humanities and Social Sciences, 60*(6-A), 1899.

Liben, L. S. (1999). Developing an understanding of external spatial representations. In I. E. Sigel (Ed.), *Development of mental representation: Theories and applications* (pp. 297–321). Mahwah, NJ: Erlbaum.

Lidstone, J. S. M., Meins, E., & Fernyhough, C. (2010). The roles of private speech and inner speech in planning during middle childhood: Evidence from a dual task paradigm. *Journal of Experimental Child Psychology, 107,* 438–451.

Light, P., & Glachan, M. (1985). Facilitation of individual problem solving through peer interaction. *Educational Psychology, Special issue: Developmental psychology and education, 5*(3–4), 217–225.

Light, R. (1990). *The Harvard assessment seminars.* Cambridge, MA: Harvard Graduate School of Education.

Lillemyr, O. F., Søbstad, F., Marder, K., & Flowerday, T. (2010). Indigenous and non-indigenous primary school students' attitudes on play, humour, learning and self-concept: A comparative perspective. *European Early Childhood Education Research Journal, 18*(2), 243–267.

Linden, W. (1973). Practicing of meditation by school children and their levels of field dependence-independence, test anxiety, and reading achievement. *Journal of Consulting and Clinical Psychology, 41,* 139–143.

Lindsay, D. (1994, July 13). The games children play. *Education Week, 13,* 37–38.

Linenbrink, E. A., & Pintrich, P. R. (2003). The role of self-efficacy beliefs in student engagement and learning in the classroom. *Reading Writing Quarterly, 19,* 119–137.

Lipton, J. S., & Spelke, E. S. (2003). Origins of number sense: Large-number discrimination in human infants. *Psychological Science, 14*(5), 396–401.

Locke, J. L. (1995). *The child's path to spoken language.* Cambridge, MA: Harvard University Press.

Loewen, J. W. (2007). *Lies my teacher told me: Everything your American history textbook got wrong* (2nd ed.). New York: Simon & Schuster.

Longo, M. R., & Bertenthal, B. I. (2006). Common coding of observation and execution of action in 9-month-old infants. *Infancy, 10,* 43–59.

Luria, A. R. (1961). The role of speech in the regulation of normal and abnormal behavior. New York: Liveright.

Lutz, A., Slagter, H. A., Dunne, J. D., & Davidson, R. J. (2008). Attention regulation and monitoring in meditation. *Trends in Cognitive Sciences, 12*(4), 163–169.

Mack-Kirschner, A. (2004). *Powerful classroom stories from accomplished teachers.* Thousand Oaks, CA: Corwin Press.

MacLean, K. A., Ferrer, E., Aichele, S. R., Bridwell, D. A., Zanesco, A. P., Jacobs, T. L., King, B. G., Rosenberg, E. L., Sahdra, B. K., Shaver, P. R., Wallace, B. A., Mangun, G. R., & Saron, C. D. (2010). Intensive meditation training improves perceptual discrimination and sustained attention. *Psychological Science, 21*(6), 829–839.

Malone, J. C. (1991). *Theories of learning: A historical approach.* Belmont, CA: Wadsworth.

Mampe, B., Friederici, A. D., Christophe, A., & Wermke, K. (2009). Newborns' cry melody is shaped by their native language. *Current Biology, 19,* 1–4.

Marcovitch, S., & Zelazo, P. D. (1999). The A-not-B error: Results from a logistic meta-analysis. *Child Development, 70,* 1297–1313.

Marsh, H., Barnes, J., Caims, L., & Tidman, M. (1984). Self-description questionnaire: Age and sex effects in the structure and level of self-concept for preadolescent children. *Journal of Educational Psychology, 76*, 940–956.

Mattson, M. P. (2004). Pathways towards and away from Alzheimer's disease. *Nature, 430*, 631–639.

Maurer, D. (1993). Neonatal synesthesia: implications for the processing of speech and faces. In B. de Boysson-Bardies, S. de Schonen, P. Jusczyk, P. McNeilage, & J. Morton (Eds.), *Developmental neurocognition: Speech and face processing in the first year of life*. Dordrecht: Kluwer Academic.

Mayer, R. E. (1999). Designing instruction for constructivist learning. In C. M. Reigeluth (Ed.), *Instructional-design theories and models: Volume II. A new paradigm of instructional theory*. Hillsdale, NJ: Erlbaum.

Mayer, R. E., & Gallini, J. K. (1990). When is an illustration worth ten thousand words? *Journal of Educational Psychology, 82*, 715–726.

McAlister, A. R., & Cornwell, B. (2010). Children's brand symbolism understanding: Links to theory of mind and executive functioning. *Psychology & Marketing, 27*(3), 203–228.

McCall, R. B., & Carriger, M. S. (1993). A meta-analysis of infant habituation and recognition memory performance as predictors of later IQ. *Child Development, 64*, 57–79.

McCall, R. B., Parke, R. D., & Kavanaugh, R. D. (1977). Imitation of live and televised models by children 1 to 3 years of age. *Monographs of the Society for Research on Child Development, 42*(5, Serial No. 173).

McCorry, N. K., & Hepper, P. G. (2007). Fetal habituation performance: Gestational age and sex effects. *British Journal of Developmental Psychology, 25*(2), 277–292.

McCrea, S. M., Mueller, J. H., & Parrila, R. K. (1999). Quantitative analyses of schooling effects on executive function in young children. *Child Neuropsychology, 5*(4), 242–250.

McDaniel, M. A., Agarwal, P. K., Huelser, B. J., McDermott, K. B., & Roediger, H. L. (in press). Test-enhanced learning in a middle school science classroom: The effects of quiz frequency and placement. *Journal of Educational Psychology*.

McDaniel, M. A., & Callender, A. A. (2008). Cognition, memory, and education. In H. L. Roediger (Ed.), *Cognitive psychology of memory*, Vol. 2 of *Learning and memory: A comprehensive reference* (pp. 819–843). Oxford: Elsevier.

McEwen, B. S., & Sapolsky, R. M. (1995). Stress and cognitive function. *Current Opinion in Neurobiology, 5*, 205–216.

Mehler, J., Dupoux, E., Nazzi, T., & Dehaene-Lambertz, G. (1996). Coping with linguistic diversity: The infant's point of view. In J. L. Morgan & K. Demuth (Eds.), *Signal to syntax*. Hillsdale, NJ: Erlbaum.

Meichenbaum, D. (1977). *Cognitive-behavior modification*. New York: Plenum Press.

Meltzoff, A. (1995a). Understanding the intentions of others: Re-enactment of intended acts by 18-month-old children. *Developmental Psychology, 31*, 838–850.

Meltzoff, A. N. (1995b). What infant memory tells us about infantile amnesia: Long-term recall and deferred imitation. *Journal of Experimental Child Psychology, 59*, 497–515.

Meltzoff, A. N., & Moore, M. K. (1977). Imitation of facial and manual gestures by human neonates. *Science, 198*, 75–78.

Miller, G. A. (1956). The magical number seven, plus or minus two: Some limits on our capacity for processing information. *The Psychological Review, 63*, 81–97.

Miller, G. A., & Gildea, P. M. (1987). How children learn words. *Scientific American, 257*(3), 94–99.

Miller, S. A., Hardin, C. A., & Montgomery, D. E. (2003). Young children's understanding of the conditions for knowledge acquisition. *Journal of Cognition and Development, 4*, 325–356.

Minick, N. (1993). Teachers' directives: The social construction of "literal meanings" and "real words" in classroom discourse. In S. Chaiklin & J. Lave (Eds.), *Understanding practice: Perspectives on activity and context* (pp. 343–374). Cambridge: Cambridge University Press.

Moely, B. E., Hart, S. S., Leal, L., Santulli, K. A., Rao, N., Johnson, T., & Hamilton, L. B. (1992). The teacher's role in facilitating memory and study strategy development in the elementary school classroom. *Child Development, 63*, 653–672.

Moore, C., Bryant, D., & Furrow, D. (1989). Mental terms and the development of certainty. *Child Development, 60*(1), 167–171.

Moshman, D., & Geil, M. (1998). Collaborative reasoning: Evidence for collective rationality. *Thinking and Reasoning, 4*(3), 231–248.

Moyles, J. (2005). *The excellence of play* (2nd ed.). New York: Open University Press.

Müller, U., Lieberman, D., Frye, D., & Zelazo, P. D. (2008). Executive function, school readiness, and school achievement. In S. K. Thurman & C. A. Fiorello (Eds.), *Applied cognitive research in K–3 classrooms* (pp. 41–83). New York: Routledge.

Mulrine, A. (2000). What's your favorite class? *U.S. News & World Report, 128*(17), 50–53.

Nadler, R. T., Rabi, R., & Minda, J. P. (2010). Better mood and better performance: Learning rule-described categories is enhanced by positive mood. *Psychological Science, 21*(12), 1770–1776.

Nagy, W. (1988). *Teaching vocabulary to improve reading comprehension*. Urbana, IL: International Reading Association.

Neisser, U. (1982). *Memory observed: Remembering in natural contexts*. San Francisco: Freeman.

Nelson, C. A., de Haan, M., & Thomas, K. M. (2006). Why should developmental psychologists be interested in the brain? Historical background. In *Neuroscience of cognitive development* (pp. 1–3). Hoboken, NJ: Wiley.

Nelson, J. R., & Frederick, L. (1994). Can children design curriculum? *Educational Leadership, 51*, 71–74.

Nelson, K. (1993). Explaining the emergence of an autobiographical memory in early childhood. In A. Collins, M. Conway, S. Gathercole, & P. Morris (Eds.), *Theories of memory*. Hillsdale, NJ: Erlbaum.

Nelson, K. (1996). *Language in cognitive development: Emergence of the mediated mind*. New York: Cambridge University Press.

Nielsen, M. (2006). Copying actions and copying outcomes: Social learning through the second year. *Developmental Psychology, 42*, 555–565.

Norman, D. (1993). *Things that make us smart*. Reading, MA: Addison-Wesley.

Ogle, D. M. (1986). K-W-L: A teaching model that develops active reading of expository text. *The Reading Teacher, 39*, 564–570.

Oliver, J. A., Edmiaston, R., & Fitzgerald, L. M. (2003, April). Regular and special education teachers' beliefs regarding the role of private speech in children's learning. In A. Winsler (Chair), *Awareness, attitudes, and beliefs concerning children's private speech*. Paper presented at the biennial meeting of the Society for Research in Child Development, Tampa, FL.

Orlick, T. (1982). *Second cooperative sports and games book*. New York: Pantheon.

Ornstein, P. A., Coffman, J. L., & McCall, L. E. (2005, April). Linking teachers' memory-relevant language and children's memory performance. In F. J. Morrison (Chair), *The socialization of cognition: Environmental influences on developmental change*. Symposium conducted at the biennial meeting of the Society for Research in Child Development, Atlanta, GA.

O'Sullivan, J. T. (1993). Preschoolers' beliefs about effort, incentives, and recall. *Journal of Experimental Child Psychology, 55*(3), 396–414.

Oudejans, R., Michaels, C. F., Bakker, F. C., & Dolne, M. (1996). The relevance of action in perceiving affordances: Perception of catchableness of fly balls. *Journal of Experimental Psychology: Human Perception and Performance, 22,* 879–891.

Palincsar, A. S. (1989). Less charted waters. *Educational Researcher, 18(4),* 5–7.

Palincsar, A., & Brown, A. (1984). Reciprocal teaching of comprehension-fostering and comprehension-monitoring activities. *Cognition and Instruction, 1,* 117–175.

Panksepp, J. (1998). Attention deficit hyperactivity disorders, psychostimulants, and intolerance of childhood playfulness: A tragedy in the making? *Current Directions in Psychological Science, 7*(3), 91–98.

Panksepp, J. (2007). Can play diminish ADHD and facilitate the construction of the social brain? *Journal of the Canadian Academy of Child and Adolescent Psychiatry, 16,* 57–66.

Panksepp, J. (2008). Play, ADHD, and the construction of the social brain: Should the first class each day be recess? *American Journal of Play, 1,* 55–79.

Papousek, H. (1977). The development of learning ability in infancy. In G. Nissen (Ed.), *Intelligence, learning, and learning disabilities* (pp. 75–93). Berlin: Springer-Co.

Pascual-Leone, A., Dang, N., Cohen, L.G., Brasil-Neto, J. P., Cammarota, A., & Hallett, M. (1995). Modulation of muscle responses evoked by transcranial magnetic stimulation during the acquisition of new fine motor skills. *Journal of Neurophysiology, 74*(3), 1037–1045.

Pashler, H., Cepeda, N. J., Wixted, J. T. & Rohrer, D. (2005). When does feedback facilitate learning of words? *Journal of Experimental Psychology: Learning, Memory, and Cognition, 31*(1), 3–8.

Pasquini, E. S., Corriveau, K. H., Koenig, M., & Harris, P. L. (2007). Preschoolers monitor the relative accuracy of informants. *Developmental Psychology, 43*(5), 1216–1226.

Pavlov, I. P. (1927). *Conditioned reflexes: An investigation of the physiological activity of the cerebral cortex* (G. V. Anrep, Ed., & Trans.). London: Oxford University Press.

Pellegrini, A. D. (1984). The social cognitive ecology of preschool classrooms. *International Journal of Behavioral Development, 7,* 321–332.

Pellegrini, A. D. (1985). Relations between preschool children's play and literate behavior. In L. Galda & A. Pellegrini (Eds.), *Play, language and story: The development of children's literate behavior.* Norwood, NJ: Ablex.

Pellegrini, A. D., & Davis, P. L. (1993). Relations between children's playground and classroom behaviour. *British Journal of Educational Psychology, 63*(1), 88–95.

Pellegrini, A. D., & Galda, L. (1993). Ten years after: A re-examination of the relations between symbolic play and literacy. *Reading Research Quarterly, 28,* 162–175.

Pellegrini, A. D., Huberty, P. D., & Jones, I. (1995). The effects of recess timing on children's playground and classroom behaviors. *American Educational Research Journal, 32*(4), 845–864.

Pellegrini, A. D., & Smith, P. K. (1993). School recess: Implications for education and development. *Review of Educational Research, 63*(1), 51–67.

Pellis, S. M., & Pellis, V. C. (2007). Rough-and-tumble play and the development of the social brain. *Current Directions in Psychological Science, 16*(2), 95–98.

Perlmutter, M., Behrend, S. D., Kuo, F., & Muller, A. (1989). Social influences on children's problem solving. *Developmental Psychology, 25,* 744–754.

Perner, J., Leekam, S. R., & Wimmer, H. (1987). Three-year-olds' difficulty with false belief: The case for a conceptual deficit. *British Journal of Developmental Psychology, 5,* 125–137.

Piaget, J. (1954). *The construction of reality in the child.* (M. Cook, Trans.). New York: Basic Books. (Original work published 1937)

Piaget, J. (1962). *Play, dreams and imitation in childhood* (C. Gattegno & F. M. Hodgson, Trans.). New York: Norton.

Piaget, J., & Inhelder, B. (1973). *Memory and intelligence.* New York: Basic Books.

Pitt, A. J., & Rose, C. B. (2007). The significance of emotions in teaching and learning: On making emotional significance. *International Journal of Leadership in Education, 10*(4), 327–337.

Plato (2008). *Phaedrus* (Benjamin Jowett, Trans.). Charleston, SC: Forgotten Books. (Original work published 360 BC).

Pogrow, S. (2009). *Teaching content outrageously: How to captivate all students and accelerate learning, grades 4–12.* San Francisco: Jossey-Bass.

Porges, S. (2003). *The polyvagal theory: Phylogenetic contributions to social behavior.* Oxford: Elsevier Science.

Posner, M. I., & Rothbart, M. K. (2002). Attention, self-regulation, and consciousness. In J. T. Cacioppo, G. G. Berntson, R. Adolphs, C. S. Carter, R. J. Davidson, M. K. McClintock, B. S. McEwen, M. J. Meaney, D. L. Schacter, E. M. Sternberg, S. S. Suomi, & S. E. Taylor (Eds.), *Foundations in social neuroscience: Social neuroscience series* (pp. 189–243). Cambridge, MA: MIT Press.

Povinelli, D. J., Landau, K. R., & Perilloux, H. K. (1996). Self-recognition in young children using delayed versus live feedback: Evidence of a developmental asynchrony. *Child Development, 67,* 1540–1554.

Pramling, I. (1998). Understanding and empowering the child as a learner. In D. R. Olson & N. Torrance (Eds.), *The handbook of education and human development* (pp. 565–592). Malden, MA: Blackwell.

PreschoolPlanner101. (2007). Preschool lesson plans: Memory game. Retrieved August 31, 2011, from http://preschoolplanner101.blogspot.com/2007/02/preschool-lesson-plans-memory-game.html

Pressley, M., & Hilden, K. (2006). Cognitive strategies. In D. Kuhn, R. S. Siegler, W. Damon, & R. M. Lerner (Eds.), *Handbook of child psychology: Vol. 2. Cognition, perception, and language* (6th ed., pp. 511–556). Hoboken, NJ: Wiley.

Pressley, M., & Levin, J. R. (1977). Developmental differences in subjects' associative learning strategies and performance: Assessing a hypothesis. *Journal of Experimental Child Psychology, 24,* 431–439.

Pressley, M., Levin, J. R., & Delaney, H. D. (1982). The mnemonic keyword strategy at two age levels. *Journal of Educational Psychology, 72,* 575–582.

Pressley, M., Wharton-McDonald, R., Mistretta-Hampton, J., & Echevarria, M. (1998). The nature of literacy instruction in 10 grade 4/5 classrooms in upstate New York. *Scientific Studies of Reading, 2,* 159–194.

Quinn, P. C., & Eimas, P. D. (1996). Perceptual organization and categorization in young infants. In C. Rovee-Collier & L. P. Lipsett (Eds.), *Advances in infancy research* (Vol. 10, pp. 1–36). Westport, CT: Ablex.

Quitadamo I. J., & Kurtz, M. J. (2007). Learning to improve: Using writing to increase critical thinking performance in general education biology. *CBE Life Sciences Education, 6*(2), 140–154.

Rakoczy, H. (2008). Taking action seriously: Young children understand the normative structure of joint pretend games. *Developmental Psychology, 44*(4), 1195–1201.

Rakoczy, H., Warneken, F., & Tomasello, M. (2009). Young children's selective learning of rule games from reliable and unreliable models. *Cognitive Development, 24,* 61–69.

Ramachandran, V. S. (2009, November). The neurons that shaped civilization. TED India [video file]. Retrieved December 20, 2010, from http://www.ted.com/talks/vs_ramachandran_the_neurons_that_shaped_civilization.html

Ranganathan, V. K., Siemionow, V., Liu, J. Z., Sahgal, V., & Yue, G. H. (2003). From mental power to muscle power—gaining strength by using the mind. *Neuropsychologia, 42*, 944–956.

Ratner, H. H. (1984). Memory demands and the development of young children's memory. *Child Development, 55*, 2173–2191.

Ratner, H. H., Foley, M. A., & Gimpert, N. (2000). Person perspectives on children's memory and learning: What do source-monitoring failures reveal? In K. P. Roberts & M. Blades (Eds.), *Children's source monitoring* (pp. 85–114). Mahwah, NJ: Erlbaum.

Ratner, H. H., Foley, M. A., & Gimpert, N. (2002). The role of collaborative planning in children's source-monitoring errors and learning. *Journal of Experimental Child Psychology, 81*, 44–73.

Redding, R. E., Harmon, R. J., & Morgan, G. A. (1990). Relationships between maternal depression and infants' mastery behaviors. *Infant Behavior and Development, 13*, 391–395.

Reeder, J. A., Martin, S. E., & Turner, G. W. (2008). Memory development in childhood. In S. K. Thurman & C. A. Fiorello (Eds.), *Applied cognitive research in K–3 classrooms* (pp. 123–138). New York: Routledge.

Reese, E., Haden, C. A., & Fivush, R. (1993). Mother-child conversations about the past: Relationships of style and memory over time. *Cognitive Development, 8*, 403–430

Renninger, K. A., Hidi, S., & Krapp, A. (1992). *The role of interest in learning and development.* Hillsdale, NJ: Erlbaum.

Richards, J. (1987). Infant visual sustained attention and respiratory sinus arrhythmia. *Child Development, 58,* 488–496.

Ridderinkhof, K. R., & van der Molen, M. W. (1995). A psychophysiological analysis of developmental differences in the ability to resist interference. *Child Development, 66*, 1040–1056.

Ridgway, A., Northup, J., Pellegrin, A., LaRue, R., & Hightshoe, A. (2003). Effects of recess on the classroom behavior of children with and without attention-deficit hyperactivity disorder. *School Psychology Quarterly, 18*(3), 253–268.

Rimm-Kaufman, S. E., Curby, T., Grimm, K., Nathanson, L., & Brock, L. (2009). The contribution of children's self-regulation and classroom quality to children's adaptive behaviors in the kindergarten classroom. *Developmental Psychology, 45*(4), 958–972.

Ringel, B. A., & Springer, C. J. (1980). On knowing how well one is remembering: The persistence of strategy use during transfer. *Journal of Experimental Child Psychology, 29*, 322–333.

Rivard L. P. (1994). A review of writing to learn in science: Implications for practice and research. *Journal of Research in Science Teaching, 31*(9), 969–983.

Robinson, K. (2010, October 14). *Changing education paradigms.* Royal Society for the Encouragement of Arts, Manufactures and Commerce [video file]. Retrieved from http://www.youtube.com/watch?v=zDZFcDGpL4U

Roediger, H. L., & Karpicke, J. D. (2006). Test-enhanced learning: Taking memory tests improves long-term retention. *Psychological Science, 17*, 249–255.

Roediger, H. L., & McDermott, K. B. (1995). Creating false memories: Remembering words not presented in lists. *Journal of Experimental Psychology: Learning, Memory, and Cognition, 21*, 803–814.

Rogoff, B. (1990). *Apprenticeships in thinking: Cognitive development in social context.* Oxford: Oxford University Press.

Rosaen, C. L. (1990). Improving writing opportunities in elementary classrooms. *Elementary School Journal, 90*, 418–434.

Rose, S. A., & Feldman, J. F. (1995). Prediction of IQ and specific cognitive abilities at 11 years from infancy measures. *Developmental Psychology, 31*(4), 685–696.

Rose, S. A., & Wallace, I. F. (1985). Visual recognition memory: A predictor of later cognitive functioning in preterms. *Child Development, 56*, 843–852.

Rosenthal, R., & Jacobson, L. (1966). Teachers' expectancies: Determinants of pupils' IQ gains. *Psychological Reports, 19*, 115–118.

Rovee-Collier C. (1996). Measuring infant memory: A critical commentary. *Developmental Review, 16*, 301–310.

Rubenstein, G. (2009, May 5). Kids feel the power of poetry in performance: Through slam poetry, students reach new heights in literacy and in life. Retrieved May 31, 2011, from http://www.edutopia.org/poetry-slam-global-writes

Rueda, M. R., Rothbart, M. K., McCandliss, B. D., Saccomanno, L., & Posner, M. I. (2005). Training, maturation, and genetic influences on the development of executive attention. *Proceedings of the National Academy of Sciences of the USA, 102*, 14931–14936.

Rumelhart, D. E. (1991). Understanding understanding. In W. Kessen, A. Ortony, & F. Craig (Eds.), *Memories, thoughts, and emotions: Essays in honor of George Mandler*. Hillsdale, NJ: Erlbaum.

Sabbagh, M. A., & Baldwin, D. A. (2001). Learning words from knowledgeable versus ignorant speakers: Links between preschoolers' theory of mind and semantic development. *Child Development, 72*(4), 1054–1070.

Saffran, J. R. (2003). Statistical language learning: Mechanisms and constraints. *Current Directions in Psychological Science, 12*(4), 110–114.

Saffran, J. R., Aslin, R. N., & Newport, E. L. (1996). Statistical learning by 8–month-old infants. *Science, 274*, 1926–1928.

Salatas, H., & Flavell, J. H. (1976). Perspective taking: The development of two components of knowledge. *Child Development, 47*, 103–109.

Samaha, N. V., & De Lisi, R. (2000). Peer collaboration on a nonverbal reasoning task by urban, minority students. *Journal of Experimental Education, 69*(1), 5–21.

Sattelmair, J., & Ratey, J. J. (2009). Physically active play and cognition: An academic matter? *American Journal of Play, 1*(3), 365–374.

Sawyer, R. K. (2006). Introduction: The new science of learning. In R. K. Sawyer (Ed.), *The Cambridge handbook of the learning sciences* (pp. 1–16). Cambridge: Cambridge University Press.

Schmidt, M. E., Pempek, T. A., Kirkorian, H. L., Lund, A. F., & Anderson, D. R. (2008). The effects of background television on the toy play behavior of very young children. *Child Development, 79*, 1137–1151.

Schmitt, K., & Anderson, D. R. (2002). Television and reality: Toddlers' use of visual information from video to guide behavior. *Media Psychology, 4*, 51–76.

Schneider, W. (1997). The impact of expertise on performance: Illustrations from developmental research on memory and sports. *High Ability Studies, 8*(1), 7–18

Schneider, W., Kron-Sperl, V., & Hünnerkopf, M. (2009). The development of young children's memory strategies: Evidence from the Würzburg Longitudinal Memory Study. *European Journal of Developmental Psychology, 6*(1), 70–99.

Schneider, W., & Lockl, K. (2002). The development of metacognitive knowledge in children and adolescents. In T. J. Perfect & B. L. Schwartz (Eds.), *Applied metacognition* (pp. 224–257). Cambridge: Cambridge University Press.

Schneider, W., & Pressley, M. (1997). *Memory development between 2 and 20*. Mahwah, NJ: Erlbaum.

Schneps, M. H. (1989). *A private universe: Misconceptions that block learning* (Video). Santa

Schuh, K. L., & Rea, J. (2001). Emotion and meaning-making: Affordances in the classroom. *Mid-Western Educational Researcher, 14*(2), 2–10.

Schurgin O'Keeffe, G., Clarke-Pearson, K., et al. (2011). The impact of social media on children, adolescents, and families. *Pediatrics, 127*, 800–804.

Schweinhart, L. J., & Weikart, D. P. (1997). Lasting differences: The HighScope preschool curriculum comparison study through age 23. *Monographs of the HighScope Educational Research Foundation, 12*. Ypsilanti, MI: HighScope Press.

Schwenck, C., Bjorklund, D. F., & Schneider, W. (2009). Developmental and individual differences in young children's use and maintenance of a selective memory strategy. *Developmental Psychology, 45*(4), 1034–1050.

Sharon, T., & DeLoache, J. S. (2003). The role of perseveration in children's symbolic understanding and skill. *Developmental Science, 6,* 289–297.

Shepherd, G. M. (2005). Perception without a thalamus. *Neuron, 46*(2), 166–168.

Shernoff, D. J., Csikszentmihalyi, M., Schneider, B., & Shernoff, E. S. (2003). Student engagement in high school classrooms from the perspective of flow theory. *School Psychology Quarterly, 18*(2), 158–176.

Shin, H. E., Bjorklund, D. F., & Beck, E. F. (2007). The adaptive nature of children's overestimation in a strategic memory task. *Cognitive Development, 22*, 197–212.

Sibley, B. A., & Etnier, J. L. (2003). The relationship between physical activity and cognition in children: A meta-analysis. *Pediatric Exercise Science, 15*, 243–256.

Siegler, R. S. (1995). How does change occur: A microgenetic study of number conservation. *Cognitive Development, 28*, 225–273.

Sigman, M., Cohen, S. E., & Beckwith, L. (1997). Why does infant attention predict adolescent intelligence? *Journal of Infant Behavior & Development, 20*, 133–140.

Signorella, M. L., Bigler, R. S., & Liben, L. S. (1993). Developmental differences in children's gender schemata about others: A meta-analytic review. *Developmental Review, 13*, 147–183

Sigman, M., Cohen, S. E., Beckwith, L., & Parmelee, A. H. (1986). Infant attention in relation to intellectual abilities in childhood. *Developmental Psychology, 22*, 788–792.

Skouteris, H., Spataro, J., & Lazaridis, M. (2006). Young children's use of a delayed video representation to solve a retrieve problem pertaining to self. *Developmental Science, 9,* 505–517.

Smith, F. (1998). *The book of learning and forgetting.* New York: Teachers College Press.

Smith, L. (1988). One-year follow-up of small preterm infants. *Infant Behavior and Development, 11,* 320.

Smith, S. M., & Vela, E. (2001). Environmental context-dependent memory: A review and a meta-analysis. *Psychonomic Bulletin & Review, 8,* 203–220.

Smith, S., Willms, D., & Johnson, N. (Eds.). (1997). *Nurtured by knowledge: Learning to do participatory action-research.* New York: Apex Press.

Smith-Donald, R., Raver, C. C., Hayes, T., & Richardson, B. (2007). Preliminary construct and concurrent validity of the Preschool Self-Regulation Assessment (PSRA) for field-based research. *Early Childhood Research Quarterly, 22*(2), 173–187.

Smotherman, W. P., & Robinson, S. R. (1988). The uterus as environment: The ecology of fetal behavior. In E. M. Blass (Ed.), *Handbook of behavioral neurobiology: Vol. 9. Developmental psychobiology and behavioral ecology.* New York: Plenum Press.

Sobel, D. M., & Sommerville, J. A. (2009). Rationales in children's causal learning from others' actions. *Cognitive Development, 24*, 70–79.

Soini, H., & Flynn, M. (2005). Emotion and rhythm in critical learning incidents. *Interchange, 36*(1–2), 73–83.

Sommerville, J. A., & Hammond, A. J. (2007). Treating another's actions as one's own: Children's memory of and learning from joint activity. *Developmental Psychology, 43*, 1003–1018.

Sommerville, J. A., Woodward, A. L., & Needham, A. (2005). Action experience alters 3-month-old infants' perception of others' actions. *Cognition, 96*, B1–B11.

Spence, M. J. (1996). Young infants' long-term auditory memory: Evidence for changes in preference as a function of delay. *Developmental Psychobiology, 29*, 685–695.

Squire, L. R., & Kandel, E. R. (2000). *Memory: From mind to molecules.* New York: Holt.

Srivastava, N. D. (1997). *Meta modern era.* New Delhi: Ritana Books.

St. Clair-Thompson, H. L., Stevens, R., Hunt, A., & Bolder, E. (2010). Improving children's working memory and classroom performance. *Educational Psychology, 30*, 203–220.

Steidl, S., Razik, F., & Anderson, A. K. (2011). Emotion enhanced retention of cognitive skill learning. *Emotion, 11*(1), 12–19.

Steiner, R. (1919). *The spirit of the Waldorf School* (R. Lathe & N. Whittaker, Trans.). Herndon, VA: SteinerBooks.

Stevanoni, E., & Salmon, K. (2005). Giving memory a hand: Instructing children to gesture enhances their event recall. *Journal of Nonverbal Behavior, 29*(4), 217–233.

Stipek, D., Recchia, S., & McClintic, S. (1992). Self-evaluation in young children. *Monographs of the Society for Research in Child Development, 57*(1, Serial No. 226).

Straub, W. F. (1989). The effect of three different methods of mental training on dart throwing performance. *The Sport Psychologist, 3*, 133–141.

Strauss, S. (2005). Teaching as a natural cognitive ability: Implications for classroom practice and teacher education. In D. B. Pillemer & W. Sheldon (Eds.), *Developmental psychology and social change: Research, history, and policy* (pp. 368–388). New York: Cambridge University Press.

Strauss, S., Ziv, M., & Stein, A. (2002). Teaching as a natural cognition and its relations to preschoolers' developing theory of mind. *Cognitive Development, 17*, 1473–1787.

Suddendorf, T. (1999). Children's understanding of the relation between delayed video representation and current reality: A test for self-awareness. *Journal of Experimental Child Psychology, 72*, 157–176.

Suddendorf, T., Simcock, G., & Nielsen, M. (2007). Visual self-recognition in mirrors and live videos: Evidence for a developmental asynchrony. *Cognitive Development, 22*, 185–196.

Sullivan, M. W., Rovee-Collier, C., & Tynes, D. M. (1979). A conditioning analysis of infant long-term memory. *Child Development, 50*, 152–162.

Sun, R., Merrill, E., & Peterson, T. (2001). From implicit skills to explicit knowledge: A bottom-up model of skill learning. *Cognitive Science, 25*, 203–244.

Sun, R., Slusarz, P., & Terry, C. (2005). The interaction of the explicit and the implicit in skill learning: A dual-process approach. *Psychological Review, 112*(1), 159–192.

Swanson, H .L., Ashbaker, M. H., & Lee, C. (1996). Learning disabled readers working memory as a function of processing demands. *Journal of Experimental Child Psychology, 61*, 242–275.

Swing, S. R, Stoiber, K. C., & Peterson, P. L. (1988). Thinking skills versus learning time: Effects of alternative classroom-based interventions on students' mathematics problem solving. *Cognition and Instruction, 5*(2), 123–191.

Symons, D., McLaughlin, E., Moore, C., & Morine, S. (1997). Integrating relationship constructs and emotional experience into false belief tasks in preschool children. *Journal of Experimental Child Psychology, 67*, 423–447.

Tamis-LeMonda, C. S., & Bornstein, M. H. (1989). Habituation and maternal encouragement of attention in infancy as predictors of toddler language, play, and representational competence. *Child Development, 60*, 738–751.

Tang, Y. Y., Ma, Y., Wang, J., Fan, Y., Feng, S., Lu, Q., Yu, Q., Sui, D., Rothbart, M. K., Fan, M., & Posner, M. I. (2007). Short-term meditation training improves attention and self-regulation. *Proceedings of the National Academy of Sciences, 104*(43), 17152–17156.

Taras, H. (2005). Physical activity and student performance at school. *Journal of School Health, 75*, 214–218.

Taylor, J. S. (2010). Learning with emotion: A powerful and effective pedagogical technique. *Academic Medicine, 85*(7), 1110.

Taylor, K., Marienau, C., & Fiddler, M. (2000). *Developing adult learners: Strategies for teachers and trainers.* San Francisco: Jossey-Bass.

Taylor, M., Esbensen, B. M., & Bennett, R. T. (1994). Children's understanding of knowledge acquisition: The tendency for children to report that they have always known what they have just learned. *Child Development, 65*, 1581–1604.

Thelen, E., & Smith, L. B. (1996). *A dynamic systems approach to the development of cognition and action.* Cambridge, MA: MIT Press.

Thomas, L. A., & LaBar, K. S. (2008). Fear-relevancy, strategy use, and probabilistic learning of cue-outcome associations. *Learning & Memory, 15*, 777–784.

Thompson, C. P. (2000). Mnemonists. In A. E. Kazdin (Ed.), *Encyclopedia of psychology* (Vol. 5, pp. 288–289). Washington, DC: American Psychological Association.

Thompson, L. A., Fagan, J. F., & Fulker, D. W. (1991). Longitudinal prediction of specific cognitive abilities from infant novelty preference. *Child Development, 62*, 530–538.

Thompson, M. (Director). (2006). *Raising Cain.* [Motion picture]. Portland, OR: PBS.

Tobin, J., Hsueh, Y., & Karasawa, M. (2009). *Preschool in three cultures revisited.* Chicago: University of Chicago Press.

Tomasello, M. (1999). *The cultural origins of human cognition.* Cambridge, MA: Harvard University Press.

Tomasello, M., Kruger, A. C., & Ratner, H. H. (1993). Cultural learning. *Behavioral and Brain Science, 16*, 495–552.

Trabasso, T., & Suh, S. (1993). Understanding text. *Discourse Processes, 16*, 3–34.

Troseth, G. L., & DeLoache, J. S. (1998). The medium can obscure the message: Young children's understanding of video. *Child Development, 69*, 950–965.

Tulving, E., & Thomson, D. M. (1973). Encoding specificity and retrieval processes in episodic memory. *Psychological Review, 80*, 352–373.

Turner, S. L., Hamilton, H., Jacobs, M., Angood, L. M., & Dwyer, D. H. (1997). The influence of fashion magazines on the body image satisfaction of college women: An exploratory analysis. *Adolescence, 32*(127), 603–614.

Twain, M. (1901, November). Speech at the 145th annual dinner of St. Andrew's Society, New York. In P. Fatout (Ed.), (1976) *Mark Twain speaking* (p. 424). Iowa City: University of Iowa Press.

Underwood, J., Underwood, G., & Wood, D. (2000). When does gender matter? Interactions during computer-based problem solving. *Learning and Instruction, 10*, 447–462.

Unestahl, L. E. (1983). *Inner mental training: A systematical self-instructional program for self-hypnosis.* Orebro, Sweden: Veje.

Vail, P. (1994). *Emotion: The off/on switch.* Rosemont, NJ: Modern Learning Press.

van Heteren, C. F., Focco Boekkooi, P., Jongsma, H. W., & Nijhuis, J. G. (2000). Fetal learning and memory. *The Lancet, 356*(9236), 1169.

Viadero, D. (2008). Exercise seen as priming the pump for students' academic success. *Education Week, 27*, 14–15.

Vygotsky, L. S. (1966). Development of the higher mental functions. In A. N. Leontiev, A. R. Luria, & A. Smirnol (Eds.), *Psychological research in the USSR* (Vol. 1, pp. 11–45). Moscow: Progressive Publishers. (Original work published 1930)

Vygotsky, L. S. (1978). *Mind in society: The development of higher psychological processes* (M. Cole, V. John-Steiner, S. Scribner, & E. Souberman, Eds.). Cambridge, MA: Harvard University Press. (Original work published 1930)

Vygotsky, L. S. (1986). *Thought and language* (rev. ed.). A. Kozulin (Ed.). Cambridge, MA: MIT Press. (Original work published 1934)

Vygotsky, L. S. (1987). *The collected works of L. S. Vygotsky, Vol. 1*. New York: Plenum. (Original work published 1934)

Walker-Andrews, A. S., & Grolnick, W. (1983). Discrimination of vocal expressions by young infants. *Infant Behavior and Development, 6*, 479–486.

Wallace, B. A. (1999). The Buddhist tradition of Samatha: Methods for refining and examining consciousness. *Journal of Consciousness Studies, 6,* 175–187.

Watson, A., Nixon, C., Wilson, A., & Capage, L. (1999). Social interaction skills and theory of mind in young children. *Developmental Psychology, 35*, 386–391.

Weinger, H. B., & Anisfeld, M. (1998). Infant social referencing: A meta-analytic review [abstract]. *Infant Behavior and Development, 21*, 751.

Wellman, H. M. (2002). Understanding the psychological world: Developing a theory of mind. In U. Goswami (Ed.), *Handbook of childhood cognitive development* (pp. 167–187). Oxford: Blackwell.

Wellman, H. M., & Lagattuta, K. H. (2004). Theory of mind for learning and teaching: The nature and role of explanation. *Cognitive Development, 19*, 479–497.

Wellman, H. M., Ritter, K., & Flavell, J. H. (1975). Deliberate memory behavior in the delayed reactions of very young children. *Developmental Psychology, 11*, 780–787.

Welsh, M. C., & Pennington, B. F. (1988). Assessing frontal lobe functioning in children: Views from developmental psychology. *Developmental Neuropsychology, 4*, 199–230.

Whalen, S. P., & Csikszentmihalyi, M. (1991). Putting flow theory into educational practice: The Key school's flow activities room. In *Report to the Benton Center for Curriculum and Instruction*. Chicago: University of Chicago Press.

What helps us learn? (2010). *Educational Leadership, 67*(5), 68–69.

White, E. B. (1952). *Charlotte's web*. New York: HarperCollins.

White, R. W. (1969). Motivation reconsidered: The concept of competence. *Psychological Review, 66*, 297–333.

Whitehead, A. N. (1932). *The aims of education and other essays*. London: Williams & Norgate.

Willingham, D., Nissen, M., & Bullemer, P. (1989). On the development of procedural knowledge. *Journal of Experimental Psychology: Learning, Memory, and Cognition, 15*, 1047–1060.

Willis, J. (2006). *Research-based strategies to ignite student learning: Insights from a neurologist and classroom teacher*. Alexandria, VA: ASCD.

Winsler, A., Diaz, R. M., & Montero, I. (1997). The role of private speech in the transition from collaborative to independent task performance in young children. *Early Childhood Research Quarterly, 12*, 55–73.

Wolfe, P. (2001). *Brain matters: Translating research into classroom practice*. Alexandria, VA: ASCD.

Wolfe, P. (2006). The role of meaning and emotion in learning. In S. Johnson & K. Taylor (Eds.), *The neuroscience of adult learning* (pp. 35–41). San Francisco: Jossey-Bass.

Wolk, E. S. B. (2008). *Getting the green light: The transformative power of participatory action-research with students as researchers*. Retrieved September 5, 2009, from http://gallery.carnegiefoundation.org/collections/castl_k12/ewolk/

Wood, K. (2008). Mathematics through movement: An investigation of the links between kinesthetic and conceptual learning. *APMC, 13*(1), 18–22.

Wood, M. (2003). *Shakespeare*. New York: Basic Books.

Wurm, J. (2005). *Working in the Reggio way: A beginner's guide for American teachers*. Minneapolis, MN: Redleaf Press.

Yerkes, R. M., & Dodson, J. D. (1908). The relation of strength of stimulus to rapidity of habit-formation. *Journal of Comparative Neurology and Psychology, 18,* 459–482.

Zajonc, R. B. (1984). On the primacy of affect. *American Psychologist, 39*, 117–123.

Zambo, D., & Brem, S. K. (2004). Emotion and cognition in students who struggle to read: New insights and ideas. *Reading Psychology, 25*, 189–204.

Zelazo, P. D., & Müller, U. (2002). Executive function in typical and atypical development. In U. Goswami (Ed.), *Handbook of childhood cognitive development*. Oxford: Blackwell.

Zelazo, P. D., Sommerville, J. A., & Nichols, S. (1999). Age-related changes in children's use of external representations. *Developmental Psychology, 35*, 1059–1071.

Zimbardo, P. G., Butler, L. D., & Wolfe, V. A. (2003). Cooperative College Examinations: More gain, less pain when students share information and grades. *Journal of Experimental Education, 71*, 101–125.

Zimmerman, F. J., Christakis, D. A., & Meltzoff, A. N. (2007). Associations between media viewing and language development in children under age 2 years. *Journal of Pediatrics, 151*, 364–368.

Zukow-Goldring, P., & Arbib, M. A. (2007). Affordances, effectivities, and assisted imitation: Caregivers and the directing of attention. *Neurocomputing, 70*, 2181–2193.

Index

Note: The letter *f* following a page number denotes a figure.

About the Author

Wendy Ostroff's expertise in cognitive psychology, child development, and metacognition stems from her research experience as a scientist in the Infant Perception Laboratory at Virginia Tech; as a visiting scientist at the Max Planck Institute for Evolutionary Anthropology in Leipzig, Germany; and as a Carnegie Scholar with the Carnegie Foundation for the Advancement of Teaching at Stanford University. She has been developing curriculum on children's learning for the past 15 years in the Hutchins School of Liberal Studies at Sonoma State University; in the Department of Education and Child Study at Smith College; and, most recently, as Associate Professor in the program for the Advancement of Learning at Curry College. Dr. Ostroff has taught more than 30 distinct university-level courses and has been granted three university *Excellence in Teaching* awards. She is deeply committed to the design and implementation of state-of-the-art education.

Related ASCD Resources: Understanding How Children Learn

At the time of publication, the following ASCD resources were available (ASCD stock numbers appear in parentheses). For up-to-date information about ASCD resources, go to www.ascd.org. You can search the complete archives of *Educational Leadership* at http://www.ascd.org/el.

ASCD EDge Group

Exchange ideas and connect with other educators interested in the brain and learning on the social networking site ASCD EDge™ at http://ascdedge.ascd.org/

DVDs

Teaching the Adolescent Brain (DVD with Facilitator's Guide) (#600237)
The Brain and Mathematics (DVD and Facilitator's Guide) (#600237

Online Courses

Go to ASCD's Home Page (www.ascd.org) and click on professional development to find the following ASCD Professional Development Online Courses: *The Brain: Memory and Learning Strategies*; *The Brain: Mind-Body Connection*; and *The Brain: Understanding the Physical Brain*

Print Products

The Brain-Compatible Classroom: Using What We Know About Learning to Improve Teaching by Laura Erlauer Myrah (#101269)
Brain Matters: Translating Research into Classroom Practice by Patricia Wolfe (#101004)
How to Teach So Students Remember by Marilee Sprenger (#105016)
Research-Based Strategies to Ignite Student Learning: Insights from a Neurologist and Classroom Teacher by Judy Willis (#107006)
Teaching to the Brain's Natural Learning Systems by Barbara K. Given (#101075)
Teaching with the Brain in Mind, 2nd edition, by Eric Jensen (#104013)

THE WHOLE CHILD The Whole Child Initiative helps schools and communities create learning environments that allow students to be healthy, safe, engaged, supported, and challenged. To learn more about other books and resources that relate to the whole child, visit www.wholechildeducation.org.

For more information: send e-mail to member@ascd.org; call 1-800-933-2723 or 703-578-9600, press 2; send a fax to 703-575-5400; or write to Information Services, ASCD, 1703 N. Beauregard St., Alexandria, VA 22311-1714 USA.